CHINESE RELIGION IN CONTEMPORARY
SINGAPORE, MALAYSIA AND TAIWAN

MANCHESTER
1824
Manchester University Press

ALTERNATIVE SINOLOGY

Series editors: Richard Madsen and Yangwen Zheng

This series provides a dedicated outlet for monographs and possibly edited volumes that take alternative views on contemporary or historical China; use alternative research methodologies to achieve unique outcomes; focus on otherwise understudied or marginalized aspects of China, Chineseness, or the Chinese state and the Chinese cultural diaspora; or generally attempt to unsettle the status quo in Chinese Studies, broadly construed. There has never been a better time to embark on such a series, as both China and the academic disciplines engaged in studying it seem ready for change.

Previously published

The advocacy trap   Stephen Noakes

Communists constructing capitalism: State, market, and the Party in China's financial reform   Julian Gruin

CHINESE RELIGION IN CONTEMPORARY SINGAPORE, MALAYSIA AND TAIWAN

The cult of the Two Grand Elders

FABIAN GRAHAM

Manchester University Press

Copyright © Fabian Graham 2020

The right of Fabian Graham to be identified as the author of this work has been asserted by him in accordance with the Copyright, Designs and Patents Act 1988.

Published by Manchester University Press
Oxford Road, Manchester M13 9PL
www.manchesteruniversitypress.co.uk

British Library Cataloguing-in-Publication Data is available

ISBN 978 1 5261 4057 9 hardback
ISBN 978 1 5261 6777 4 paperback

First published by Manchester University Press in hardback 2020

This edition published 2022

The publisher has no responsibility for the persistence or accuracy of URLs for any external or third-party internet websites referred to in this book, and does not guarantee that any content on such websites is, or will remain, accurate or appropriate.

Typeset by Servis Filmsetting Ltd, Stockport, Cheshire

Contents

List of plates and figures	*page* vii
Series editors' foreword	ix
Preface and acknowledgements	x
List of abbreviations	xv
Introduction	1

Part I: Setting the scene

1	The modern Underworld tradition	15
2	Analysis: a baseline of comparison	21
3	The historical development of Underworld cosmology	32

Part II: The Underworld tradition in Singapore

4	Yu Feng Nan Fu Xuanshan Miao: setting a baseline of comparison	41
5	A new Underworld God of Wealth, and foetus assistance rituals in Singapore	62
6	Lunar Seventh Month: the centrality of graveyards in the Underworld tradition	83

Part III: The Underworld tradition in Malaysia

7	Malaysia and the party spirit: *guanxi* and the creation of 'intentional' communities	113
8	Seventh Month rituals in southern Malaysia: salvation rituals and Ah Pek parties	141
9	Seventh Month rituals in central Malaysia: coffin rituals and the releasing of exorcised spirits	164

Part IV: Tracing the origins of the modern Underworld tradition

10 Anxi Chenghuangmiao and cultural flows of local mythology   189
11 Penang: the earliest recollections of Tua Di Ya Pek embodied   202
12 Analysis and conclusions   214

Appendix of Chinese names   230
References   237
Index   244

Plates and figures

Plates
1. Yu Feng Nan Fu Xuanshan Miao
2. Oil wok ritual
3. Tua Ya Pek splices his tongue
4. Cemetery plot for foetuses, babies and young children
5. Offerings before the foetus ghost's altar
6. Guan Gong paying respects to a Datuk Gong, Malaysia
7. The 'Hell of Severing in Two'
8. Ah Boon resting in Di Ya Pek's altar room
9. Di Ya Pek and *luk thep* dolls
10. Dasheng Gong Chenghuang Dian's Underworld altar
11. One pair of Tua Di Ya Pek at the conference
12. My coffin ritual at Brickfields Chenghuangmiao
13. Miniature coffins frequently found on Singapore's Underworld altars
14. Anxi Chenghuangmiao's Tua Di Ya Pek (top) compared to their common depiction in Singapore and Malaysia (bottom)
15. Inviting the temple's deities at Anxi Chenghuangmiao
16. Feeding Tua Ya Pek opium at Penang's City God Temple

Figures

5.1	Bao Bei Ya in Geylang	*page* 67
5.2	Tua Ya Pek at Sanzhong Gong	75
6.1	Central to the foetus ghost's altar	91
6.2	Tua Ya Pek preparing to cast coins	92
6.3	Pierced with skewers representing the Eight Underworld Generals	100
7.1	The Third Court of King Songdi	120
7.2	Tua Di Ya Pek dancing	136
8.1	Dizangwang's 'huashen'	146
8.2	Tua Di Ya Pek's wardrobe	154
9.1	The prison cell	176
9.2	Di Ya Pek patrolling the area	178

10.1 Ba Ye Gong (Xie Bian) and Jiu Ye Gong's (Fan Wujiu's) new graves 194
10.2 The lowest section of the new staircase 198
11.1 Underworld throne in Penang 213

All images in this book are the property of the author.

Series editors' foreword

The study of China has in recent decades seen an explosion as many universities began to offer modules ranging from Chinese history, politics and sociology to urban, cultural and Diaspora studies. This is welcome news; the field grows when the world is hungry for knowledge about China. Chinese studies as a result have moved further away from the interdisciplinary tradition of Sinology towards more discipline-based teaching and research. This is significant because it has helped integrate the once-marginalised Chinese subjects into firmly established academic disciplines; practitioners should learn and grow within their own fields. This has also, however, compartmentalised Chinese studies as China scholars communicate much less with each other than before since they now teach and research in different departments; the study of China has lost some of its exceptionalism and former sheen.

Alternative Sinology calls for a more nuanced way forward. China scholars can firmly ground themselves in their own perspective fields; they still have the advantage of Sinology, the more holistic approach. The combination of disciplinary and area studies can help us innovate and lead. Now is an exciting time to take the study of China to new heights as the country has seen unprecedented change and offers us both hindsight and new observations. Alternative Sinology challenges China scholars. It calls on them to think creatively and unsettle the status quo by using new and alternative materials and methods to dissect China. It encourages them to take on understudied and marginalised aspects of China at a time when the field is growing and expanding rapidly. The case of China can promote the field and strengthen the individual discipline as well.

Zheng Yangwen and Richard Madsen

Preface and acknowledgements

In 2005 I enrolled in an MA programme in Taiwan studies in National Chengchi University in Taipei, Taiwan. As a part of the coursework for a 'qualitative research methods' module I led a small research team at Taipei's oldest Buddhist temple with the aim of establishing the extent of local practitioners' knowledge of historical Buddhism. I was in for a shock. While the depth of devotion to the temple's Guanyin and the sincerity of devotees' ritual practices were unparalleled in my experience, interviewees' historical knowledge of Buddhism was minimal. Most respondents suggested I refer my questions to the temple's information counter. The disparity between the intensity of beliefs and practices and lack of doctrinal knowledge, coupled with my passion for Chinese temple culture, provided the inspiration for my first MA thesis, which focused on four of Taiwan's oldest temples, their deities and the role each temple played in the local and wider religious landscape.

Leading ethnographies on modern Chinese religion which had been carried out by anthropologists in Taiwan from the 1960s to 1980s, when China was closed to Western academics, were essential reading. However, many of Taiwan's post-1980s ritual practices which I encountered between 2005 and 2007 required a broader study. One tradition in particular, Taiwan's new Money God temples, led me to a journal article titled 'A free gift makes no friends' by James Laidlaw, concerning non-reciprocity among Jain renunciants. The depth and brilliance of the analysis came as an epiphany which inspired me to move from area studies to anthropology. I was lucky enough to study under Professor Laidlaw for a year at Cambridge, where, much to his credit, he tried his uttermost to educate me in anthropological analysis before I moved on to research for my doctorate at SOAS, University of London.

Chinese temple culture is an immense field of study and my first PhD supervisor Dr Fiona Bowie and I shared an interest in mediumship and spirituality. She encouraged me to specialise in the former while keeping an open mind on the latter. Her guidance proved invaluable, for which I remain sincerely grateful. For me as a new researcher, Chinese spirit possession resonated with my continuing exploration of the numinous and provided an academic path allowing for enquiry into one instance, albeit culturally bound, of the continuity of some element of 'the self' or 'soul' surviving physiological death. The social life of the dead is a topic that is explored in detail in this volume.

At the age of nineteen, I first became interested in the spiritual nature of religious traditions through Chinese chi kung taught by a Taoist master and from Hindu meditation techniques learned from my first Indian guru. Soon after, on a quest for experiential knowledge, I began an overland trek from London to Nairobi, during which I engaged with Tuaregs in the western Sahara, lived for a month with the Mbuti pygmies in the Ituri rain forests of what was then the Republic of Zaire, shared food, shelter and stories with Nigerian refugees while travelling through Cameroon and first encountered witch doctors in candle-lit villages in the Central African Republic. From Kenya I journeyed to Sri Lanka. It was 1989 and pre-internet and, ignorant of the fact that the second armed revolt between the Janatha Vimukthi Peramuna and the government raged on, I saw the dead burned bodies of young Singhalese left by the roadside before dawn as I rode my motorcycle around the island.

Towards the end of 1989 I finally arrived in India, where my interest in spiritual traditions was further stimulated by interactions with sadhus at sacred sites. Shiva's sacred mountain in Tiruvannamalai; Pushkar's holy lake; Rishikesh's ashrams and at Mount Abu in Rajasthan, the home of Raja yoga, where I eagerly immersed myself in the Bhagavad Gita and learned commentaries on the text. My religious and spiritual horizons were then expanded by participating in multiple ten-day silent vipassana meditation retreats in Thai monasteries, which would later lead to longer periods of retreat. During my twenties I had therefore traversed the world, crossing Africa, Asia and North America.

My travels were financed by selling jewellery which I had hand-crafted from stones and silver using rudimentary tools and techniques. In the process I became well acquainted with gemstones ranging from natural quartzes and bi-coloured tourmaline crystals to Indian star rubies and facet-cut emeralds haggled for with merchants on my travels. On my return to the UK, a meeting at London's Central Saint Martin's college with a department head to discuss studying gemmology with her husband led to an offer of a place on their BA programme in jewellery design, which I accepted on impulse.

My undergraduate degree nurtured a real-world comprehension of the creative process and an appreciation of history, artistry and form in material culture. This served me well in identifying the inventive elements of spirit medium rituals and in distinguishing the sometimes-subtle nuances of differing material cultures in contrasting temple landscapes.

Initially researching in two locations, Singapore and Taiwan, my intention was to integrate myself into the religious landscapes and, through participation, to gain experiential knowledge that would enable me to describe the lesser-known life-worlds of practitioners in both academic and local terms. I soon realised that, like myself, the spirit mediums and their followers were ordinary people facing similar trials and tribulations to those living in other developed countries beyond Asia. Most pursued conventional careers or ran small businesses, spirit mediums commonly working in related industries including geomancy and selling religious paraphernalia, while practitioners' professions traversed the social spectrum. With this in mind, I compiled a comparative analysis accounting for differences between the two temple landscapes, most notably, the popularity of Underworld deity worship in Singapore versus Heaven deity worship in Taiwan. However, this book focuses primarily on contrasts between Underworld deity worship in Singapore and Malaysia. While I demonstrate that there has been a remarkable upsurge in Underworld deity worship in Singapore and Malaysia, this does not mean that Heaven deities have entirely disappeared. On the contrary, there is still an active spirit medium scene in both countries channelling these deities. Nonetheless, the contrast with Taiwan is striking.

After obtaining my PhD in 2014 I continued researching independently in Southeast Asia. While participating in Singapore's Nine Emperor God festival in the enviable position as sword bearer for the First Emperor God as channelled through his medium, I first met Professors Peter van der Veer and Kenneth Dean, the former offering me a two-year postdoctoral fellowship at the Max Planck Institute for the Study of Religious Diversity. Based in Malaysia, my research would contribute to the 'Temples, rituals and the transformation of transnational networks' project in which the two professors were collaborating. Already well known among Singapore's spirit medium networks through my prior research and contributions to online Underworld deity and Taoist forums, by 2015 I was receiving up to ten invitations a month to visit and research at spirit medium temples in Singapore and Malaysia. These commonly came from spirit mediums, their closest followers or temple committee members, and, accepting as many invitations as was viable, I came into contact with many of the mediums, temples and ritual events featured in this book. My reputation as a non-judgemental scholar eager to participate in temple life preceded me, and spirit mediums and their devotees invited me to join in and to record their temples' events.

Led by encounters with spirit mediums channelling Underworld deities, my research agenda evolved reflexively, prompting the rapid refinement of and increased focus on my dialogic approach of consulting spirit mediums in trance possession states. In this manner, as significant divergences between

Malaysia and Singapore's Underworld traditions and interpretations of afterlife cosmology became apparent, I determined to undertake a detailed comparative study of the Underworld traditions in the two locations. To maintain consistency, questions previously put to mediums in Singapore were repeated in Malaysia, the answers providing further lines of enquiry which were then followed up with mediums in both locations.

By mid-2016 it became clear that locating the origins of the modern Underworld tradition was both fundamental to the study and of keen interest to numerous practitioners whom I had interviewed. My research thus expanded to include a key overseas temple, Anxi City God Temple in Fujian Province, China, and, towards the end, brought me back to Malaysia's oldest City God and Underworld temples located in George Town, Penang State.

As in my earlier travels, throughout my research I was drawn to active participation in cultural and ritual events. I experienced many and sometimes conflicting emotions during these, from the thrill verging on terror of collecting cemetery 'medicines' from open graves in the dead of night in Singapore to the surreal yet meditative experience of being guided to the gates of the Underworld by a spirit medium while in a semi-trance state in Malaysia. From interviewing possessed spirit mediums to playing an active role in the preparation and performance of rituals, the trust placed in me by my hosts was humbling and something I never took for granted. I therefore acted with the uttermost integrity, both as a sign of respect and to leave a door open for other researchers to conduct fieldwork in the same geographical locations.

The best way to have a friend is to be a friend, and many of the friendships that formed over a decade of fieldwork have been maintained. These relationships were reciprocal, and whenever possible I gave something back, from offering my services as a temple's chef or photographer during major events, to sharing the knowledge that I had previously accumulated. Given our close relations, my research was undertaken in collaboration with members of temple communities, thereby giving the research subjects a say in how the research was conducted and reported on. The process of informed consent was therefore continuous, my intention to write this book was known to all and my active participation in ritual events was by invitation. On my explaining the custom and merits of maintaining anonymity in anthropological texts and the possible repercussions of using the real names of people and places, almost without exception, spirit mediums and temple representatives requested that their own and their temples' names should receive recognition in the final book. Permissions granted, their requests have been respected.

Moving on, this book details my observations from a decade of interactive fieldwork, whereas the traditions described belong to a larger temporal continuum. However, as ongoing needs require innovative means and new rituals continue to be invented, and further transnational cultural flows continue to exert influence on local temple cultures, the essential features of the contemporary Underworld tradition described remain consistent even as they are being passed down to the next generation of religious specialists. Therefore, while specific information pertaining to individual temples may become out of date with shifts in the temple landscapes, the ritual and material cultures described should remain relevant for the foreseeable future. Moreover, the alternative ontological method proffered, the narrational style and lexicon of terms introduced, my dialogic approach to mediumship and the framework of analysis should remain significant to future academics researching the world's evolving spiritual and religious traditions.

This book has been a labour of love which could not have been accomplished without the cooperation and guidance of numerous individuals who deserve acknowledgement as a measure of my gratitude. In academia, I would like to thank James Laidlaw, Fiona Bowie, Peter van der Veer and Kenneth Dean for their inspiration, patience, unwavering support and friendship. I would like to extend this thanks to Thomas Dark from Manchester University Press for supporting this project and bringing its publication to fruition. I also wish to thank the huge number of religious practitioners and specialists for their selfless hospitality and for allowing me to participate so fully in their religious life-worlds. Of these, I would like to articulate my heartfelt thanks to the following people in particular. In Singapore, Lim Tau-Ching, Chen Jun-Cheng, Chen Qi-Zan, Tan Ah-Loon, Master Liang, Chung Kwang-Tong, Alvin Goh and Victor Yue. From Malaysia, Low Chee-Boon, Chen Wen-Fai, Ng Meng-Chung, Chen Xue-Le, Chew Kean-Nam, Goh Kum-Hoong, Christopher Lee, Daryl Lee Ming-Woei, Joshua Lam and Professor Wang Chen-Fa. Lastly, I would like to thank Wu Pei-Chien for her superb transcriptions from multiple Hokkien dialects into English, and Wang Chien-Chuan for her help and support throughout my research.

Abbreviations

CCP	Communist Party of China
HDB	Housing Development Board
KMT	Kuomintang
NDP	National Development Policy
NEA	National Environmental Agency
NEP	New Economic Policy
PAP	People's Action Party

Introduction

Chinese religion in contemporary Singapore, Malaysia and Taiwan is an in-depth study of the contemporary Underworld tradition in Singapore and Malaysia (with comparisons to religious developments in Taiwan), where Hell deities are venerated in statue form and freely interacted with while embodied in their spirit mediums, *tang-ki* (童乩).[1] The ethnography focuses on the temple-based, spirit medium-centric ritual and material cultures that have come to prominence in these two locations since the turn of the century. The Chinese Underworld[2] and its sub-hells are populated by a bureaucracy drawn from the Buddhist, Taoist and vernacular pantheons. Under the watchful eye of Hell's 'enforcers', the lower echelons of demon soldiers impose post-mortal punishments on the souls of the recently deceased for moral transgressions perpetrated during their prior incarnations. Inspired by Buddhist cosmology, the tortures inflicted are karmic retributions, a necessary precursor to the transmigration of souls into a new form, human or otherwise. As such, the Chinese Underworld or Hell[3] is distinct from the biblical Hell, and from Hells recognised by other religious traditions.

The contemporary Underworld tradition centres on two of Hell's most feared demon enforcers, Tua Ya Pek and Di Ya Pek, together known as Tua Di Ya Pek. Previously obscure figures in Chinese vernacular cosmology, following an inversion of religious antecedents from Heaven to Hell deity worship, and gradually rising to prominence in the second half of the twentieth century, Tua Di Ya Pek have now become the most frequently channelled deities in Singapore and Malaysia.

1 A Hokkien term literally meaning 'child diviner'.
2 As distinct from the Chinese 'criminal underworld'.
3 The two terms are used synonymously throughout the book, with 'sub-hells denoting individual locations of post-mortal punishments.

Their unrivalled popularity in the local ritual arenas is therefore a twenty-first-century phenomenon, but is singular to these two locations. This raises the questions of how and why the worship of practitioners' own post-mortal torturers has become among the most predominant forms of contemporary religious expression in Singapore and Malaysia, while elsewhere in the wider present-day Chinese religious diaspora the Underworld and its pantheon remain ostensibly taboo. Addressing these questions, and with the intention of contributing to anthropological theory, I have applied a framework of analysis labelled 'self-perpetuating technologies of religious synthesis' which links developments in the religious landscapes to specific socio-political catalysts triggering the change. Thus, taking the comparative ethnography from Singapore and Malaysia as a single extended case study, the Underworld tradition serves as a vehicle to demonstrate an analytical framework which may be employed in diverse social, political, ethnic and geographic settings linking societal catalysts to new and evolving religious and esoteric trends. A full working explanation of self-perpetuating technologies of religious synthesis will follow in Chapter 2. As the modern[4] Underworld tradition has evolved over approximately seven decades, the theoretical framework incorporates van der Veer's (2016) 'historical sociology'. That is, as "An anthropological perspective [...] based on historical materials as well as fieldwork that raises new questions and highlights differential patterns and their causes" (van der Veer, 2016: 9).

Throughout the book, while carrying the analysis, the ethnographic narrative is intended to provide the reader with unique insights into the lived tradition and into the cosmology upon which contemporary ritual practices are based. To achieve this, what have previously been regarded as conflicting approaches in the study of Chinese vernacular religion have been embraced. These include ontological and dialogic[5] approaches to religious phenomena including *tang-ki* in trance possession states, combined with historical sociology and an interpretative societal analysis. The rationale behind adopting these methodologies and how they become complementary requires elucidation.

While there has been a convergence of anthropological discourses focused on the concept of ontology, there is still no one cohesive approach within the ontological turn (Holbraad & Pedersen, 2017). Instead, one finds a gen-

---

4 'Modern' does not equate to 'modernity' in Hannerz's (1996) vision of a 'global ecumene' with a 'centre and periphery' but is used in a comparative sense to local religious antecedents.
5 See Tedlock & Mannheim's (1995) *The dialogic emergence of culture* for earlier examples, especially the 'Introduction', and DeBernardi's chapter 'Tasting the water' based on two chance encounters with Tua Di Ya Pek between 1979 and 1981.

eralisation of approaches which have been described as 'the anthropology of ontology' (Scott, M. W., 2013). This diversity allows for the selectivity of appropriate theories from within ontological discourse relevant to the subject studied and for further experimentation with ontological methodologies. Inspired by Descola (2013, 2014), M. W. Scott (2007, 2013, 2013a, 2016) and Pedersen's (2012) recent discussions concerning ethnographic research into non-human worlds, I have adopted an ontological approach as an underlying methodological principle in researching efficacy in ritual, but *not* in the analysis of societal influences on the religious landscapes themselves, nor in the interpretation of meaning within them. Analytically, then, I am conceptually opposed to some positions taken by key proponents of the ontological turn, most notably to the notion that meanings "No longer need to be excavated, illuminated, decoded and interpreted" (Henare, Holbraad & Wastell, 2007: 4), and to "An anthropology that holds issues of interpretation at bay" (Henare, Holbraad & Wastell, 2007: 4). In contrast, I maintain that interpretation and meaning are integral both for practitioners and for academics researching systems of religious knowledge, and I do so for the following reasons. The differences in emic interpretations of cosmology between the Underworld traditions in Singapore and Malaysia; divergences in meaning actuated through the influence of distinct transnational cultural flows; and comparisons with developments in Chinese vernacular religion in Taiwan over a similar period all illustrate that meaning is time and location specific, and that interpretation is dependent on differing social and historical circumstances. Both meaning and interpretation are therefore entirely relevant to a comparative study.

Returning then to the ontological influences from which I have drawn, and the rationale behind these choices. Descola (2013, 2014) argues that cultural variation is not dependent of how a universal reality is represented but, rather, by which qualities and interrelationships traverse humans' ontological filters and become actualised at any given time or place. This process of 'ontological predication', rather than producing multiple worldviews of the same complete reality (i.e., the social construction of reality), produces different 'styles of worlding'. In other words, 'ontological filters' determine initial suppositions of what the world contains, including the numerous kinds of beings which populate it, and how these beings interact. As ontological predication involves only piecing together fragmentary elements from all possible existents, it effectively precludes multiple-worlds hypotheses and, in metaphysical terms, the hierarchical domination of one form of ontology or cosmology over another. Adding traction to this last statement, Paleček and Risjord (2012) have noted that if 'things' are the product of interactions between the human and non-human worlds, so too are ontologies, and therefore "No one set of interactions could be regarded as the True Ontology" (Paleček & Risjord, 2012: 12). Applying this understanding ethnographically allows emic ontologies to maintain their integrity, meaning that alterity is to be taken seriously and, as far as possible, understood and represented on its own terms. With this in mind, I feel that rejecting emic perceptions of spiritual efficacy would render practitioners' own claims absurd, thus alienating the social actors, and disengaging them from the discourse that emerges from the research. This, as Escolar notes, "Steals dignity from the events and from the subjects" (Escolar, 2012: 38), and this is a path I have chosen not to tread.

An approximation of this ontological approach has been labelled by Scott (2013) as 'relational non-dualism' or 'flat-ontology', where objects in the broadest sense, from humans to the discarnate, are relational and can metaphysically transform from one thing to another, thus negating the Cartesian law of non-contradiction. A human may therefore be a vessel for deities (a *tang-ki*); a deity (*shen* / 神) may animate an object through embodiment; and the embodied object may transform into a conduit for a deity's efficacy. In contrast to anthropological dualism, which "Has helped to assert the cultural transcendence and political ascendency of Cartesian-based truth claims over much of the rest of the world" (Scott, 2013: 863), relational non-dualism levels the playing-field and prevents the theft of integrity from practitioners, their cosmologies and ritual practices. In Descola's terms, a religious tradition is "A system of incompletely actualised properties, saturated with meaning and replete with agency" (Descola, 2014: 277–278), and I treat Chinese vernacular religion as one such system.

In *Voices from the Underworld*, acknowledging relational non-dualism as an underlying principle while researching *tang-ki* in trance possession states allows the emic voice to be *literally* heard, and to be incorporated constructively into the ethnography. Moreover, this approach readdresses alterity in a way that removes the need to distance oneself philosophically from the religious and ritual phenomena studied. Within Sinology, and in regard to deities and *tang-ki* spirit possession in particular, the academic antecedent has been a denial of emic ontologies, from *tang-ki* "Who claim to have the ability to embody spirits of divine beings" (DeBernardi, 2006: 4) to "There is a kind of role-playing of what the gods might be saying if there were gods" (Jordan, 1972: 84). While utilising these quotes as examples, I mean in no way to detract either from the excellence of the two monographs or from their authors' outstanding contributions to the field, but instead to highlight the potential of an alternative Sinology in the study of Chinese religion. In offering an alternative point of academic departure, this study aims to contribute to wider present-day anthropological discourse concern-

INTRODUCTION 5

ing the interrelationships between sociocultural and spiritual worlds; human agency and the religious objectivation of cosmology; and to discourse related to de-stigmatising the very notion of spirit possession in the contemporary study of esoteric and religious traditions.

Allowing the emic voice to be heard is further facilitated by being "Prepared to learn theoretical lessons from the concepts used by the groups studied, and to adopt (perhaps modified) local concepts into anthropological theory" (Paleček & Risjord, 2012: 3). Otherwise put, by applying ontological and dialogic approaches to the study of religious phenomena, the ethnography is transformed from "Finding ways to question or otherwise qualify presuppositions that stand in the way of 'grasping the native's point of view'" (Holbraad & Pedersen, 2017: 6), into a source of original anthropological theorisation. In this vein, inspired by Pedersen's understanding of the ontological turn as being "Concerned with how anthropologists might get their ethnographic descriptions right [...] a technology of description which allows anthropologists to make sense of their ethnographic material in new and experimental ways" (Pedersen, 2012: 1–2), by analysing the emic voice, a new lexicon of terms to codify the multiplicity of emic descriptions which I encountered in the field has emerged.

For instance, in Chinese vernacular religion deities are depicted in statue form with specific identifiers, these commonly being weapons, decorative items and functional objects. In the Underworld tradition, Tua Ya Pek carries a rattan fan which is wielded as a power-object by *tang-ki* when channelling him. However, when asked, practitioners variously described Tua Ya Pek as "using his fan like a weapon" and replied that "Ghosts fear his fan – it has his power in it", that "It is only powerful when held by Tua Ya Pek" and that "It contains *yin* energy". When I pressed for clarification, in common with Jean DeBernardi's earlier experience in Penang (DeBernardi 1995), I was most commonly advised to 'ask the deity' myself. Similarly, when discussing Tua Di Ya Pek's efficacy, it was variously referred to as '*qi*' (气) or invisible power, *ling hun* (灵魂)[6] or soul, or simply as power drawn from the Underworld. Evaluating practitioners' contrasting responses provided a starting-point for an analysis to locate appropriate terms for active agency within the tradition and for its transmission in ritual. Encapsulating the essence of these emic explanations, new terminology including 'deific efficacy', 'discarnate efficacy' and 'deific embodiment' arose recursively from the research.

This lexicon broadly offers a new and distinct set of descriptive phrases

---

6 *Ling hun* suggests the animating nature of the self, sometimes described as 'life force' or 'vital' energy'; see for example Wikan (1989) and Hook *et al.* (2004).

to concisely frame the metaphysical in religious and esoteric traditions in academic terms. From 'deific efficacy' to 'post-mortal journeys of the soul', the terminology generated may resonate within Sinology and the anthropology of religion, and in related subfields including the 'anthropology of consciousness' and the fledgling field of paranthropology. My hope is that this lexicon will be drawn on and further expanded by Sinologists, and by academics researching ritual, religion and spiritual, new age, occult and esoteric practices, to more uniformly describe emic understandings of the discarnate forces around which such traditions revolve.

The term 'ethnography' itself carries a multiplicity of methods and meanings and therefore requires clarification in regard to my fieldwork among *tang-ki* in trance possession states. I feel that first-hand experience of ritual is a crucial factor alongside observation, active participation leading to a contextual appreciation of a lived ritual tradition. Therefore, from the outset, rather than relying on second-person narratives, wherever possible, often stepping outside of my own comfort zone, I actively participated in *tang-ki*'s rituals either as the subject of a ritual or as an assistant. However, while Edith Turner claimed that to fully understand the religious experience researched, "'Participant observation' in the fullest sense requires taking the final leap and 'going native' in the most complete way possible" (Turner, 1993: 9), I consider this a leap too far, a leap inhibiting the likelihood of a subsequent objective analysis. Instead, alongside experiential participation, I have adopted a dialogic approach to the study of trance possession, "To engage intelligently, empathetically and respectfully" (Bowie, 2013: 25) with Underworld deities as channelled through their *tang-ki*. Influenced by "Cognitive empathetic engagement" (Bowie, 2013), a research methodology intended "To elucidate the object of study rather than become an exercise in self-reflection" (Bowie, 2013: 4), the dialogic approach has been utilised as a fundamental research tool allowing for personal communication and interaction with *tang-ki* before, during and after rituals. Intriguingly, once employed in the field, after *tang-ki* entered a trance possession state, the almost prerequisite social classifications of 'the enthusiastic researcher' and 'the research subject' became largely redundant alongside 'the ontological other'.

A depth of familiarity with this ontological other was mutually nurtured over an eight-year period and has been rendered into print through the use of italics to indicate where I have both observed and participated in a ritual, and where recorded consultations, interviews and discussions with *tang-ki* in trance possession states have been reproduced in print. These dialogues have been included to variously illustrate the principles underlying Underworld deities' popularity; recent developments in Underworld cosmology; the psychological and physiological effects of trance possession; and to contextualise Tua Di Ya Pek's role as channelled through their *tang-ki* in the development of the ritual and material cultures built up around their veneration.

Their inclusion also attempts to respond to Tedlock & Mannheim's (1995) claim of a hierarchical imbalance between 'disciplinary discourse' and 'field discourse' in academic literature, and tries to do so on several levels. First, their reproduction clearly illustrates the dialogic practices upon which most ethnography is based. Second, they demonstrate how alterity may be thematically inversed in dialogue with possessed *tang-ki*, in effect, the ontological other rendering both practitioners and the trained academic the 'relative native'. Third, and of key import, the inclusion of extensive dialogues on issues, objects, rituals and cosmologies directly related to the study facilitates the possibility of further interpretations, insights and theorisations on the part of the reader after the event.

The emphasis on first-person dialogues in the ethnography also evokes insights into both the mindsets and the vibrant and often intense life-worlds of the religious practitioners described, thus affording the reader with as complete a picture as possible of the lived Underworld tradition. To further this end, the monochrome photographs and colour plates add a visual dimension to the ethnography. The dazzling colours of Chinese temple culture provide a visual feast, especially so the lingering images of *tang-ki* rituals, which are graphically and emotionally compelling. In 1973 Margaret Mead argued that it is an ethical responsibility of anthropology as a discipline to preserve records of disappearing 'irreproducible behaviours', and, given the rapidity of development in Singapore and Malaysia's social and religious arenas, the images reproduced capture a temporal snapshot of a lived tradition which is itself in an ongoing process of reinvention.

The book is based on over eight years of research, with continuous periods of fieldwork undertaken in Singapore in 2010, 2011 and 2014 and, sponsored by the Max Planck Institute for the Study of Religious and Ethnic Diversity, in Malaysia in 2015 and 2016. Anxi Chenghuangmiao in Fujian Province, China was visited in 2014 and 2018, and the primary fieldwork sites were all revisited during shorter research trips in 2017 and 2018. Where possible, the fieldwork was undertaken in Mandarin and English. However, in trance possession states the native dialects of the possessing deities become the medium of communication, and I encountered various forms of Hokkien, including a seventeenth-century Anxi variation, as well as Hainanese, Cantonese, Tamil and Malay. As practitioners and temple visitors also hail from multiple dialect groups, several interpreters are commonly on hand during consultations and at major ritual events. Therefore, to ensure the accuracy of on-the-night translations, every interview cited was recorded and later transcribed by local academics fluent in the particular dialect spoken and familiar with the religious tradition. A precise record of the dialogues was therefore produced incorporating the sometimes subtle nuances of insinuation, humour and irony, accompanied by detailed explanations of religious references to which *tang-ki* had alluded.

The structure of the book and outline of chapters

Voices from the Underworld is divided into four parts, each containing three chapters. Following a brief summary of the historical development of Underworld cosmology in Part I, Part II focuses on the Underworld tradition, its cosmology, rituals and material culture in Singapore. This sets a baseline of comparison against which the Malaysian tradition can be contrasted. Part III moves north to Malaysia and concentrates on the evolution of difference between the two Underworld traditions, and the unities and diversities in their ritual and material cultures, and illustrates differing interpretations of Underworld cosmology. Part IV brings together the histography and ethnography to draw conclusions regarding the where and why of the modern Underworld tradition's inception and the timeline of its subsequent geographic diffusion.

Part II: The Underworld tradition in Singapore

Chapter 4 begins by contextualising Underworld deity worship within the broader context of vernacular religion in the Chinese diaspora, and then presents a compendium of Tua Di Ya Pek's contrasting mythologies. The ethnographic narrative begins with an 'oil wok' ritual to prepare medicines for the elderly in Jurong, Singapore, introduces the Underworld tradition's material and ritual cultures and emic perceptions of Hell, and presents a detailed description of a *tang-ki* entering a state of trance possession. The analysis focuses on alcohol consumption and gambling as self-perpetuating mechanisms and, contrasting ethical codes, draws comparisons with Taiwan's ghost temples (Weller, 1999), which became popularised during a similar time period.

Chapter 5 contains two ethnographies emphasising the dialogic approach. The first revolves around a conversation with Tua Ya Pek discussing a new Underworld God of Wealth, and the internal logic underlying the creation of new deities in the expanding Underworld pantheon. The second details a ritual performed by Tua Ya Pek to speed the journey of an aborted 'foetus spirit' (*taishen* / 胎神) through the Underworld, and serves as a comparison to the manipulation of malicious foetus ghosts (*ying ling* / 婴灵) in Malaysia in Chapter 8.[7] Following the foetus ritual, Tua Ya Pek's self-perceptions and physiological sensations while possessing his *tang-ki* are then discussed, providing first-person insights into altered states of perception during trance possession. Analytically, the chapter weighs up the effects of urban redevelopment and governmental promotion of religious harmony as catalysts to unique forms of temple networking and to Tua Di Ya Pek's far-reaching reinvention to explain why, in Singapore's contemporary religious landscape, Hell's enforcers are perceived as the most appropriate deities to approach for assistance both to the living and to the souls of the recently deceased.

Chapter 6 connects the Underworld tradition to graveyards through Lunar Seventh Month (Ghost Month) 'salvation rituals' performed in cemeteries for the souls of ancestors, aborted foetuses and wandering spirits. After outlining the Buddhist origins of Ghost Month and various taboos now associated with it, the ethnography moves to Singapore's Choa Chu Kang Cemetery. The narrative contains two sections, the first describing two distinct rituals in a cemetery plot set aside for babies and aborted foetuses, and the second following a temple's Seventh Month rituals, from applying for cemetery permits to the *tang-ki*-centric conclusion of their Seventh Month rituals. Analytically, the presence of Taoist priests in Singapore's Underworld tradition is assessed with reference to the decennial census, and revisions to the 'Master Plan' (1965) concerning cemeteries are explored as societal catalysts both to the popularisation of the Underworld tradition and to 2017's cemetery rituals in particular. These rituals are analysed in the context of Foucault's 'heterotopias' as 'everyday forms of resistance' (Scott, 1985, 1990) to new and controversial national land policies.

Part III: The Underworld tradition in Malaysia

Providing details from the 'Jade Record' (*Yuli chao chuan*), Chapter 7's ethnography is focused on a model reconstruction of the Underworld illustrating its Ten Courts and a selection of tortures in their sub-hells which has been built as a ritual space and place of worship. Located in Klang, Selangor State, Malaysia, Di Ya Pek's three-day birthday celebrations, which attracted approximately one thousand devotees, provides the chapter's ethnographic setting for the mass channelling of Underworld deities and their subsequent consumption of opium and alcohol alongside the channelling of multiple Chinese Heaven deities and Malay Datuk Gong. The two features

---

[7] The distinction between 'foetus spirits' (*taishen*) and malevolent / malicious or vindictive 'foetus ghosts' (*ying ling*) is important in the context of the two Underworld traditions and will be discussed further in Chapter 8.

of analytical interest which arise from this are the transfiguration of religious norms and the formation of extensive ethno-religious communities based around Underworld deity veneration. The transfiguration materialises in two guises, the first being an inversion of authority in the 'Heaven–human–Underworld' hierarchy seen reflected in the interactions between the possessed *tang-ki*, and second being the mass consumption of intoxicants in temple settings. Both are analysed in the broader context of changing moralities and the role of ethnic self-identity in Malaysia's religious landscape and how, in addressing these issues, the Underworld tradition has become a locus of local community formation.

Moving south to the Muar district of Johor State during Ghost Month, Chapter 8 focuses on the comparative importance of City God temples in Malaysia, and the active role played by Anxi Chenghuangmiao in promoting the contemporary tradition. The first ethnography follows the finale of an elaborate Seventh Month salvation ritual at Muar City God Temple, with particular attention paid to the influence of Mahayana Buddhism and Thai vernacular religion on Malaysia's ritual and material culture. The latter manifests in the use of Thai *luk thep* dolls, appropriated to accommodate the souls of malicious foetus ghosts enlisted into the temple's Underworld spirit army during Ghost Month. As the Malaysian malicious foetus ghost is a reinvention both of vulnerable foetus spirits described in Chapter 5 and of foetus ghosts appropriated into Taiwan's vernacular tradition from Japan (Moskowitz, 1998, 2001), transnational cultural flows and the sociopolitical catalysts affecting them are introduced into the analysis. Returning to the creation of community, the second ethnography focuses on an event formally titled 'Anxi City God's cultural exchange'. Bringing together ten pairs of Tua Di Ya Pek, one pair from each Underworld court, channelled through their *tang-ki*, discussions with them reveal perceptions of postmortal cosmology which are in conflict with their Singaporean counterparts. The analysis therefore compares societal catalysts triggered by Singapore and Malaysia's competing post-1965 political agendas to account for the divergences between the two Underworld traditions' cosmologies.

Returning to central Malaysia to describe two events, Chapter 9 serves to compare south and central Malaysia's Seventh Month ritual traditions. The first ethnography recounts a night-time luck-promoting 'coffin ritual' in Kuala Lumpur where participants lie in a coffin, symbolically dying and entering the Underworld when the coffin lid is closed and re-entering the world of the living as the coffin lid is removed. The ritual is described from the perspective of both participant and observer. As the coffin ritual was appropriated from contemporary Thai Theravada Buddhism, the analysis further examines transnational cultural flows. The second ethnography revisits Klang to recount the ritual release of exorcised spirits which have been trapped in Guinness bottles and stored in the prison cell in the temple's Underworld recreation. Following their release, the chapter concludes by discussing Di Ya Pek's perceptions of the relative passing of time in the Underworld, and an alternative interpretation of the Chinese Underworld's creation.

Part IV: Tracing the origins of the modern Underworld tradition

Relocating to China, Chapter 10 centres on Anxi Chenghuangmiao. The temple's early history and its 1990 relocation from Anxi city centre to the Fengshan Scenic Tourism Area below the graves of Xie Bian and Fan Wujiu are critically investigated, as are its atypical Tua Di Ya Pek mythologies. Analysed in the context of the invention and commoditisation of tradition and of China's changing cultural policies, Anxi Chenghuangmiao's reinvention is associated with self-perpetuating its own City God tradition, and with Tua Di Ya Pek's recent overseas popularisation. Continuing this line of enquiry, the chapter concludes by describing the opening of a new annex in front of Xie Bian and Fan Wujiu's graves, an annex first conceptualised in Klang, Malaysia, and evaluating the contestation of meaning and counter-claims to provenance of the new ritual site.

Owing to the implausibility of Anxi Chenghuangmiao providing the tradition's genesis, Chapter 11 returns to Malaysia to trace the modern Underworld tradition's origins. Following a historical trail of oral accounts, the ethnography turns to 1950s George Town, Penang, and to legends surrounding Malaysia's eldest City God temple. In the absence of textual records, oral narratives present the earliest recollections of not only where but also how the modern Underworld tradition most likely began. Substantiated by a Tua Di Ya Pek mythology from George Town's eldest Underworld temple, local history and folklore converge, suggesting George Town as the modern Underworld tradition's most likely point of origin.

As neither Xie Bian nor Fan Wujiu's popular mythology originated in either Anxi or Penang, and allowing for the complexities of cultural transmission, Chapter 12, the final chapter, begins by proposing the most likely timeline and trajectory of the Underworld tradition's geographical spread, both in and between Malaysia and Singapore. The versatility of the framework of analysis is then demonstrated by being applied to religious developments over a corresponding timeframe in Taiwan to explain why a similar Underworld tradition has not developed there. The potential benefits of combining ontological, dialogic, participatory and interpretative approaches to the study of religious and esoteric traditions are then clarified and discussed, and final conclusions are drawn.

On a final note, Hanyu Pinyin has been used for the romanisation of both Mandarin and Hokkien terms, the choice of language coinciding with current local usage. Proper nouns, including the Chinese names of deities and their titles, of individuals and places, as well as the English names of scriptures, are printed in regular font. Other non-English terms, including the names of festivals, rituals, religious texts, key ritual objects and emic philosophical concepts, have been reproduced in italics, and for common nouns Chinese characters have been provided in parentheses on their first use.

Part I
Setting the scene

1

異

The modern Underworld tradition

Multiple narratives

In Chinese vernacular religion the central factor around which all else revolves is identifiable deities, 'identification' being a defining factor of 'deity', as, in its absence, the specific ritual and material cultures built up around their worship would crumble. In the vernacular tradition, consulting deities in anthropomorphic form or embodied through their *tang-ki* is an ordinary practice, much in the same manner as attending liturgical religious services in world religions. Both the individual and congregational approaches are fundamental to the way in which humans interact with discarnate entities, as is the intentionality to change material or emotional circumstances through deific intervention. While the external trappings and cosmologies[1] on which rituals are based may be observed and analysed, in Chinese vernacular religion the key element for practitioners is the existence of deific efficacy, ostensibly as manifested and directed through *tang-ki* in ritual. From the emic perspective, a *tang-ki* in trance possession is a deity incarnate and, through the *tang-ki*, devotees can freely communicate directly with their deities.

In both Singapore and Malaysia the majority of practitioners are descendants of Minnan speakers[2] from Fujian Province and coastal regions of

---

[1] The terms 'cosmology' and 'cosmological' are used in this book in the context of Chinese religious beliefs, practices and philosophies relating to "The world as a totality of all phenomena in space and time" (Howell, 1996: 157).
[2] The largest Minnan group speaks local variations of the Hokkien dialect, with smaller Teochew, Hainanese and Cantonese linguistic groups. The presence of multiple dialect groups and the lack of a unified culture with established lineages and ritual specialists has given *tang-ki* more scope to innovate in the Chinese diaspora.

southeast China. Therefore, while two political systems and different combinations of cultural influences have affected the development of religious trends in each location, practitioners would have originally shared similar cosmologies and traditions based around ancestral halls and the worship of Heaven deities. Until the early 1970s their primary religious cosmologies and associated material and ritual cultures were largely analogous with those of Taiwan and other locations in Southeast Asia's Chinese diaspora. However, changes in the religious landscapes have become increasingly diverse, with a growing emphasis on Underworld deity worship, and modifications have been occurring with ever-increasing rapidity.

While the private worship of ancestors and deities at home or temple altars remains the most widespread religious practice in both locations, Underworld altars and their *tang-ki* have now become a major locus of group ritual activities in Singapore and Malaysia. The primary ethnographic narrative is therefore centred on the pivotal role of Underworld deities as channelled through their *tang-ki* and the rituals they perform, which support the invention, reinterpretation and inversion of religious antecedents which Hell deity worship has entailed.

The second narrative contextualises the contemporary Underworld tradition's ritual and material cultures in a historic framework by outlining the long-term development of Chinese post-mortal cosmology. A summary beginning from the Shang dynasty (1600–1046 BCE) 'Yellow Springs' era, encompassing the first-century CE import of Buddhism and its subsequent influence on early Taoist cosmology, and an introduction to significant medieval morality tracts are therefore provided in Chapter 3. This narrative continues in the ethnography, Chapter 6 charting the evolution of Ghost Month cosmology, and, returning to the influence of morality tracts, most notably the Qing dynasty 'Jade record'[3], analysing its recent reinterpretation in the Underworld tradition in the context of present-day criminality and ethics in Malaysia.

Prior to Tua Di Ya Pek's popularisation, Underworld deities were depicted in statue form in City God temples, and in a small number of temples dedicated to the Underworld deity Dongyue Dadi,[4] but were not channelled through *tang-ki*. I therefore use the term 'modern Underworld tradition' to distinguish the post-1950s tradition centred on the channelling of Underworld deities in front of altars dedicated to the Underworld pantheon, or in temples devoted entirely to the worship of Hell deities, from

---

3 Anonymous author, also referred to as 'The Jade Register'.
4 Currently in Singapore there are seven City God temples of varying importance (four built before 1970) and one dedicated to Dongyue Dadi; and in Malaysia, eleven City God temples (two predating 1970) and one Dongyue Dadi temple.

earlier forms of Chinese vernacular religious practice. As Hell's two most illustrious enforcers are now most commonly identified as the posthumously promoted souls of two individuals, Xie Bian and Fan Wujiu, whose graves now lie above the present-day location of Anxi City God Temple (Anxi Chenghuangmiao) in Fujian, China, the third narrative revolves around Anxi Chenghuangmiao's influence on and participation in the modern Underworld tradition.

The structure of and developments in temple landscapes are inevitably influenced by the changing political and economic characteristics of the societies in which they are located. The analytical framework therefore looks to recent societal catalysts to account for the move away from the worship of Heaven deities and to explain the increasing popularity and channelling of Underworld deities. Therefore, and at the core of the analysis, the fourth narrative encompasses Singapore and Malaysia's own post-independence development, where two contrasting approaches to social cohesion and the construction of strong nation-states have furnished the socio-political and ethnocultural catalysts for the inversion of religious antecedents required to render the veneration of Hell deities not only among the most popular forms of temple worship, but also as normative. The framework of analysis and an overview of recent socio-political developments influencing the two temple landscapes are detailed in Chapter 2.

Locating appropriate terminology to describe the 'religion of the masses'

Academics have coined a variety of terms to describe the religion practised by the lay masses. These include '*shenism*'[5] (Elliott, 1990); 'popular religion' (Bell, 1992; Chau, 2006; Teiser, 1995); the worship of 'gods, ghosts and ancestors' (Ahern, 1973; Jordan, 1972; Wolf, 1974); and perhaps most commonly, 'folk religion' (Cohen, 1977; Harrell, 1979). Primiano (1995) suggested that in relation to institutionalised orthodox traditions, by designating non-orthodox traditions with an 'unofficial religious status', such terminology "Residualizes the religious lives of believers and at the same time reifies the authenticity of religious institutions as the exemplar of human religiosity" (Primiano, 1995: 39). In regard to religiosity and the vernacular tradition, lay religious practitioners outnumber the orthodox Taoist and Buddhist clergies in Singapore and Malaysia by many thousands to one, and it is the lived rather than the textual traditions which dominate practitioners' religious lives. In light of this, Primiano's definition of 'vernacular religion' most closely matches my own approach to research, that is, "As it

[5] Deity worship.

is lived: as human beings encounter, understand, interpret, and practice it [...] with special attention to the process of religious belief [...] the verbal, behavioural, and material expressions of religious belief [...] and the ultimate object of religious belief" (Primiano, 1995: 44–45). I have therefore employed Primiano's term to describe the broader religion of which the Underworld tradition is a part, namely, 'Chinese vernacular religion'.[6] This choice is in no way intended to devalue either previous scholarship or the orthodox traditions themselves. In practice, orthodox rituals are still performed at many vernacular religious temples' events, and their metaphysical contributions which have filtered, albeit in a diluted and renegotiated form, into Chinese vernacular religion and its temple culture are still relevant today.

However, while the orthodox traditions have provided a scriptural foundation underlying the development of contemporary Chinese vernacular religion and Underworld cosmology, as the vernacular tradition is predominantly based on the transmission of oral traditions (Chan, 2006; Elliott, 1990; Tong, 1989), the 'knowledge buffet'[7] from which it draws is far broader. Present-day vernacular religion variously incorporates aspects of Animism; indigenous and local deities and imported ritual traditions; imperial deities and traditions dating back to the Shang dynasty (Adler, 2002); Confucian ethics; elements derived from the diverse schools of Mahayana Buddhism and orthodox Taoism (DeBernardi, 2002; Harrell & Perry, 1982; Pas, 1979); and reconceptualised and newly invented rituals, material objects and cosmologies. In total, these represent a veritable knowledge buffet where inconsistent and sometimes conflicting varieties of knowledge which are "Only partly consciously and rationally planned or reasoned" (Aspen, 2001: 17) may be selected by a diner where there is no definitive correct meal. In other words, unrestricted by institutional or scriptural directives, vernacular religion may diversify easily, establishing new cosmological and ritual precedents in the process.

Deification and pantheons: the centrality of the human soul

While philosophically it is possible to analyse the nature of deities in terms of their efficacy (*ling* / 灵) or spiritual nature (*hun* / 魂), the constituent

---

6 The terms 'popular religion', '*shenism*', 'folk religion' and now 'Chinese vernacular religion' have been coined in academia to distinguish between the orthodox and lay traditions and are not used by Chinese religionists themselves. Instead, most Chinese religionists in Singapore, and increasingly so in post-2000 Malaysia, refer to themselves as Taoist, with a diminishing number self-identifying with Buddhism even though Buddhists still outnumber Taoists in the latest census.
7 A term first coined by Aspen (2001).

elements are variable and separable and therefore as unquantifiable as the whole. Historically, the soul has been conceptualised as being divisible in nature, the earliest archaeological evidence of this hailing from approximately 100,000 Shang dynasty oracle bones. It was during this era that the distinction between the earthly *po* / 魄 (*yin* / 阴) and numinous *hun* (*yang* / 阳) elements of the soul were first postulated (Thompson, 1979). Following death, the spiritual *hun* essence of the soul was thought to ascend to Heaven as an ancestral spirit and, if provided with sufficient offerings, to dispense blessings and operate as an intermediary between Heaven's elite and its own descendants. The deceased, in effect, acquired more efficacy in ancestral form than they had possessed when alive. With the power to positively affect the lives of their descendants, they were therefore attributed with capacities akin to, but weaker than, deities (Thompson, 1979). This aspect of Shang cosmology has endured into the present.

The *hun* or 'soul' of ancestors and of deities both consist of *yang* energy, thus allowing for the deification of humans and the promotion of ancestral spirits to the rank of deity. The distinction between the two is that deities possess greater efficacy, meaning that while ancestors can influence the lives of their descendants, deities can affect the lives of any individual and, with sufficient efficacy, potentially benefit entire communities, regions, professions and nations. Once deified, a stylised anthropomorphic image is created and worshipped in statue form on home and temple altars and two-way communication may then be initiated through divination whereby a deity may answer simple 'yes' 'no' questions by manipulating divination blocks (*bue* / 筊). Complex human–deity interactions occur when the latter are channelled through their *tang-ki*.

Spirit possession depends on the philosophical concept of the divisible nature of the soul, and on a spirit medium's *hun* soul (the *yang* element) leaving their body, thus creating a vacuum to be occupied by the *hun* of a deity. Elliott (1990) noted that the *tang-ki*'s own *hun* are taken care of by other Heaven deities, and *tang-ki* that I interviewed variously reported that their soul remains in a receptacle in the temple, for instance, the deity's censer or statue, or is guarded by the temple's deities, most often by their own Underworld generals.

Ling is accumulative and diminishing in nature, thereby allowing a deity to increase in power relative to sacrifices and worship received. The process of transference is activated by the offering of incense (*baibai* / 拜拜) when a small portion of the worshipper's own *ling*,[8] carried by incense smoke, is transferred through highly focused concentration on the object of worship.

---

8 Sometimes referred to as '*qi*' by practitioners.

Conversely, in the absence of worship, a deity's efficacy diminishes. When its *ling* is virtually exhausted it may revert to a lower status as ancestor or ghost, reincarnate, or cease to exist. Deities may therefore emerge and later disappear from the religious landscape, a fact attested to by the absence of those mentioned in historical texts or represented on artefacts but no longer present on contemporary temple altars.

The expansion of and appropriation between Chinese religious pantheons is historically documented, and the pragmatic appearance of new deities to fulfil contemporary needs is ongoing. The latter is now most apparent in the Underworld tradition and, in comparison to historical precedents, is distinctive due to the cosmological inversion of emphasis involved. In an essentially pragmatic tradition, *tang-ki* spirit possession illustrates how discarnate forces have been moulded by human design in such a way as to allow for human control over them through ritual and symbolic means. In the Underworld tradition, the no-nonsense elevation in rank of Tua Di Ya Pek on temple altars, and when channelled through their *tang-ki*, adheres to this imperative. Spirit possession by Hell's enforcers may therefore be seen as illustrative of the capacity of human ingenuity to incorporate eschatological convictions centred on post-mortal punishments into the religious life-worlds of practitioners as a means of positively influencing the occurrences and episodes that characterise everyday human existence. These deities and the rituals they perform now lie at the heart of vernacular religious practice in Singapore and Malaysia, and, therefore, of this book. However, it is the inversion of cosmological emphasis allowing for the promotion, centrality and channelling of Hell deities, and the character of Underworld deity's rituals and paraphernalia that renders the modern Underworld tradition a unique and new field of study.

2

Analysis: a baseline of comparison

Framework of analysis

The framework of analysis contributes methodologically to the study of Chinese vernacular religion through the contextualisation of causality, linking developments in the Underworld tradition, through the ethnographic narrative, to Singapore and Malaysia's differing socio-political and ethnocultural agendas. In doing so, specific societal catalysts are isolated which, intentionally or inadvertently, have triggered reactions within the religious traditions, leading to singular developments in each religious landscape. These include new patterns of temple networking and community formation, and innovations in the material culture which require additional or adapted ritual forms for their incorporation. The book's key argument is therefore that specific historic and ongoing socio-political developments in Singapore and Malaysia have been conducive to an atypical inversion of religious emphasis in Chinese vernacular religion, resulting in the gradual transition from the worship and channelling of Heaven deities in Chinese temples to the worship and channelling of predominantly Hell deities in Singapore and Malaysia's contemporary religious landscapes.

As noted in the Introduction, the technologies employed in the diversification of religious antecedents are located within an analytical framework labelled as 'self-perpetuating technologies of religious synthesis', a theory which considers the combinations of possible societal catalysts for the development of specific religious trends. In this instance, the theory is applied to account for the founding and popularisation of the modern Underworld tradition; for its continuation; and for the evolution of difference between the traditions in Singapore and Malaysia.

The individual 'technologies of religious synthesis' are drawn from two existing discourses. First, from the politics of syncretism incorporating 'appropriation', where "Members of one culture are taking something that originates in another cultural context [...] Sometimes items are freely transferred from one culture to another" (Young & Brunk, 2009: 3–4); 'absorption', where in the process of acculturation "Incorporation involves some kind of transformation, some kind of deconstruction and reconstruction which converts them to people's own meanings and projects" (Stewart & Shaw, 1994: 18–19); and transfiguration, hybridisation and transfiguring hybridisation (Goh, 2009), where "Transfiguration refers to the changing of forms of practices without the shift in essential meanings [and] hybridisation refers to the change in meaning with little change to forms of religious practice" (Goh, 2009: 113). Second, from a broadening interpretation of Hobsbawm and Ranger's (1983) 'invention of tradition' to include the reinvention, reinterpretation, inversion and the Sinification of tradition. In addition, variations in the selectivity of, and emphasis on, differing cosmological and ritual precedents and the influence of transnational cultural flows have been integrated into the framework. Analysis of the ethnographic data illustrates that these various technologies of religious synthesis have been triggered in reaction to societal catalysts resulting in religious transformation, and that, as such, as forms of adaptation to either opportunity or adversity, these technologies function as 'self-perpetuating mechanisms' for the wider religious tradition. Moreover, in some instances it is not only possible to link individual societal catalysts to specific developments in the material culture, but also to illustrate how the new material elements are themselves catalysts to the development of additional ritual forms to accommodate them. As causality plays a hand in the addition of material objects, causal connections may be traced back to specific societal catalysts triggering their inclusion. Incorporating historical sociology into the analytical framework allows macro-level societal stimuli, including nationalism, urban redevelopment, legislative directives, ethnic prejudice and transnational cultural flows, via technologies of religious synthesis, to be connected to specific religious developments, the effects of which can be observed on the micro level, manifested in the ritual and material cultures of each religious landscape. The following example is illustrative of this process.

Historically, whips were the first man-made object to cross the sound barrier and, as with lightning, where the heat generated causes the rapid expansion of surrounding air to accelerate past the speed of sound, both result in a shock wave causing a sharp crack – the latter followed by the rumble of thunder as the sound dissipates. Currently, dragon-handled whips, an element of material culture incorporated from orthodox Taoism, are now used for multiple purposes, but their *extensive* use in Singapore's vernacular tradition to dispel malevolent forces dates back only to the 1970s. In the intervening period, new ritual forms have developed around the material objects, culminating in present-day ritual performances of elaborately choreographed synchronised whipping. Now ubiquitous in Singapore's *tang-ki* temple culture, the most complex displays are seen during 'tours of the borders' (*yew keng* / 游境), when deity statues are taken out of their temples to pay respects to other temples' deities. On arrival, between one and ten members of each temple meet at the visited temple's threshold and an intricate performance ensues where each group in turn steps forward, whips the air with a flourish, steps back and bows. Following established etiquette, there is now a 'correct' way to hold and flourish the whip, to move to and fro and to genuflect, all being new conventions in Singapore's ritual culture. These new ritual forms developed, and then did so rapidly, only after the Dangerous Fireworks Act of 1972, which prohibited the possession and discharge of fireworks in Singapore. Prior to this, as is still the case among affluent temples in Malaysia and throughout Taiwan, firecrackers serve the same purpose. However, the active agency in dispelling malevolent forces is neither the whips nor the explosive power of gunpowder, but their imitation of thunder, the weapon used by the deity Leigong to dispel evil and punish wrongdoers in orthodox and vernacular mythology (Werner, 1922). A clear link can therefore be drawn from the development of new ritual forms to accommodate, legitimise and normalise the use of dragon-headed whips, back to the Dangerous Fireworks Act of 1972, which provided the initial societal catalyst to change.

Returning to the importance of van der Veer's (2016) historical sociology, the two introductions that follow provide a historical baseline of comparison and an initial analysis of societal catalysts that have triggered technologies of religious synthesis. These provide a starting point to account for the inversion of tradition vis-à-vis Heaven deity worship, and for the idiosyncratic diversities of tradition described in Parts II and III of the book, which Hell deity worship engenders and validates.

Introduction to Singapore's secular and religious landscapes

Following the election victory of the People's Action Party (PAP) in 1959, while the British maintained control of military and foreign affairs, under the leadership of Lee Kuan Yew, Singapore became in effect an internally self-governing state. On 9 August 1965, following expulsion from an unsuccessful twenty-three-month merger with Malaysia, Singapore gained formal independence as the Republic of Singapore. Based on revisions to the Master Plan of 1958, the PAP, adopting a multicultural and nationalistic agenda, embarked on the nationwide modernisation of industry, agriculture, commerce, transportation, public housing, education, public services, land use, the military and central administrative bureaucracy. Clause 11.15, 'Planning for rapid expansion and growth'[1] listed three primary objectives, each of which would require the relocation or destruction of religious buildings, thus initiating the reconstruction of a reshaped temple landscape. These were "(1) The comprehensive redevelopment of the central parts of the city ... (2) the containment of the existing city by a green belt to combat urban sprawl ... (3) the construction of new towns well removed from the existing city".[2] Thus, in Singapore self-perpetuating technologies of religious synthesis were catalysed largely in reaction to governmental engineering implemented to reshape the multi-ethnic social and religious landscapes.

A priority of the PAP was to promote a primary sense of Singaporean identity (Tan, 2002, 2008), and it therefore undertook "Elaborate measures to ensure that nationalism and nationhood are intrinsic values woven into cultural and community discourse" (Gomes, 2009: 37). With this goal in sight, the PAP promoted religious harmony through urban relocation by bringing multi-ethnic communities together in Housing Development Board (HDB) estates. The ethnic integration policy of HDB ownership required the destruction of older villages and was intended to create a patriotic nation-state where "If one owns an asset in the country, one would stand to defend it" (Teo et al., 2004: 98). These policies were not intended to act as catalysts for technologies of religious synthesis; nonetheless, their implementation, as will be shown, has reshaped the religious landscape, especially so in regard to *tang-ki* temples. Prior to urban redevelopment, the Chinese religious landscape and its temple networks closely resembled contemporaneous 'ceremonial circles' observed in Taiwan (Lin, 1986, 1989; Skoggard, 1996), dominated by village temples financially supported by local residents who worshipped the Heaven and local tutelary deities housed in them.

Prior to urban relocation, long-established village temples hosted resident *tang-ki*, most commonly channelling one of their temple's main deities. During the relocation process unregistered temples, that is to say, the majority of temples, were demolished, thus removing prior ceremonial circles from Singapore's religious landscape and leaving a pool of itinerant *tang-ki* free to affiliate with temples and deities of their choice. Ironically, relocating Singapore's temples and population, coupled with restrictions

---

1 *State of Singapore Master Plan first review, 1965. Report of survey.* Ministry of National Development Planning Department, http://eservice.nlb.gov.sg/data2/BookSG/publish/b/b8e0c6ac-7ea4-4e81-8db4-e437d70b5097/web/html5/index.html?opf=tablet/BOOKSG.xml&launchlogo=tablet/BOOKSG_BrandingLogo_.png&pn=8
2 *State of Singapore Master Plan first review, 1965.*

on land available for religious buildings, resulted in the construction of numerous unofficial temples. Hue summarised that "Village temples have become a thing of the past, replaced by spirit medium altars set up within the government-built HDB apartment buildings" (Hue, 2012: 165). *Tang-ki* temples have also been established in unconventional ritual spaces ranging from discarded cargo containers to industrial warehouses and, to date, many have remained unregistered. These unofficial temples, initially founded by *tang-ki* who had managed to secure temple relics from their villages to legitimise their new altars, and later by their assistants-become-*tang-ki*, soon evolved as experimental ritual grounds. Here, Underworld deity cults and their associated material culture, including the mass consumption of alcohol, opium[3] and cigarettes by possessed *tang-ki*, developed largely beneath the political radar of the state.

While the material developments in Singapore's temple landscape are self-evident, noting the singular inversion of cosmological emphasis involved in the radical choice of Hell over Heaven deities by *tang-ki* and devotees alike requires contextual explanations. These will come to light as the multiple narratives unfold, but as a preliminary observation, I propose that a pre-existing factor in Singapore is a collective historic memory, namely, of the perpetration of massacres by the Japanese military police (*kempeitai*) in their 'purge through purification' (*suqing* / 肅清[4]) during the 1941–1945 occupation. In the popular consciousness this contributed to the perception of an overabundance of wandering and malevolent spirits that needed to be controlled. Thus, early in the Underworld tradition's development, historical memory and fear of wandering spirits became a common, though perhaps subliminal, contributing factor behind the gradual rise to dominance of Underworld over the Heaven deities in the temple landscape. After all, who better to control malevolent spirits than the deities charged with their capture and subsequent return to the Underworld?

The Underworld is associated with death, and death with graveyards. Elliott claims that when the first burial grounds in Singapore were removed in the 1950s, possibly due to the death of immediate family members during the war, there was little resistance from local residents, with only a few cases of bones being claimed by survivors for reinterment (Elliott, 1990: 36). However, in the following decades several related societal catalysts were brought into play. First, in 1965 the Master Plan for land use identified cemeteries as available land for new developments, and in 1972 laws were passed

---

3 The religious consumption of opium in Singapore rapidly diminished after the implementation of the 1973 Misuse of Drugs Act, and opium use by *tang-ki* is now negligible.
4 Japanese, *Kakyō Shukusei*, meaning 'purging of Overseas Chinese'.

empowering the government to close cemeteries without giving any reason (Kong & Yeoh, 2003: 57). Thereafter, the HDB removed graves to make space for new urban housing. This was a case of institutional pragmatism backed by government directives prevailing over the dominant religious tradition, as, in vernacular religious perception, one portion of the soul remains in the grave so long as the body has been buried with correct ritual and sacrifices continue to be offered to it. If these conditions are not met, the soul becomes restless and transforms into a malevolent spirit or vengeful ghost, *gui* (鬼), to haunt its descendants. Compounding the perceived threat of malevolent spirits, in 1998 the National Environment Agency (NEA) implemented a regulation requiring cadavers to be exhumed after fifteen years for cremation, to make room for new burials to take place. Together, I argue, at least in Singapore's collective consciousness, these factors generated a demand for religious specialists to control malevolent ghosts; a collective consciousness which voted with its collective feet and decided that Underworld deities were best qualified to perform this task. While this 'grave' issue is brought up to date in Chapter 6 with examples of Ghost Month cemetery rituals, this particular factor is, metaphorically speaking, only scraping the analytical surface, and further societal catalysts fuelling the rapid popularisation of Singapore's Underworld tradition will be examined within the ethnography.

Introduction to Malaysia's secular and religious landscapes

Following the Second World War, in 1946 the territories on Peninsular Malaysia were unified as the Malayan Union, later becoming the Federation of Malaya in 1948, the gaining independence on 31 August 1957. On 16 September 1963, after integrating North Borneo, Sarawak and Singapore into the union, it renamed itself Malaysia. Amid ethnic tensions, Singapore, as mentioned, was expelled from Malaysia in 1965. While both countries had multi-ethnic and multi-religious populations, in contrast to Singapore, the approach implemented to nation building in post-1969 Malaysia, rather than being based on multiculturalism, focused instead on ethnic exclusion and the socio-political promotion of ethnic Malays, the *bumiputra*.[5]

Looking back first to the Japanese occupation, and then to the Malayan Union and early Federation of Malaya post-war periods, two interrelated events occurred which drastically changed the population's demographics. These led to the widespread dispersion of new ethnic Chinese villages, thus

---

5 A term coined by the second Prime Minister of Malaysia, Abdul Razak Hussein, to describe those with one or both parents being Muslim Malay, and indigenous natives of Sabah and Sarawak.

forming the foundations from which much of Malaysia's present-day Chinese temple landscape has grown. The first event transpired during the Japanese occupation, when the mass execution of ethnic Chinese which began in Singapore was followed by the widespread and indiscriminate massacres of ethnic Chinese across Malaysia's urban and more densely populated rural areas (Blackburn, 2009). This provided the catalyst for those who could to flee the execution squads and join the Malayan Communist Party's (MCP) guerrilla forces in the jungle (Strauch, 1981). Even though the MCP was operating in cooperation with the British colonial administration, in the eyes of the post-war colonial bureaucracy the dispersed Chinese MCP fighters, displaced and lacking land deeds, became 'squatters' (Strauch, 1981). Robinson (1956) estimated their total number to have risen to 400,000 by the end of the war. Had they then returned to their homes, the following string of events might not have unravelled, but most chose to remain in the jungle and to continue fighting alongside the MCP.

The second event was triggered by the transformation of the anti-Japanese MCP's guerrilla army into an anti-colonial movement which targeted isolated European estates and remote vestiges of the colonial administration (Winzeler, 2010). Adopting a predominantly non-violent strategy, the British colonial government declared a state of 'Emergency' under which it implemented the 'Briggs Plan' (1948). Based on the concept of removing the MCP's supply lines, in a two-year programme Chinese 'squatter' villages were destroyed and their populations were placed in enclosed guarded settlements. By the time the fences were removed in 1958, permanent houses, shops and schools had already been established, and most of the 574 compounds remained as new, single-ethnicity villages. Over half of these villages had populations exceeding 1,000, which, in the Malaysian context, distinguished them as urban rather than rural populations. In later years, as the expansion of these villages into townships was boosted by the urbanisation of ethnic Malays and Indians from nearby plantations, multi-ethnic townships developed, many of which now contain Malay majority populations. Nonetheless, this early period of forced relocation accounts for the large ethnic Chinese population and temple networks now running down Malaysia's west coast from Selangor State and Kuala Lumpur (Chapters 7 and 9) to southern Malaysia, and includes a major concentration of Chinese temples in Johor State (Chapter 8). In contrast to post-relocation in Singapore, these temples, many of which moved from plantations into villages, characterise the organisational structure of Singapore's pre-urban-renewal ceremonial circles.

The villages themselves had been well equipped by the colonial authorities, and "Many Malays tended to resent that the amenities – schools, houselots, electricity (necessary to illuminate the barbed wire perimeter fences by night), piped or well water" (Strauch, 1981: 63) provided by the British were retained by the squatters. This contributed to the increasing resentment felt among Malays regarding Chinese social and economic dominance – a dominance which, Freedman argued, "Led to the institutionalisation of Malay special rights in the Independence Constitution of 1957" (Freedman, 2001: 416). However, the inequalities were real, not imagined. For instance, in 1947 the average per capita income among Chinese was 656 Malaysian dollars,[6] as compared to the average income of 258 Malaysian dollars among Malays (Tajuddin, 2012). In terms of commercial land capital, 299 estates covering 26,927 acres were Chinese owned, as compared to 23 Malay-owned estates comprising under 5,000 acres in total (Tajuddin, 2012). The disparities extended beyond land ownership and wealth. For instance, in higher education, during the 1960s, before preferential admission policies were granted to Malays, 1,596 bachelor's degrees were awarded to Chinese students graduating in mathematics, engineering, technology and the natural sciences, as compared to only 73 received by Malays (Sowell, 2016).

Malay 'special rights' enshrined in the constitution would soon lead to the active promotion of Malay interests under the New Economic Policy (NEP) of 1971, and the National Development Policy (NDP) which superseded it in 1990 (Carstens, 2005). First though, a catalyst to change was required, and this was furnished by the race riots of 13 May 1969. Sparked by a post-election parade by the defeated opposition parties[7] to celebrate unexpected electoral gains, the procession was "Perceived as abusive to Malay sensibilities" (Freedman, 2001: 417) and as "A challenge to Malay political supremacy"[8] (DeBernardi, 2004: 114) and, as a result, "Violent anti-Chinese race riots erupted in Kuala Lumpur" (Landa, 2016: 3). "After dozens had been killed and many shops and houses had been attacked ... violence started to spread to the nearby state of Selangor and other parts of the country in the following days and weeks" (Mueller, 2014: 13), moving to Penang State in the north and as far as Johor State in the south. It still remains unclear how many Chinese were killed or displaced.

Following the race riots, the Malay nationalist Mahathir Mohamad wrote *The Malay Dilemma* (1970), in which he posited that the Malay race are the indigenous people (*bumiputras*) of Malaysia; that the sole national language is the Malay language and all other races must learn it; and that a programme of affirmative action was required to correct the imbalance created

---

6 The official name of the Malaysian currency until 1975.
7 The Democratic Action Party, which had campaigned against *bumiputra* privileges, and the Chinese-dominated Malaysian People's Movement Party.
8 The interpretation of Malay leaders addressing a pro-government demonstration staged in response to the parade.

by Malaysian Chinese hegemony in business. Meanwhile, Malaysia's largest political party, the Islamic-based United Malays National Organisation (UMNO) "Embarked on a path of reconstructing the political system to reinforce its power" (Lee, 2002: 178), a cause for concern among the ethnic Chinese population, as the party's purpose included "Defending and developing Islam, the official religion of the country ... advancing the economy of the Malays and *bumiputera* especially, [and to] guarantee the position of the National Language (Bahasa Melayu) as the sole official language".[9] The 1969 riots had provided the necessary socio-political catalyst to make this a reality, and this materialised in the formulation and enactment of the NEP from 1971 to 1990 and in the political recognition and rise to power of Mahathir Mohamad as Malaysia's fourth Prime Minister (1981–2003), to implement the second phase of the NEP. In the words of the soon-to-be Minister of Home affairs (1973–1981) Muhammad Ghazali bin Shafi, "The politics of this country has been, and must remain for the foreseeable future, native [i.e. Malay] based: that was the secret of our stability and our prosperity and that is a fact of political life which no one can simply wish away" (Lee, 2002: 178).

Under the NEP, Malaysia's ethnic Chinese became "Acutely aware that language, education and employment policies favouring Malays, or *bumiputra*, have impacted Chinese communal political influence and economic opportunities" (Freedman, 2001: 418) as the UMNO systematically took control of the state apparatus, including the police, judiciary and armed forces. Having been marginalised in the economic and political realms, the next political assault was intended to impact on Chinese cultural identity through official attempts to eradicate Chinese language as a medium of secondary and higher education. This was undertaken by consecutive measures prohibiting the use of Chinese language in the classroom, including the temporary promotion of English to replace Chinese as a medium of education. Chinese language, as Cao notes, clearly plays "A vital role in maintaining continuity and transmitting Chinese cultural values" (Cao, 2006: 44), and, after the removal of English from the education system, "The Malay language became the exclusive language of both secondary and university education" (Carstens, 2005: 150). As expressed by one Chinese school teacher, "The Malays were united by Islam and the Malay language, but Malaysian Chinese lacked any single unifying symbol" (Carstens, 2005: 175–176). Clearly, the teacher was not yet a Chinese religionist.

As religion permeates most areas of Chinese life, from the placing of the

---

9 UMNO constitution clause 3, subclauses 3.3, 3.4 and 3.5; web.archive.org/web/20120229132114/http://umno-online.com/?page_id=2787

Kitchen God over the family stove to choosing auspicious dates for naming a baby and burying the dead, I would suggest that in Malaysia the reproduction of a Chinese religious identity significantly overlaps with the reproduction of a Chinese cultural identity, as Chinese language, whether Mandarin or other local dialect, is a prerequisite of the religious tradition. The gradual erosion of the Chinese education system thus provided a powerful societal catalyst, the reaction to which has been the gradual promotion of Chinese religion in lieu of Chinese-language education as a means of cultural transmission. Based on faith in the discarnate, an intangible commodity rather than a quantifiable measure of socio-political dominance, temples began to substitute for classrooms in the production and perpetuation of a Chinese cultural identity. In contrast to Singapore, ethnic inequality and the gradual erosion of the Chinese education system have led both to an increase in the overall number of temples and to the cultural significance attached to them. Catalysed by cultural adversity, Malaysia's temples have played an increasing role in maintaining the internal cohesion and integrity of ethnic Chinese communities, the communities themselves thus becoming the self-perpetuating mechanism sustaining a temple culture in which the Underworld tradition has flourished. The role of temples in cementing ethno-religious communities and, in particular, the appeal of Underworld temples in community formation will be illustrated ethnographically in Chapters 7 and 8.

Referring back to the 1969 race riots, their significance, as summarised by Jean DeBernardi, is that "The event profoundly traumatized Chinese Malaysians, leaving many with a mistrust of Malays" (DeBernardi, 2004: 114). Casting this in a positive light, I would suggest that this mistrust has reinforced the need for social cohesion and the cross-generational transmission of Chinese culture in urban centres and among village-based and emerging rural ethnic Chinese communities. In a comparative context, while disparate socio-political influences in Singapore and Malaysia have produced differing attitudes among their ethnic Chinese populations towards their respective nation-states, an ethnic identity rooted in the Chinese language and the vernacular religious tradition has remained a constant in both locations. Both in pre-urbanisation Singapore and in Taiwan, village temples provided a focal point for single-ethnic religious communities. As noted, Singapore's ceremonial circles have all but been replaced by new temple networks; in Taiwan they have been displaced by 'belief circles', that is, island-wide temple networks linked to a 'parent' temple by *fenling* (分灵), these being 'replicas' of elder and often famous statues from 'parent' temples attributed with possessing the same *ling* or spirit as the original deity statue. In belief circles, ritual networks are therefore maintained through the worship of the parent temple's primary deity in multiple temple locations. In

Malaysia, in both rural and urban settings, Underworld temples have taken on a central role in the formation of new ethno-religious communities based around individual temples where a wide variety of different Tua Di Ya Pek and other low-ranking Hell deities are venerated or channelled.

3

The historical development of Underworld cosmology

The Shang dynasty oracle bones discovered in Henan province provide the earliest archaeological evidence from China supporting a belief in the afterlife. They show that, while on Earth the Shang emperors had supreme command over their dominions and subjects, in Heaven, Shangdi, the 'Emperor Above', had ultimate authority over the celestial domains. Returning to the bipartite *yin* and *yang* nature of the soul, at some time between the Shang dynasty and the Spring and Autumn period (770–476 BCE), the concept of a subterranean post-mortal destination for the *yin* element of the soul developed, a location referred to as the 'Yellow Springs' (*Huangquan*). The earliest surviving references to the Yellow Springs appeared in the Warring States period (403–221 BCE) *Exegesis of the Spring and Autumn Annals*, a chronicle of the State of Lu, and one of the five Confucian classics (*Wu Jing*). A second location also became associated with the afterlife: Mount Tai (Tai Shan), which, by the end of the first century BCE, was ruled by Taishan Fu Jun, the Lord of Mount Tai, also known as Dongyue Dadi; the deceased registered their names in his capital, located close by at Liangfu (Yu, 1987). Significantly, while both the Yellow Springs and Mount Tai were associated with coldness and darkness, and prior to the introduction of Buddhism, "Hell was yet to be judgemental and there are no explicit mentions of punishments" (Miller, 2008: 70) in either the Yellow Springs or Mount Tai.

Historically, "It was Buddhism which furnished a completely worked out theory of sin and punishment to the Chinese" (Thompson, 1989: 35). With the arrival of Buddhism came the concepts of karma, merit transfer and post-mortal punishments in a judgemental Hell. Buddhism's effect on Chinese religiosity was huge; in John Lagerwey's words, "It steamrolled

China" and "laid the groundwork for what would later become popular religion" (Lagerway, 2009: 46).

In the *Mahavastu-Avanda Sutra*[1] the Buddha described eight fiery hells piled on top of each other, with the deepest hell for the most grievous of sins. Goodrich elucidates this, explaining that by the addition of an entrance and an exit "The number ten was established" (Goodrich, 1981: 70). However, in the second century 'Sutra on the Eighteen Hells' (*Shiba nili jing*) the Buddha describes eight fiery and ten cold hells, each a place of torture, and the torture in each consecutive hell equaling twenty times that of the previous. In the sutra, time in each hell moves at a different speed relative to Earth time. For instance, in the Pangzu Hell, where people were boiled and then flung into a pit of fire to be beaten with iron sticks, "A total of 60,000 human years is just one day. For 16,000 such years is a person tortured here, and that equals 2,160 billion years on Earth" (Young, 1981: 131). Returning to Goodrich's 'ten', and providing a salient temporal reinvention, in the illustrated morality text the 'Scripture of the Ten Kings' (*Shiwang jing*), most likely composed between 720 and 908 CE, the focus is on the passage through and tortures endured in ten chambers of purgatory, "Beginning with the first court seven days after death and ending three years later in rebirth" (Teiser, 2003: 7).

While Buddhist perceptions of a judgemental Underworld had started filtering down into vernacular religious consciousness from around the third century CE, Taoist Underworld cosmology was still in its infancy. In the Celestial Masters school of cosmology,[2] three officers, *Sanguan*, representing Heaven, earth and water, lived in three higher heavens and, after passing judgement on the living, sent demonic officials to afflict the unvirtuous with sickness while still alive. The founder of the Celestial Masters, Zhang Daoling, compiled a register of gods and demons, passed down in the form of a revelation from Lord Lao (Laojun), the deified Laozi, in which deities from the existing vernacular pantheon were identified as demons. They were thus demoted and condemned to reside in the lower Six Heavens, where they "Were enlisted as generals and administrators of the dead" (Dean, 2000: 663). As Miller explains, the Six Heavens (*Liutian*) were "an abode for non-initiates, in contrast to Taoists who inhabit the Three Heavens (*Santian*)" (Miller, 2008: 70). However, the term 'Six Heavens' is deceptive, as is its description as "an abode for non-initiates" (Miller, 2008: 70). First, these heavens were subterranean; and second, 'non-initiates' included most earlier deities,[3] the souls of past emperors from pre-Han dynasties and souls

---

[1] Likely begun in the second century BCE and completed by the fourth century CE (Jones, 1949).
[2] Among the first schools of Taoism, founded in 142 CE.
[3] Earth gods and the Gods of the Five Sacred Mountains being notable exceptions.

of the general populace – in essence, all non-Taoists, whether human or discarnate (Wang, 2012). Opposed to the Han dynasty imperial religion's blood sacrifices to past emperors, the Celestial Masters installed the spirits of five previous Zhou dynasty rulers and "The Duke of Eastern Light Qi of Xia" (Wang, 2012: 137) as rulers of the Underworld's Six Palaces. Six Heavens cosmology was thus constructed by the Celestial Masters in opposition to the official imperial religion and represents the first scriptural Taoist interpretation of Hell. Taoist conceptions of the Underworld would soon evolve in the Shangqing school of Taoism, but the Underworld would retain its negative political and anti-vernacular-tradition connotations until it was transformed into a place of post-mortal punishment through the addition of the Buddhist concept of post-mortal karmic retribution by the Lingbao school of Taoism.[4]

The second attempt to construct a unified Taoist pantheon from previous scriptural sources was undertaken by Tao Hongjing (456–536) of the Shangqing school of Taoism in his 'Chart of the ranks and functions of the real numinous beings' (*Zhenling weiye tu*), where the lowest rank encompassed the Underworld bureaucracy consisting of demonic officers (*guiguan* / 鬼官) answerable to higher-ranking Underworld deities. The Shangqing Taoist administration of the dead was based on the Six Heavens of Fengdu, an increasingly complex system recorded in Tao Hongjing's 'Declarations of the Perfected' (*Zhengao*), a corpus of Shangqing revelations completed in 499 CE. Drawing on Han dynasty notions of Mount Tai as the Underworld's location, and coupled with the Six Heavens cosmology, the Underworld's primary function was commanding demonic armies to subdue forces of evil (Nickerson, 2008). Tao Hongjing's Underworld was "divided into six great chambers, the Palaces of Fengdu, each supervised by its own complement of record keepers and inquisitors, all under the ultimate authority of Beidi, Thearch of the North" (von Glahn, 2004: 135). In this way, drawing on earlier post-mortal concepts whereby individuals could become more powerful in death than in life, the Palaces of Fengdu provided a scriptural foundation for the promotion of human souls in the Underworld to higher spiritual levels – a system which was far more pliable than in the contemporary Underworld tradition. Following punishment, individual souls entered the immortal hierarchy on its lowest rung, as demons to police the palaces of Fengdu. The hierarchical structure in ascending order then progressed to demon officer, Underworld ruler (*dixia zhuzhe* / 地下主者), sage (*shengren*

---

4 The concept of *chengfu* (承负), inherited burden or guilt, was introduced in the second century 'Scriptures of the Great Peace' (Taipingjing), but applied to the living rather than the dead.

/ 圣人), immortal (*xian* / 仙) and a perfected being (*zhenren* / 真人), each rank attainable through the gaining of merit by virtuous actions, or via ritual assistance from the human realms (Kohn, 2001). Immortality in the afterlife had thus become bureaucratised.

The first major development in Taoism from which illustrated medieval morality tracts would later spring, was the introduction of the Buddhist doctrine of karmic retribution and "Torture chambers for the dead" (Kohn, 2009: 91). These were first incorporated by the Lingbao school of Taoism in the fifth century. Moving away from Six Heavens cosmology, the Lingbao scriptures refer to the Underworld as 'earth prisons' (*diyu* / 地狱) and, combining punishments practised in the Han dynasty with those appropriated from Buddhist sutras, they provide the basis for sub-hells described in the later 'Jade Record'. The Lingbao school also appropriated the Buddhist concepts of universal salvation and the transmigration of the soul along one of the 'six paths' of reincarnation. Dependent on merit, the six paths included reincarnation as a god, demigod, human, animal, hungry-ghost, or Hellbeing. The most influential Lingbao scripture on the development of later Chinese Underworld cosmology was the 'Scripture of Karmic Retribution' (*Yinyuan jing*), which, drawing on Mahayana Buddhism, introduced judgemental hells and post-mortal punishments into Taoism (Yamada, 2000). The 'Scripture of Karmic Retribution' also appropriated and then reinvented an obscure Buddhist doctrine, the "Numerous worlds in the ten directions" (Xing, 2010: 65), described in the *Neicang Baibao jing*[5] as "The countless Buddhas of the ten directions" (Xing, 2010: 65) but reinvented as new Taoist deities, "The Ten Worthies Who Save From Suffering (Taiyi Jiuku Tianzun)" (Kohn & Kirkland, 2008: 373). By appropriating and Sinicising multiple elements from Buddhist cosmology, the Lingbao school "shaped the direction of Taoism itself" (Bokenkamp, 2008: 664) and provided the 'Ten Worthies', later reinterpreted to inhabit the Underworld in the 'Scripture of the Ten Kings'. Early Chinese conceptions of the post-mortal journey of the soul were therefore permanently transformed by the appropriation of Buddhist cosmology into Taoism. The pre-Buddhist beliefs in a non-judgemental Underworld had thus been replaced by the Buddhist principle of multiple hells, each administered by a king.

By the Ming dynasty period (1368–1644 CE), when non-orthodox morality tracts increased in circulation, the widespread acceptance of a judgemental Underworld was already prevalent among the masses, the most widely circulated morality tracts adding a degree of uniformity to the existing belief system. The 'Scripture of the Ten Kings' made two major contributions

---

5 Lokanuvartanasutra.

to Underworld cosmology. It reduced time spent in Hell from billions of years to just three, thus providing a realistic and comprehensible timeframe consistent with prevailing vernacular beliefs regarding ancestor worship and reincarnation, and provided a systematic framework of Ten Courts, which would be expanded upon in the hugely influential 'Jade Record'.

In the 'Jade Record', each of the Ten Courts is governed by one of the 'Yama-Kings of Ten Tribunals', *Shi Dian Yenwang*. The first king and overlord, Qinguang Wang, with the authority bestowed on him by the Jade Emperor, passes judgement on individual souls upon arrival, and, based on their iniquities, decrees which of the remaining courts each soul must report to. The kings of courts two to nine then implement Qinguang Wang's judgements, directing each soul to specific sub-hells under their jurisdiction for punishment. Karmic retribution complete, assisted by eighty offices where the 'ledgers of reincarnation' (*zhuanjie suo* / 转劫所) are maintained, the tenth king, Zhuanlun Wang, weighs up previous misdeeds to calculate the appropriate level of transmigration for each soul. The Tenth Court also houses Lady Meng, commonly referred to as Meng Po, in charge of producing the 'Broth of Oblivion' (*mi tang* / 迷汤),[6] and is where "Demons divide the spirits of men from those of women; they then make them drink willy-nilly, so that all memory of the nether world is abolished at the moment of their return upon earth to be reborn in some shape or another" (Maspero, 1932: 368). Each soul is then flung into a crimson river from the 'Bridge of Pain' (*Kuzhu qiao*), where it is washed away to its next incarnation.

This necessarily brief historical summary has illustrated the progression of Underworld cosmology incorporating Shang dynasty and pre-Taoist notions of the afterlife; the Taoist reaction to Han imperial sacrifices resulting in Six Heavens cosmology; the appropriation of Buddhist post-mortal doctrines into Taoism; and their subsequent influence on afterlife beliefs in the vernacular tradition. It has also illustrated how morality tracts rendered complex cosmologies comprehensible through the selective absorption and rejection of elements appropriated from the orthodox traditions. In doing so, they provided the foundation from which the modern Underworld tradition has evolved.

Prior to the advent of the contemporary Underworld tradition, Henri Maspero described the 'Jade Record' as the basis from which "common folk and, generally speaking, all who are not members of religious orders, whether Buddhists or Taoists, take most of their notions about the hells and the judges of the lower world" (Maspero, 1932: 364). In regard to the organisational structure of the Ten Courts of the Underworld and their sub-hells,

---

6 Or 'Five flavoured tea of forgetfulness'.

this remains largely true, and while the similarities between the Underworld of the 'Jade Record' and that of the contemporary tradition outweigh the differences, they do so amid the now ubiquitous images of Tua Di Ya Pek central in every court, sub-hell and nook and cranny of the Underworld.

Times have changed both figuratively and literally, with technological advances, social change and cosmological developments all occurring with increasing speed. In contrast to the gradual historical processes described, in the modern Underworld tradition the evolution of religious convictions into lived ritual and material cultures has been swift, mirroring rapid socio-political change in the secular arena. Swifter still have been the advancements in technology, outpacing while recording ongoing societal developments and radical transformations in the religious landscapes. Increasingly dramatic and digitally personalised representations of Tua Di Ya Pek now appear in JPEG and animated GIF formats, and *tang-ki* captured in high-resolution 4K video on practitioners' mobiles are uploaded daily and viewed. Through this process of sharing digitalised history in the making, power structures within the developmental process have themselves been redefined. Since the 2010s, with camera-wielding photographers superseded by smartphone-ready devotees, and TV broadcasts dwarfed by view counts of Tua Di Ya Pek videos on popular websites, in a *modus operandi* best described as 'the vernacularisation of tradition', the control over and dissemination of reinvented rituals and cosmologies has been transferred from the hands of religious specialists into the public domain.

Part II
The Underworld tradition in Singapore

4

Yu Feng Nan Fu Xuanshan Miao: setting a baseline of comparison

A baseline of comparison

The atypical nature of the popularisation and channelling of Underworld deities needs to be emphasised, as the significance of the contemporary Underworld tradition only becomes fully apparent in a comparative context.

Elsewhere in the Chinese cultural universe, with two notable exceptions, Underworld deities remain largely feared, a taboo subject where even discussions of them will be hushed, as these deities are widely perceived as harbingers of misfortune or death. The first exception is in temple parades of the kind known as 'tours of the borders',[1] where they are sometimes portrayed as giant puppets or by two members of the Eight Infernal Generals (*Ba Jiajiang*) performance troupes.[2] In both instances they walk in sombre silence along parade routes in order to clear the path of malevolent spirits before a temple's deity statues pass. As the Eight Infernal Generals, the performers sport painted faces and don imitation fangs to look fearsome, but their mouths must stay closed, otherwise the malevolent ghosts will recognise the deception. The second exception is their anthropomorphic inclusion in City God temples and in temples dedicated to an Underworld king, Dongyue Dadi.

In other temples in the Asia Pacific region and China, Underworld deities are not accorded their own temple altars, so they are neither publicly worshipped nor channelled by *tang-ki*, thus rendering their presence minimal

---

1 This refers to the borders of a temple's or temple deity's spiritual jurisdiction, which are important in urban areas where there are many temples. Not all temple parades are 'tours of the borders', nor are all 'tours of the borders' temple parades.
2 Originating in Taiwan (see Sutton, 2003) and popularised in Singapore since around 2010.

in the religious landscape. In Chinese vernacular religion the relationship between humans and deities is not one of supplication, but one of contractual agreements, and beyond the Malay Peninsula it would be extremely improbable for a practitioner to enter into an agreement with a Hell deity. Elsewhere, temple altars are adorned with statues of Heaven deities, and it is rare to visit a temple in all but the remotest locations without seeing devotees worshipping through the offering of incense or consulting them for advice by casting divination blocks.

Thus, on the evening that I arrived in Singapore, on entering my first Singaporean temple, even though the altars were lined with rows of familiar Heaven deities, I was quite taken aback to find that the censers dedicated to the primary deities were devoid of the smouldering incense sticks customarily left by worshippers, and by the absence of the devotees themselves. It was a sizeable temple and, while I admired the ritual objects on the various deity altars, a slow chant in a minor key became audible, emanating from the rear of the temple. I wandered towards the sound and found a back door leading to a dark altar room lit by only two candles where, in front of an altar containing unfamiliar deity images, a *tang-ki* was rocking violently in a wooden throne decorated only with the faces of Ox Head (Niutou) and Horse Face (Mamian), Buddhist Hell deities based on Hindu *yaksa* and *raksasa* which elsewhere are said to escort the soul to the Underworld after death. The heady aroma of incense and the rhythmic chant to invoke the deity were also intended to assist the *tang-ki*'s attainment of a trance state, allowing the human soul to leave his body and a deity spirit to enter. Only later did I discover the purpose of the powerful rocking movements that, as the *tang-ki*'s body doubled up, repeatedly brought his head towards the ground before he recoiled with a dull thud back into the hefty throne. The Underworld is located below, and the moment when the *tang-ki*'s head goes down coincides with the attainment of a full physiological trance; the Hell deity enters the *tang-ki* through the floor, directly into his skull, the force displacing the *tang-ki*'s soul into various receptacles in and around the Underworld altar. Although I was in a Chinese temple and five years into my research, I felt as if I had entered a new and mysterious world far removed from the variations of Chinese vernacular religion that I had become familiar with in other locations. To put my sentiments into perspective, the contrast was *almost* equivalent to a seasoned theologian visiting a Christian country in Europe and finding a church congregation hidden in a room behind the sanctuary worshipping images of and invoking the Devil, and then finding this pattern repeated in multiple churches each adorned with crucifixes, but where Satan and his minions are channelled through spirit mediums after dark. Churches where practitioners sincerely love God and worship Jesus, but say that for them, Satan is just easier to get along with. I emphasised the word '*almost*', as Underworld deities do not represent evil (as in the struggle between the forces of light and darkness), but are enforcers of karmic punishments; and, unlike the biblical Hell associated with everlasting damnation, the Chinese Underworld is a place of temporal punishment before a subsequent reincarnation is possible. However, the irony of the affection felt by devotees towards deities who will inflict tortures on them in their post-mortal journey through the Underworld ranks high among the complexities of the deities' new-found popularity.

Tua Di Ya Pek's mythologies

Underworld altars in Singapore and Malaysia are dominated by Tua Ya Pek (Great Grand Elder) and Di Ya Pek (Second Grand Elder), the deities whose original human names were Xie Bian and Fan Wujiu. Most Chinese deities have multiple conflicting historiographies and mythologies, with the most complex being those belonging to several or competing pantheons and those whose stories have been passed down through oral or theatrical traditions or recorded in epic tomes of romantic fiction. Tua Di Ya Pek belong to the vernacular pantheon,[3] their origins being placed in the Tang, Song, Ming and Qing dynasties by various informants, the Ming period being the most prevalent theory. One commonality running though their mythologies is that they lived in Fujian Province, China, and this is supported by their graves being located on a hill overlooking Anxi City God Temple in Fujian.

They are affectionately portrayed either as mercenaries employed by a magistrate to bring opium traders and other criminals to justice or as righteous criminals who trafficked opium and avoided the magistrate's sheriffs. When asked, many devotees espouse the first interpretation of them as upholders of justice and then, in hushed tones often accompanied by a wink and a smile, may add, "but we know they were gangsters really". In both mythologies, and accounting for their anthropomorphic representations and the comportment of their *tang-ki* when channelled, is the legend of their deaths. This version contains the most common and essential elements of their mythos and is therefore the story most often recalled.

During the early Ming dynasty in Fujian Province there lived two men who were the closest of friends. One was very short and the other very tall and, due to the depth of their friendship, in time, they became sworn blood brothers, a relationship based on honour and implicit trust. The short man

---

3 They are now recognised in Taoism through their association with the imperial city god cult, city gods only later being associated with Taoism.

was named Fan Wujiu (Di Ya Pek) and his tall friend was Xie Bian (Tua Ya Pek). They were both skilled martial artists, and worked as runners at a local magistrate's office, serving warrants and hauling in criminals for judgement, but never harming honest folk.

On one occasion they were caught in a torrential storm, and great curtains of rain beat down on their heads. They had reached the South Platform Bridge, when Xie Bian told Fan Wujiu to wait under the bridge while he went to fetch a large umbrella. He was gone a long time, the storm did not abate and the water under the bridge rose higher and higher. Fan Wujiu did not leave to seek higher ground as he had given his word that he would wait for Xie Bian under the shelter of the bridge, and his word was his bond. Suddenly, a colossal wall of water swept over him and, unable to hold his footing, he was swept along the river, where he drowned, and his body was washed far downstream.

By the time Xie Bian returned with the umbrella, the storm was coming to an end, but he could not find his blood brother. He knew that Fan Wujiu would not have left unless some calamity had befallen him, so he searched for several days. At last, he found Fan's dead body, bloated and already turning reddish black, entangled in the roots of a fallen tree. Overcome with grief and remorse, he promptly hanged himself from a bough of the same tree. When their bodies were found, Xie Bian's face was chalky white and puffed up and his long tongue was protruding between his lips, while Fan's stout, bloated body was doubled over and rotting in the roots below him. No one knew if they had any family, so they were buried by the local villagers. Their extraordinary affection and loyalty moved the local City God, Chenghuang, who had them appointed as his assistants, working together to protect people from the ghosts of bandits and malicious spirits that wander the Earth.

Regarding their deification, another legend tells that Chenghuang was unaware of them until Li Shimin, the second Emperor of the Tang dynasty, visited the land of the dead in a dream in which Fan Wujiu and Xie Bian served as his guides. The Emperor subsequently rewarded them by appointing them as assistants to the City God. However, in the Li Shimin version, and contrary to popular opinion, they would have lived over six centuries before the Ming dynasty. In another mythology, Dongyue Dadi, a Taoist King of the Underworld, was so impressed by their sense of honour and devotion to justice that he promoted them to the rank of generals, thus making them responsible for capturing the souls of criminals. To assist them, they received three magic treasures, a soul-chaining lock and two demon-summoning plaques, the chain eventually being acquired by Fan Wujiu.

A Qing dynasty variation of the traditional story was related to me by a Tua Ya Pek *tang-ki* in Malaysia.

At the height of opium addiction in China caused by the importation and sale of opium by the British, a drug lord approached Xie Bian and Fan Wujiu to bribe them into letting him continue with his illegal activities in the province in exchange for free opium. The two constables, who were known for their righteousness, refused the offer. This infuriated the drug lord, and this made him turn on Xie Bian, and so he reported to the local Magistrate that Xie Bian was taking bribes from opium traders. The magistrate immediately launched investigations into the allegations against him. To prove his own innocence, Xie Bian resolved to hang himself outside the magistrate's office, along with an oath that he was loyal and innocent.

Early the next morning, when Fan Wujiu was reporting for duty, he found the body of Xie Bian hanging outside the magistrate's door. Devastated by his death and angered by the accusations brought against his sworn brother, after burying him, he decided to join his brother in death by drowning himself in the sea.

The loyalty and brotherly love displayed by Xie Bian and Fan Wujiu touched the hearts of the deities in the Underworld, and they were thus promoted and became known as Hei Bai Wuchang, the Black and White Lords.[4]

A variation of this second account is that the magistrate ordered them to investigate a local tycoon who was suspected of distributing opium. On uncovering a large amount of evidence, they were offered a sizeable bribe to turn a blind eye, but they refused. Before being arrested, the tycoon told his followers to deliver false evidence to the magistrate indicating that Xie Bian and Fan Wujiu were arresting him only because they were opium dealers themselves and wanted to eliminate their competition.

The relationship between Underworld deities and opium can be seen in the material culture surrounding their veneration. The anthropomorphic images of Tua Di Ya Pek on temple altars often have a piece of black-stained plastic stuck to their tongues, and these are opium wraps from which Tua Di Ya Pek have previously consumed opium through their *tang-ki*. Jean DeBernardi notes that across the border, in Malaysia, *tang-ki* temples had relationships with 'black societies', secret crime organisations which would have given them a source of illegal opium (DeBernardi, 1987: 312–313), and it is reasonable to assume that similar ties existed in Singapore. I was also informed that in 'the old days' (1960s–1970s) Singapore's Underworld *tang-ki* smoked opium, but now opium consumption during trance possession is a rarity,

---

4 Literal translation being 'Black and White Impermanence'.

while in Malaysia the contemporary chanelling of Underworld deities and consumption of opium has become ubiquitous.

Opium's popularity in Singapore can be traced back to British rule, where, by 1904, 59% of the administration's revenue came from the opium trade (Cheng, 1961). Smuggling of opium was illegal then as it is now. However, it was prohibited in colonial times because it interfered with the government's monopoly, as chests of opium imported from India were sold by the government to Chinese merchants who bid for the rights to retail it through opium 'farms'. It was not until 1934 that opium possession without a medical prescription was banned in Singapore. Even so, during the Japanese occupation (February 1942–September 1945) the number of opium addicts reached a record high, and it was not until the passing of the Misuse of Drugs Act in 1973 that opium possession became punishable by caning and imprisonment. Article 19 of the Act states that if drug paraphernalia are found, it will be presumed that the premises have been used for the consumption of the drug. Therefore, when opium is consumed it is smeared on the outside of ordinary cigarettes so as to leave no physical evidence of the event.

When Tua Di Ya Pek are represented in anthropomorphic form, and relating back to their mythologies, each has distinctive identifying features. Tua Ya Pek is tall and slim and depicted with a lolling tongue characteristic of death by hanging. He is dressed in white robes and has a white or pale-skinned face. He wears a tall hat bearing the words *yijian daji* (一见大吉), meaning 'one glimpse, great felicity' – an intentionally grim and ironic reminder of the tortures he will inflict on individuals' souls in their post-mortal journey. In his right hand he carries a fan which in the discarnate realms operates as a weapon to control and capture souls, and on the material plane provides a physical link between the human world and the Underworld. In his left hand he wields his demon-summoning plaque in a martial posture, usually at waist height. Tua Ya Pek is thought of as 'first' or 'eldest' brother[5] and has additional names and titles. These include his human name Xie Bian; Xie Jiangjun, meaning 'General Xie'; Bai Wuchang, meaning 'White Impermanence'; and, in Taiwan, Qi Ye, meaning 'Seventh Uncle'.

In contrast, Di Ya Pek is portrayed as short and stout, his face blackened and bloated as when discovered by Xie Bian enmeshed in the tree roots. Both deities are therefore represented, quite fittingly, in the guise of death. His robes and square hat are pitch black and, playing on the same sardonic humour, the latter bears the words *tianxia taiping* (天下太平) meaning

---

[5] 'Tua' means 'big', hence 'eldest brother', and 'Di' means 'second'. While 'Ya Pek' literally means 'grandfather', it is used as an informal term of respect, commonly translated as 'elder' or 'uncle'.

'Omnipresent Peace'. His demon-summoning plaque is held aloft in his left hand, and in his right hand his soul-catching chain hangs down to the floor in preparation to strike. In temples with an upper and lower Underworld altar, each containing Tua Di Ya Pek statues, the far end of his chain on the lower altar rests at the gateway to Hell, once again providing a tangible link between the two realms. Regarded as 'second brother', though of equal rank to the first, he shares similar titles with Tua Ya Pek, including Fan Jiangjun, meaning 'General Fan'; Hei Wuchang, meaning 'Black Impermanence'; and, in Taiwan, Ba Ye, meaning 'Eighth Uncle'.

When channelled through *tang-ki*, Tua Ya Pek is usually good natured, with a sharp sense of humour, while Di Ya Pek is short tempered and comparatively stern. Frequently their *tang-ki* fit the physical stature of the deity they trance,[6] and in cases where a *tang-ki* channels both, their temperament and physiognomy transform as does their posture and deportment depending on which deity is being channelled.

Goh proposed that in Chinese religion, 'deity' "Is an almost-empty sign, a signifier referring to nothing else except the meaning of 'the spiritual other'" (Goh, 2009: 112), and that the 'sign' can be attributed various associations only limited "by the historical discursive conditions of Chinese religion in a specific social context" (Goh, 2009: 112). However, among local practitioners of Chinese vernacular religion this etic interpretation of 'deity' is not an element of their own socio-religious understanding, and distinguishing deities through interactions with ritual objects plays an essential role in their life-worlds. As opposed to being 'signifiers of the spiritual other', Tua Di Ya Pek are each understood to be a distinct post-mortal incarnation of the human souls either of Xie Bian and Fan Wujiu who reside in the Fourth Court of the Underworld, or of another Underworld enforcer of the same rank. Therefore, in practice, Tua Ya Pek and Di Ya Pek may refer to Xie Bian and Fan Wujiu, or to other Hell deities, also referred to as Tua Ya Pek and Di Ya Pek, that perform the same duties in different courts of the Underworld. The courts, punishments and Underworld hierarchy will be detailed in Chapter 7. Each Tua Di Ya Pek that possesses a *tang-ki* therefore has their own family name, which is stitched onto a hat or headband as a part of their attire, and each Ah Pek[7] holds the same rank as policeman or enforcer in the Underworld pantheon. It is therefore understood that each Underworld enforcer is a different spiritual entity, each a spirit of an individual who died in a different time and place, but shares the task of

---

6 The term most commonly used in Singaporean English (Singlish) meaning 'to channel a deity in a trance possession state'.
7 'Ah Pek' is an informal form of address for low-ranking Underworld deities.

enforcing punishments in the various torture chambers of the Underworld's sub-hells.

Their plaques, fans and chains, when wielded by a possessed *tang-ki*, can be used to direct their deific efficacy as blessings, or as weapons against malevolent spirits, but they possess no independent agency as objects, and in the absence of a *tang-ki* they merely represent the deity by association. Therefore, from the emic perspective there is a collapse in the dichotomy between object and symbol when the object is animated by a deific presence. The erstwhile symbolic object ceases to be symbolic, as, once embodied, the inherent nature of the object's qualities, be it a fan, plaque or abacus, is reimagined by practitioners to correspond in a state of equivalence to the efficacy of the deity embodying it.

Paleček and Risjord have examined the implications of the 'extended mind hypothesis'[8] on the relationship between object and mind, suggesting that "The mind is not limited to the activities of the brain (or Cartesian mind). Rather, objects and bodily actions in the environment are legitimately thought of as parts of the mind, and their use is part of thinking" (Paleček & Risjord, 2013: 8). The inference of this is that if the self is partially constituted by objects interacted with, then the 'deity self' is reliant on interactions with the ritual objects in the environment for its identifiability as 'deity'.

While this raises the paradoxical notion of a deity constituting a 'self' while possessing another's body, deities as discarnate entities do require material objects to interact with, to direct their efficacy through and thus to impart a subsequent effect upon the physical world. Therefore, during ritual processes the relationship between *tang-ki* and Underworld deities is one of interdependence, the former requiring the latter to provide efficacy in the material world and the latter requiring the former to provide the materiality through which efficacy is recognised to operate. In this way, the relevance of ritual vessels in the Underworld tradition – including Tua Di Ya Pek's black abacuses; green talisman papers and black ink;[9] rattan fans; smoking pipes; dragon-headed whips; an assortment of flags and name chops; deity-headed skewers for self-piercing; and a selection of weapons to draw their own blood – is to serve the needs of deities during rituals. Methodologically, this divides the anthropological gaze between the movement of deific efficacy between vessels and the interactions of social actors in close proximity to them.

---

8 First proposed by Clark and Chalmers (1998).
9 *Tang-ki* channelling Heaven deities and Taoist priests commonly use yellow talisman papers and a scarlet-coloured cinnabar solution (sometimes replaced by red ink) for talismans used in rituals, and for those used as medicine which are burned and the ashes either bathed in or drunk with water.

Meeting Tua Ya Pek at Yu Feng Nan Fu Xuanshan Miao, Singapore, 10 December 2010

"Follow me, blue-eyed boy," were the first words that Tua Ya Pek, the Underworld enforcer, half-deity, half-ghost,[10] spoke to me as he cleaned the blood from his chin.

He then returned to his accustomed position in front of a desk containing talisman papers, ink, a selection of calligraphy brushes and a plentiful supply of alcohol and cigarettes. His chair was carried there for him: he is 600 years old and revered by his followers.

"Blue-eyed boy ... never tell the exact time, place and date of your birth to a 'tang-ki', it can be used in black magic against you."

I considered the advice sound and followed him into the temple's interior which was shrouded in thick clouds of benzoin incense smoke issuing from the Malay Datuk Gong's and the temple's central altars. He perched on the edge of his wooden throne, its arms decorated with painted effigies of Ox Head and Horse Face, and eyed me with amusement and curiosity and noted in a disapproving tone:

"You have taken many photographs but haven't paid respects to the deities in the temple."

This was true, and I assured him that I would pay respects by offering incense to them immediately. However, he continued the conversation, and asked me if there was anything I would like to ask, and delighted with the opportunity, I began to question him about the Underworld, sin and the nature of the afterlife.

"I am not Chinese. Do Western people go to the Chinese Underworld, or is the Underworld ethnically exclusive?" I asked curiously.

I did not consider it my role as a researcher to test the authenticity of phenomena but, rather, to learn about the culture from the perspective of the actors, to gain experiential knowledge where possible and then to analyse the whys and wherefores of ongoing ritual and cosmological developments in the context of the broader and rapidly changing socio-political landscape. My intentions, in an hour-long dialogue which will be continued towards the end of the chapter, were to familiarise myself with emic understandings of the Underworld; to contextualise the *tang-ki*'s status in the temple community both in and out of trance states; to account for the normative perception among devotees towards Hell deity worship and their ritual alcohol

---

10 'Half-deity, half-ghost' is this specific Tu Ya Pek's self-description. Underworld enforcer, policeman and deity are more common.

consumption;[11] and, lastly, to explore the physiological sensations associated with alcohol and trance possession from the perspective of an Underworld *tang-ki* in a trance state.

> *"Everyone must visit the Underworld to take responsibility (punishment) for their acts and deeds and evil thoughts," Tua Ya Pek replied.*
> *"So," I asked, "if French and German and Spanish people all go to the Underworld after death, are there also French-, German- and Spanish-speaking Tua Di Ya Pek?"*
> *"Spoken language, as you understand it, is not required in the Underworld." He paused momentarily to accept and drain a small can of Guinness opened and handed to him by a devotee. Then, returning his attention to our conversation, with a knowing look on his face he enquired "Are you afraid?"*
> *"No," I replied, "just curious, and thirsting for more knowledge."*

The influence of Singapore's racial integration and religious harmony policies

The 10 December 2010 'oil wok' ritual marked the tenth anniversary of the temple in its present location. Every Saturday night and on the first and fifteenth of every lunar month at 8 p.m., the gates to Yu Feng Nan Fu Xuanshan Miao are opened, and within half an hour both temple members and those eager to consult the deity throng to this rare and beautiful yet hidden and remote temple situated high above Singapore's bustling metropolis. Lily Kong has suggested that "The structure and architecture of religious buildings influence the ambience of the setting and can play a large role in contributing to or detracting from the divine experience" (Kong, 1992: 23–24). In this temple's case, being constructed in an industrial setting and lacking the palatial structure, architectural trappings and history that lends temples in Malaysia, Taiwan and downtown Singapore their religious ambience, the divine experience is created instead by charismatic *tang-ki*; multiple deity altars throughout the temple; incense smoke radiating from these altar's censers; the multi-ethnic participation of spirit mediums in rituals; and the inclusion of Malay and Hindu deities and their ritual paraphernalia in the temple's interior. This multi-ethnic approach to sacred space represents a socio-religious transformation where Chinese temple traditions are being modified, reinterpreted and adapted to fulfil contemporary demands, processes that

---

11 As a *tang-ki*'s body must be pure before a deity can enter, and alcohol is considered a physical defilement.

"entail significant reconceptualizations and reconstructions of space" (Tong & Kong, 2000: 29–30). The process is ongoing, and has provisioned Singapore with a temple environment in which Underworld deities, their temples, altars, rituals, material culture and post-mortal cosmology have thrived.

The temple is accessed by car up a kilometre-long circular ramp, or by lift past seven floors of industrial manufacturers and warehouse space employing migrant workers from Thailand, Malaysia and India (Plate 1). Its location on the top floor of an industrial building creates an impression of remoteness that adds to, rather than subtracts from, the ambience surrounding the manifestation of deities through their mediums, and the elaborate rituals designed to evoke an experience of the numinous. Placed discreetly outside the red industrial gates is an external altar to the Underworld Camps of the Five Directions (*wai wu ying* / 外五营)[12] to prevent mischievous spirits from interfering with activities conducted within the temple's external ritual space. These spirit armies are commanded by Underworld generals who are represented by their flags outside the temple, and again inside the temple at the Underworld altar, as anthropomorphic images placed beneath higher-ranking Underworld officials.

The temple has three sections, though there are no physical divides between them. Inside the threshold, there are statues of Nan Bei Dou Xingjun (the Lords of the Northern and Southern Dipper) portrayed as childlike deities standing either side of a large copper censer dedicated to the Jade Emperor. Beyond this there is a sacred space employed for impromptu rituals, where, twenty metres above, hangs a carved *bagua* (八卦), an octagon constructed from eight trigrams representing combinations of *yin* and *yang*. On the right of this is a small shrine to a Malay Datuk Gong, from where benzoin incense fills the air with its exotic aroma. Moving further in, on the right, is the altar to Ganesh, which is littered with Hindu ritual paraphernalia including limes, candles, garlands of flowers and coloured powders[13] and next to this is an altar to the Taisui.[14] Placed in the centre of the temple is the desk in front of which a heavy throne is placed, upon which the Chinese deities are tranced. On the desk are the ritual implements employed by the deities: ink and talisman papers of different colours; brushes and pens; an abacus; a censer; snake whips; temple and deity name chops; and bottles of and utensils for consuming alcohol.

12 Placed outside only on the temple's anniversary and during Lunar Seventh Month.
13 Traditionally made from natural sandalwood or *buras* flowers (red), lime (white), *mehendi* and henna powder (green), beetroot (magenta), turmeric powder, marigolds or chrysanthemums (yellow) and hibiscus (blue).
14 There are sixty Taisui, each a general representing a star, one for each of the sixty-year cycle of the stem-branch zodiac calendar.

At the rear of the temple is the main tri-level altar extending from the floor to the ceiling, each level illuminated by coloured fluorescent tubes. The altar was organised in a unique self-styled manner by the temple's founding *tang-ki*, who was instructed in the details while channelling 'The Boss', the Emperor of the Dark Heavens (Xuantian Shangdi), the highest-ranking deity that he channels. The top level houses deities that have existed since pre-history and includes Lord Lao, who is the deified philosopher Laozi, the Three Pure Ones (Sanqing Zushi), one of several creator gods (depending on which mythology is adopted by a temple) Pangu Xianshi, and the mother of the Nine Emperor Gods Doumu Niang-niang. The middle section contains humans and animals deified in human times, including Guan Gong, Jigong, Guanyin, Shancai Tongzi, Sun Wukong and the Emperor of the Dark Heavens, and the bottom level accommodates an expansive Underworld pantheon. At its centre is a large censer, behind which are a City God, to his right a King of the Underworld Dongyue Dadi and then the Bodhisattva Dizangwang,[15] and to the left, Bao Gong the God of Justice, and the king of the Underworld's Fifth Court, Yanluo Wang. Their relative positions are indicative of rank in a temple's local hierarchy, the central position being reserved for the most senior deity,[16] the first positions to the right and left for the second and third highest-ranking deities, and to the right and left of these for the fourth- and fifth-ranking deities and so forth. In conjunction with this, the highest-ranking deities are placed on a higher level on each altar, above lower-ranking deities, as displayed in the overall design of the tri-level altar representing Heaven, Earth and the Underworld. The main deities on the Underworld altar are flanked by the City God's helpers, the twenty-four Underworld bureaucrats (*ershisi si* / 二十四司), and scattered between them all are many statues of Tua Di Ya Pek, as well as anthropomorphic representations of Underworld generals and ghosts. As Underworld deities are accustomed to darkness, the altar is lit with 'black light' and therefore fluoresces purple-blue compared to the Heaven altars above, bathed in red flourescence.

None of these deity statues is a replica from other temples, and their eyes were ritually opened (*kaiguang* / 开光) by the resident *tang-ki*, thus allowing the deities to enter.[17] On each level benzoin, as opposed to Chinese incense, is continually burned, serving as a reminder that this was once Malay land under the protection of a Datuk Gong, and that this temple caters to ethnic

---

15 A Bodhisattva who vowed not to achieve full enlightenment until the halls of the Underworld were emptied.
16 A temple's main deity takes the central position even when, as in this instance, it holds a lower pantheonic rank than the deities flanking it.
17 One exception is a pair of Fourth Court Tua Di Ya Pek, discussed in Chapter 6.

Malay, Indian and Chinese devotees. The ethnically inclusive nature of the post-mortal cosmology common to Singapore mirrors the official line on religious harmony which requires that all religions are respected, and Chinese, Malay and Indian spirit mediums all channel deities at this temple. The deities most frequently channelled include the Underworld enforcers Tua Di Ya Pek and Jigong, all of whom are channelled by the same *tang-ki*. From the Tamil Hindu popular pantheon, and illustrating the reinterpretation of cosmologies at temple level, Madurai Veeran was introduced to me by Tamil Hindus at the temple as Tua Ya Pek's Tamil counterpart in the Underworld. Elsewhere, Madurai Veeran, the 'Warrior of Madurai', is associated with the Heaven pantheon, and the reinvention of the deity's status has served to integrate this erstwhile Tamil deity into the temple's Underworld hierarchy as subordinate to Tua Ya Pek himself. As noted, Tua Ya Pek may refer to Xie Bian, or to another soul holding the rank of Underworld enforcer, and this temple's Tua Ya Pek bears the family name 'So' and resides in the Seventh Court of the Underworld. Ethnic Chinese and Malay devotees consult and receive blessings from the Indian deity and offer incense at the Indian altar and, likewise, Indian visitors pay respects and receive blessings from the Chinese deities channelled through their *tang-ki* and offer incense both to the Chinese deities and to the Malay Datuk Gong.

Returning to my initial conversation with Tua Ya Pek, the notion of an ethnically diverse Underworld that Tua Ya Pek proposed mirrors the multi-ethnic and multi-religious composition of the temple's deities and patrons. Similar worship patterns are found at numerous *tang-ki* altars, as well as in Singapore's larger United temples, some of which contain places of worship drawn from multiple religious traditions. The universal nature of the Underworld as espoused by Tua Ya Pek, where communication does not require the spoken word, is sympathetically incorporative of the temple's diverse community and highly pragmatic, with visitors representing Singapore's four official language groups of English, Mandarin, Malay and Tamil, as well native Thai and Hindi speakers, and devotees from Hokkien, Hainanese and Teochew dialect groups. Furthermore, the emic understanding of a judgemental Underworld as a post-mortal inevitability irrespective of ethnicity or religion is also pragmatic when ethically framed as a universal and inescapable consequence of one's own thoughts, words and deeds. Lastly, Tua Ya Pek's advice not to share my birth details illustrates that in the Underworld tradition a distinction based on intentionality is made between religious ritual and harmful 'black' magic, which, alongside the influence of malevolent spirits, provides the cosmological prerequisite for the deific protection of sacred space in ritual.

The 'oil wok' ritual

Having previously heard of 'oil wok' rituals, I was keen to experience the sensation of dipping my hands into boiling oil which, according to temple members, does not burn, as devotees are protected by their deities. I therefore arrived early to observe the preparations. The medicines to be cooked had been laid in boxes on the ground, and the wok was about to be placed in position in the area immediately outside the temple. There were eight spirit mediums already in trance, including two Hindu mediums, one channelling Madurai Veeran and the other the Chinese Underworld God of Wealth, Bao Bei Ya; two Malay mediums, one channelling Di Ya Pek and the other a Datuk Gong; and four Chinese *tang-ki* trancing Jigong, the Third Prince San Taizi and Tua Di Ya Pek, respectively. Unlike in Taiwan, where *tang-ki* from different temples rarely collaborate in rituals, these *tang-ki* were friends of the temple's founder, and ritual links are maintained by reciprocal participation in each other's annual festivities.

> *The oil used was a mixture of sesame and vegetable oil, and before the oil wok ritual could commence, a sacred space had to be created outside the temple proper in what is essentially a high-rise industrial car park. This was accomplished by the placing of efficacious objects to demarcate the borders of the sacred space. The outer ritual markers consisted of eight wooden blocks, each holding two candles, an offering of tea wrapped in paper as a sign of respect, and three incense sticks to attract the attention of deities. These marked each of the primary compass points thus corresponding to the eight sides of the 'bagua', each set of incense and candles invoking the protection of a deity: Heaven, Earth, the Lord of the Southern Dipper, the Lord of the Northern Dipper, the gods of the North, South, East and West, and simultaneously, the Eight Taoist Immortals. A temple member cracked a dragon whip in the air multiple times over the outer markers to dispel malevolent spirits lurking in the immediate area, and then reinforced each of the markers with a silent invocation to the deity and immortal it represented requesting their presence.*
>
> *An inner ritual space was then created by the spirit mediums dancing around the wok of hot oil, and using towels, splashing the oil over themselves, onlookers, and unwittingly over both of my cameras. The innermost sacred space was created within the wok itself, and this was accomplished by laying joss money covered in lime and 'vibhuti'[18] in the*

---

18 'Lime' being calcium hydroxide, and *vibhuti* the sacred ash used in Hinduism made from dried burned wood.

base of the wok before the oil was added. The herbs used to make the medicine, including ginger, lemon grass, holy basil, wild fungi, aromatic fern and pepper roots, were then added, and each of the visiting 'tang-ki' climbed into the wok and sat precariously on top of the hot herb and oil mixture, as in the bathing, blessings were passed from the possessing deities into the medicine (Plate 2). After the 'tang-ki' had finished, the public were allowed to put their hands in the oil which was fairly hot with a pleasant sesame aroma, but not boiling at this point. It was then covered, and the event continued inside the temple. Meanwhile, as Jigong had left the primary 'tang-ki's body, his characteristic patched yellow monastic robes had been removed and been replaced by the silver-grey silken trousers belonging to Tua Ya Pek.

Temple members, all dressed alike in yellow polo shirts decorated with the temple's logo, then began chanting an invocation to invite Tua Ya Pek into the body of their 'tang-ki'. This was accompanied by loud rhythmic drumming interspersed with cymbals and gongs, while the billows of incense smoke mushrooming out from each of the temple's eleven censers made the eyes smart amid the impassioned chants of followers.

"Gray and vast Underworld, a vast expanse of Hell;
Your followers invite Tua Ya Pek, come quickly hither to your altar.
There is opium, good tea, good wine and black cakes awaiting,
And Ox Head and Horse Face stand on both sides,
Underworld soldiers follow thee."

As the crescendo's tempo intensified, the medium rocked with increasing violence back and forth in the throne, each time bringing his head closer to the ground. The force of his momentum was so great that three sturdy helpers held the chair steady so that the 'tang-ki's velocity would not overturn it. As the 'tang-ki' entered a full state of trance, he slapped the floor with both hands, and the chanting reached an ecstatic high.

"Walk to the front of the altar to show thy power!
Incense smoke rising up to open the gates of the Underworld,
Your followers invite you again, our Tua Ya Pek, to come to the front of the altar.
Underworld soldiers come to help soon, Underworld soldiers come to Him."

The 'tang-ki' swung forward and stood up in a rigid martial posture, and helpers dressed him in ceremonial robes completing the transformation from human to Hell deity. Tua Ya Pek then led members of the temple and public in paying respects to the Jade Emperor, to Heaven deities and to the Underworld pantheon by prostrating themselves and *offering incense in front of each altar, and then he shuffled outside to inspect the medicine.*

When the lid was taken off the wok, a heady aromatic aroma filled the ritual space, and the oil was bubbling fiercely. After stirring the oil and medicines with a cloth, he laid his hands on the oil and proceeded to rub it on his arms. A queue formed and Tua Ya Pek, holding each person's wrists, touched the palms of their hands onto the surface of the boiling oil. I joined the queue, and when my turn came, Tua Ya Pek lowered my palms towards the boiling oil. The sting was immediate, and my hands recoiled instinctively, but Tua Ya Pek smiled and nodded towards the fiercely boiling concoction which helped me to focus, and then dipped my hands firmly into the top layer of oil again. Hands smarting from the heat, with an elated sense of satisfaction, I rubbed the hot aromatic oil on my wrists and spread it along my forearms.

After this, Tua Ya Pek returned to his chair at the threshold of the temple, and sitting in his throne, used a jagged shard of purposely smashed porcelain taken from a cup on the Underworld altar to slash his tongue until it bled (Plate 3). He did this with zest, and yellow scarves, personal clothing and artefacts were then passed to him, and, using his tongue, he smeared blood on each item. When the flow of blood stopped, he picked up another shard, and in long slashing movements cut fresh lacerations splitting open the tip of his tongue, thus blessing all of the objects passed to him. I recalled Margaret Chan (2006) had noted that a 'tang-ki's blood doubles the potency of a talisman or charm by charging it with 'yang' energy to overwhelm 'yin' negativity, while temple members held that the blood of a possessed 'tang-ki' carries the blessings of the deity channelled, in this instance a 'yin' deity. I asked the 'tang-ki' why such spectacle was required to let the blood required for the event, and he replied that it is natural to 'display what one cherishes' and that the gift of blood was to 'present a treasure' to the deity's devotees.

He then beckoned me, and the 'blue eyed boy' re-entered his temple.

When deities are tranced through mediums, the intensity of their stare, the dense incense smoke and hubbub of activity that surrounds them all contribute towards an environment receptive to Kong's (1992) 'divine experience'. My 'inner anthropologist' was aware of this and, as this Underworld enforcer emanated more power and charisma than any deity I had previously consulted, the prospect of cross-examining him at my leisure was enthralling. Standing under the shadow of the *bagua*, I pressed on with more questions.

"*Taking into account that different countries and religions follow diverse sets of laws and prohibitions, are there universal sins that everyone will be punished for?*"

"*Yes, there are!*"

"*If you commit these universal sins, is it possible to reincarnate as an animal?*"

He nodded indicating 'yes' and sternly replied "*You should concentrate on being good to make sure that it is not you!*" Then more jovially he repeated "*Follow me blue-eyed boy,*" and observing his stooped frame and limping gait, both suggestive of a physiological age far in advance of the 'tang-ki's own, I followed him back to his desk where he encouraged me to ask more questions.

How many souls do we have? Is the soul divisible? Where is the Underworld? Where were you before you came into the 'tang-ki's body and on and on. Underworld deities love to drink and smoke, and during the course of our conversation he drank nine small cans of Guinness washed down with large Martell Cognac chasers as he chain-smoked filterless cigarettes handed to him and then lit by temple assistants. After perhaps an hour I was becoming increasingly self-conscious as there were other people waiting to consult him, but he pressed me for more questions.

"*Okay*" I said, hoping that my next question might conclude our interview, "*Can you tell me why a Chinese Underworld enforcer drinks Irish stout?*"

He laughed heartily and told his helpers to open cupboards, thus revealing bottles of Cognac, Scotch, Saki, rice wine, red wine, sparkling wine and a dozen different beers.

"*You think I only drink Guinness? Ha ha ha! I drink Guinness because I like it,*" he replied as one of his helpers lit another cigarette and handed it to him.

"*You think I am getting drunk?*" he enquired. His eyes were red, his speech slightly slurred, and, with a drunken smile, he was swaying back and forth in his throne, so I gave it my best diplomatic guess.

"*Well, maybe just a little bit tipsy!*"

"*Wait until I return to the Underworld, and then ask the 'tang-ki' to breathe on you. Smell his breath. You won't smell alcohol or cigarettes. I am taking all of that with me back to the Underworld!*"

He then tried to cajole me into making a bet with him, suggesting that all my photographs would be out of focus as I had not lit incense and paid respects to the temple deities before taking them. I reasoned that it would be foolhardy to gamble with deities, especially so a highly *charismatic Underworld deity, so I politely declined. Then he challenged me to take out my camera there and then and look at the photos as proof that he was right. I had a high-end Nikon DSLR which I used to record my research, and I was sorely tempted to take him up on the challenge, but noticed several people shake their heads, and once again, politely eschewed the invitation.*

He then offered me a can of Guinness which I finished in a gulp and then another. With the second can, raising it to his good health, I paid my respects to him, after which he said,

"Okay, now that you have paid your respects, your photos will all be in focus!"

I considered this a fitting end to the interview.

I waited for the medium to come out of trance and immediately approached him and asked if I could smell his breath.

"Why, who are you?" he asked, in a genuinely sceptical manner.

I noted that his eyes were clear, his speech perfect, and his body language said, 'boxer in good training; round one', not '10 cans of Guinness and a dozen Cognac chasers later', so I explained. He laughed, breathed out heavily into my face, and to my astonishment, there was absolutely no trace of either alcohol or tobacco on his breath.

His return to a non-trance state was accompanied by an immediate attitude shift in both temple members and the visiting public. No longer Underworld enforcer incarnate, normative relationships reasserted themselves in his various roles as husband, father, friend, temple owner, religious specialist and businessman. Among visitors who were unfamiliar with the temple, once out of costume and character of the deity, he merged in with the crowd and, if recognised as the *tang-ki*, was addressed as an equal. In common with both groups, he treated other *tang-ki* still channelling deities with great reverence, bowing to them and, if directed, unquestioningly following their instructions as others had followed those of Tua Ya Pek just a short time before.

Our conversation had proved informative and illustrative, and provided an initial framework of comparison of Underworld deity's concepts and behaviour, both of which were consistently reconfirmed with minor variations in subsequent consultations with Tua Di Ya Pek at other temples, altars and festivals in Singapore. However, these would differ significantly from those of Tua Di Ya Pek *tang-ki* in Malaysia. Comparisons in the interpretation of post-mortal cosmology and actual ritual practices between the Underworld traditions in the two locations will be addressed and analysed in Part III.

Conclusion: Underworld deities and ghosts – analysing degrees of morality

Continuing on from the earlier discussion of a multi-ethnic, multi-faith and therefore inescapable Underworld, Tua Ya Pek's notions of universal sins and, by extension, practitioners' emic understandings of the interrelationship between morality and post-mortal punishments are strongly influenced by a universal morality which stands separate from and operates independently of local secular laws. The brief mention of animal incarnations resulting from infringements of this universal morality, and the way in which Tua Ya Pek immediately personalised the context suggested (and this was later confirmed during interviews) that the actuality of a future animal incarnation does not enter the mind-sets or religious life-worlds of practitioners. Rather, in the Underworld tradition it is commonly held that once an individual had received the correct punishments for iniquities in their previous incarnation, they were reincarnated into their present human form, and after death the same process would be repeated.

The conversation also highlighted the centrality of alcohol and tobacco in the Singaporean tradition and, in the process, illustrated the cosmological separation of dual moralities, the first applied to Underworld deities as channelled through their *tang-ki*, and the latter to their followers. In essence, deities may consume alcohol excessively, as it is held that when they return to the Underworld the alcohol will be removed from the *tang-ki*'s body. It is therefore 'as if' the *tang-ki* has not drunk any alcohol, their body staying pure, thus allowing deities to re-enter when required. That Tua Ya Pek handed out occasional cans of Guinness shows that the moderate consumption of alcohol in a temple environment is not considered unethical. The ongoing late-night consumption of alcohol in and around Underworld temples after the PAP passed the 2015 Liquor Control (Supply and Consumption) Act, prohibiting the public[19] consumption of alcohol between 10:30 p.m. and 7 a.m., reiterates the distinction between what is considered ethical and legitimate in the religious versus the secular arenas. The Underworld tradition thus encompasses three distinct moralities: as judged post-mortally in the Underworld; as stipulated by secular law; and as different behavioural codes for channelled deities and for their devotees in temple settings. The ethical dimensions of ritual intoxication will be explored further in relation to Tua Di Ya Pek's mass consumption of opium in Malaysia.

Moving on to physiological sensations and trance states, it was evident

---

19 Defined as "Any place (whether open-air or enclosed) to which members of the public have access".

that the *tang-ki* was intoxicated at the time of our conversation, though he appeared sober immediately after exiting the trance state. While the possible effects of trance states on the absorption of alcohol are beyond the scope of this research, within the internal logic of the tradition the emic understanding of an Underworld deity's ability to transfer alcohol to the Underworld validates the custom of placing used opium wraps on deity statues' tongues. The two concepts are mutually reinforcing, both illustrating technologies of transference through contiguity as practised in the Underworld tradition.

Lastly, Tua Ya Pek's cajoling me into a wager illustrates Underworld deities' willingness and enthusiasm for gambling, an eagerness most commonly expressed by proffering possible combinations of winning numbers for the four-digit (4D) lotto at temples in both locations. With several thousand combinations being offered monthly by Tua Di Ya Pek's *tang-ki*, and lottery providers offering multiple winning combinations each week, practitioners invariably know someone who has won money in this fashion. Depending on the amount of their winnings, practitioners customarily reciprocate with gifts ranging from cans of Guinness to lavish banquets. This renders the practice self-perpetuating, as each correct prediction reinforces emic perceptions of a particular Tua Di Ya Pek's efficacy, thereby increasing their popularity and following, and the subsequent demand for and willingness of the deity to provide further predictions.

The combination of tobacco, alcohol and gambling allows for parallels to be drawn with the rise in notoriety of ghost temples in Taiwan that occurred simultaneously with the popularisation of Underworld deities in the 1980s. Weller (2000) claimed ghost temples to be an indigenous example of religious expression in Taiwan, and largely attributed their success to a surplus of disposable wealth created by restrictions placed on the export of Taiwan's currency, resulting in mass speculation in stocks and shares and in real estate. "Taiwan became a gambler's economy in which earlier values of hard work and savings no longer explained profits" (Weller, 2000: 481). The most famous of these temples, Shiba Wang Gong, was dedicated to the ghosts of seventeen drowned sailors and their faithful dog. Local folklore tells that the dog was still alive when the sailors were buried, and it jumped into the grave with them. The sailors were attributed with the habit of heavy smoking, and a custom developed whereby, instead of burning incense, cigarettes were offered at the altar, and, in common with the channelling of Underworld deities, Shiba Wang Gong were most commonly approached at night. In contrast to the Heaven deities that filled other temple altars in Taiwan, in return for sufficient offerings of money or goods, the venerated ghosts (Wanshan Ye) would grant their devotees immoral favours. By the late 1980s, "Ghost shrines gained national popularity" (Weller, 1999: 355) and, as Shi Ba Wang Gong's ghosts had become famed for choosing winning lottery numbers and profitable investments on the stock market, it became among the most visited temples in Taiwan.

Looking then to degrees of morality, Underworld deities, located between Heaven deities and venerated ghosts, are perceived to have a flexible sense of values and, bound by Hell's own ethical codes, to possess their *tang-ki* to preach universal laws of morality. In essence, be virtuous in this life, or suffer me and the post-mortal consequences in the Underworld. In consultations they provide advice and spiritual assistance, and perform exorcistic, luck-changing and healing rituals for their devotees. The combination of these positive attributes, coupled with their association with gambling and the de-stigmatisation of smoking and alcohol consumption, has rendered them easily approachable when channelled through a *tang-ki*. This very approachability has proven to be a major factor in their popularisation and rise to dominance in Singapore's religious landscape.

5

異

A new Underworld God of Wealth, and foetus assistance rituals in Singapore

Following on from rituals performed at a privately owned *tang-ki* temple in Chapter 4, the ethnographic focus now moves to two linked public temples integrated into a new 'united temple' complex. After detailing a form of temple networking unique to Singapore, and in the context of the recently expanding Underworld pantheon, I reproduce a discussion with the case-study temple's *tang-ki* concerning the new Underworld God of Wealth, Bao Bei Ya. The analysis of the discussion draws on parallels made by Tua Ya Pek, comparing Bao Bei Ya to the 'Laughing Buddha' Mile Pusa, thus linking the contemporary promotion of a new Underworld deity in Singapore with the Han dynasty absorption of Buddhist cosmology. The second ethnography follows a 'foetus assistance' ritual performed by Tua Ya Pek, channelled by the same *tang-ki*, to speed the passage of its soul through the Underworld. The chapter concludes with an analysis of this Underworld deity's own sense perceptions while possessing his *tang-ki*. This final discussion covers the autocratic nature of government legislation, technologies of religious synthesis and the inversion of tradition in the context of Confucian and Buddhist influences on contrasting ethical codes in Singapore's contemporary Underworld tradition.

The case-study temples

As well as the creation and expansion of Underworld temple networks based on reciprocity by individual *tang-ki*, and distinctive to Singapore's religious landscape, ritual connections based on temples' prior locations pre-urban redevelopment have been constructed in Singapore by the post-relocation generation of *tang-ki*. This chapter features two such temples, Choa Chu

Kang (the name of the area) Doumu Gong and Sanzhong Gong. These temples, although occupying two units in a large united temple consisting of five temples, for all practical intents and purposes act as a single religious and ritual unit, visitors offering incense to deities at both temple altars. The three other resident temples that together comprise Choa Chu Kang United Temple, though not ritually linked, share equally proportioned areas within the temple's long, narrow courtyard. Acting as distinct ritual and social units, each has a *tang-ki* channelling their own Tua Di Ya Pek on different nights of the week.

Doumu Gong and Sanzhong Gong were originally situated in the same street in the now defunct village of Lai Dong Sen, before being relocated during the government's city restructuring programme in the 1970s. At Lai Dong Sen, most families had kinship ties both within the village and with those living in neighbouring villages, many practitioners sharing a family name, in this case Tan.[1] After the original village was demolished its businesses, temples and inhabitants were relocated to districts in the northwest of Singapore – present-day Yew Tee, Choa Chu Kang and Bukit Batok. A large proportion of Lai Dong Sen's past residents and their descendants continue to worship at the surviving relocated temples, many being active members of Doumu Gong and Sanzhong Gong, which originally were separate temples but now share the same sacred space with no dividing wall between them.

Linked by past proximity and kinship ties from the village era, new and ongoing ritual links between Lai Dong Sen's temples thus mirror social relations not only within and between participating temples but also between Singapore's past and present in terms of locations and generations. While ritual connections between competing village temples were uncommon, Lai Dong Sen's relocated temples[2] have formed new ritual networks based on their past proximity, maintained through reciprocal participation by their *tang-ki* in each other's annual festivals. Of Lai Dong Sen's original village temples, Jin Shui Gang has relocated to Yio Chu Kang, Laisheng Gong to Bukit Batok, Nanlai Dian to Yew Tee and Sanzhong Gong and Doumu Gong to Choa Chu Kang. Tua Di Ya Pek are channelled at all of these temples by elder *tang-ki* who previously channelled only Heaven deities, and by a host of younger *tang-ki* whom they have mentored and trained. In this regard, by reshaping the temple landscape, urban relocation has acted as a catalyst to ongoing religious synergy. Understanding tradition as a continual process of development, a progression Charles Stewart described as "the outcome,

1 'Tan' is the Hokkien pronunciation of 'Chen'.
2 This applies to public temples registered with local authorities. Unregistered 'residential temples' were not officially relocated, but some re-formed in the limited space that HDB accommodation had to offer.

at any particular moment, of historical and social processes" (Stewart, 2004: 274), the latest generation of *tang-ki* and their apprentices may be seen as one of several 'self-perpetuating mechanisms' resulting from the urban renewal programme, thus sustaining Singapore's currently flourishing Underworld tradition.

The expanding Underworld pantheon in Singapore

The appropriation of deities between Chinese religious pantheons is a historically documented phenomenon, and the creation of new deities from natural objects and human souls is ongoing. For instance, I have observed the deification and subsequent anthropomorphising of a large boulder venerated at Yilan Jinxing Gong in Taiwan as the anthropomorphic deity Mr Blackstone (Heishi Xiansheng), and recent location-specific, politically motivated post-mortal pantheonic additions including Chiang Kai-shek, who is worshipped at several temples in Taiwan, and the widespread religious veneration of Mao Zedong in state-sponsored temples across China. In contrast to deities in the Underworld tradition, each of these examples conforms to long-established traditions either of deifying inanimate objects – for example, local rivers and mountains to local river and mountain gods (*heshen* / 河神 and *shanshen* / 山神) – or of the post-mortal promotion of powerful or meritorious individuals to the rank of deity.

However, until some time in the late 1990s there have been no significant additions to the Underworld pantheon in Singapore. While the earlier channelling of Underworld deities may have occurred in isolated historical instances, the genesis of the contemporary Singaporean tradition dates only from the late 1950s,[3] and it is only since the early 1990s that Tua Di Ya Pek began to emerge, and dynamically so, as among the most frequently channelled deities in Singapore. However, even though the local Underworld pantheon remained unchanged until the 1990s, Tua Di Ya Pek's increasing veneration has been accompanied by changing associations within the Underworld tradition itself. While the Underworld has remained the locus of post-mortal punishments, a hypothetical free-association 'Rorschach'-style test among Singapore's young adult devotees may now play out as follows: Death–Underworld; Underworld–Tua Di Ya Pek; Tua Di Ya Pek–Guinness; Guinness–alcohol; alcohol–Tua Di Ya Pek; Tua Di Ya Pek–Underworld; Underworld–punishment, and so forth. While this simulation is intentionally exaggerated and not intended as a serious analytical commentary on Underworld temple culture or beliefs, it provides an indication of changing

3 Discussed in detail in Chapter 11.

associations based on the inversion of religious practices unaccompanied by a change in cosmology. In the process of popularisation, the creative portrayals of the Underworld courts and post-mortal tortures which commonly adorn purpose-built tents during festivals, or placed around Underworld temple altars, reinforced by Tua Di Ya Pek's sombre warnings of 'behave now, or endure me later', have, perhaps contrary to intuition, served to enthuse an alienated youth to associate more proactively with Underworld *sintua* (神坛).[4] Contributing to this phenomenon are Tua Di Ya Pek's increasingly jovial demeanour and escalating consumption of alcohol, factors which together have made them easily accessible 'people's deities' who, in return for devotion, worship and assistance, endeavour to solve their devotees' problems and ills and supply them with predictions of possible winning combinations for the national four-digit (4D) lottery.

However, owing to the promotion of erstwhile Hell spirits to the rank of deity, the Underworld pantheons in Singapore, and more so in Malaysia, have recently expanded, and continue to do so. Previously unknown Underworld deities are now being channelled with increasing frequency, from Singapore to Kuala Lumpur and Penang. Among these, and unique in originating from Singapore rather than Malaysia, is a new Underworld God of Wealth, Bao Bei Ya.

Money: the new gods on the block

I first came across the Underworld deity Bao Bei Ya in a small shop-front temple in Geylang, a traditional business district of Singapore, and had been planning to ask Sanzhong Gong's Tua Ya Pek more about him. According to informants, statues of this deity first appeared in the 1990s, and there is a general consensus among Singapore's religionists that even by 2010 this deity was rarely channelled by *tang-ki*. He is, for all intents and purposes, the new deity on the block. The appearance and spread of his iconography were followed within a decade by *tang-ki* channelling the deity, suggesting that requests made to Bao Bei Ya's statues yielded sufficiently successful results to create both a demand for, and supply of, *tang-ki* to channel him.

However, the precise relationship between anthropomorphisation, iconography and human embodiment remains speculative. For instance, Margaret Chan (2008) claims that an anthropomorphised form is necessary in order to worship and bargain with deities and Jordan Paper notes that "Nature and other spirits over time became transformed into dead humans so that they too can possess us" (Paper, 2009: 344). He suggests that anthropomorphising

[4] Religious groups based around a specific altar.

is necessary before a deity can enter a human form, and this may be because a human spirit is more likely to fit into a human body than is a spirit with a different shape (Paper, 2009: 334). Chan goes further, arguing that "The anthropomorphic image, as against the aniconic, gives a spirit the body it needs for an existence in the human world" (Chan, 2008: 23). Putting these speculations aside, the idea of a 'new' deity of wealth was intriguing, especially so because in Taiwan in a similar period, money god (*caishen* / 财神) temples also increased in popularity, though they are populated by Heaven deities and there are contrasting methods of bargaining with them for wealth. I therefore consulted Tua Ya Pek to learn more about the creation of deities in the Underworld, and specifically about the Underworld God of Wealth, Bao Bei Ya.

Each *tang-ki* has a specific style of calling their 'Boss' to possess them, some using secret signals to indicate to the possessing deity that they are ready, though for most *tang-ki* the movements have become stylised. For Underworld deities, *tang-ki* generally enter a trance state in a throne held down by assistants to prevent it from tipping over under the medium's momentum as an invocation is chanted. Illustrating the appropriation of Taiwan's music culture into Singapore's religious landscape, the tune used most frequently to invoke Underworld deities was first popularised as a Taiwanese folk song called 'Mrs Green Oyster' (*Qi e'ah So*), written by Guo Dacheng in 1970 and first recorded by the singer Lina. While Guo's song lyric is about a woman with an ugly husband who sells oysters for a living, the words have been replaced with an invocation to the Underworld, which varies from temple to temple. Replacing the violins and keyboards are traditional *shougu* (手鼓) hand drums and *tongluo* (铜锣) brass gongs, all struck in a mesmerising rhythm by groups of temple volunteers who are devotees of the Underworld deities they summon. At Sanzhong Gong, the original lyrics, "Other people's husbands are wearing suits, my husband is selling green oysters, so everyone calls me Mrs Green Oyster", have been replaced with "Incense smoke raising up slowly to open the gates of the Underworld, we invite Tua Ya Pek up from the Underworld [...] to decide the good and bad of this world resolutely, to reward goodness and punish evil." The percussion and chant grow in rapidity and volume as the *tang-ki*'s motions intensify, rising to a dramatic crescendo as the experienced eyes of the assistants recognise that the deity will soon possess the medium. The drums and chants usually continue until the medium has been ceremonially dressed in their appropriate attire, the chant at Sanzhong Gong ending in energetic choruses of "Followers focus and invite, invite Tua Ya Pek of the East Prison. Five Generals approach the front of the altar, your Underworld armies are arriving soon."

5.1 Bao Bei Ya in Geylang

Discussing Bao Bei Ya at Sanzhong Gong

On 4 January 2011, at around 9 p.m., the 'tang-ki's heavy wooden throne was placed just outside the Underworld altar room at the rear of the temple with three burly assistants holding it secure. The medium faced the altar on which the three most senior deities, Dizangwang, Chenghuang and Bao Gong, sat majestically above and behind assorted statues of Tua Di Ya Pek and Underworld ghosts. In front of the deities was a large altar table littered with Underworld paraphernalia including a black abacus which Tua Ya Pek uses to calculate one's sins, karma, future, fortune and luck, and a variety of alcohol including cans of Guinness and Ah Pek's favourite cognac, Martell Cordon Bleu. Behind the 'tang-ki' stood his closest devotees performing the invocation, and I stood close by to observe the proceedings.

After sitting in the Underworld throne the 'tang-ki' yawned, and soon his legs began to shake. Then he started swaying towards the floor and crashing back into the throne with increasing violence as three assistants battled to hold it steady. As the medium's body came up for the umpteenth time, a 'Hell scream' arose from deep in the 'tang-ki's throat. In the darkness, humidity and heat of the equatorial night, this scream sent a spine-tingling chill down to the soles of my feet, and I felt goose bumps rise on my neck as I watched his body crumple forward again with a ferocious momentum propelling his head to within centimetres of the floor from where another piercing scream emanated. When he rocked back he was in a trance state and possessed by Tua Ya Pek. In moments, he was skilfully dressed by his assistants in a white patterned gown, a fan placed in one hand, three incense sticks in the other, and his hat rested on and secured to his head. The transformation of Mr Chen into Tua Ya Pek was compelling, not only visually, but also physically and mentally as it was clear that there had been a dramatic change in the physical posture, voice and personality of the 'tang-ki'. Falling to his knees with a Hell scream, Tua Ya Pek prostrated himself before the deities on the altar and then again before images of the Underworld Generals of the Five Directions housed in a small ground-level shrine beneath the auspices of the temple's black flag (ohr leng / 黑令). The flag is both a signifier of 'tang-ki' temples, and considered to be a ritual vessel embodied with independent efficacy. Whether embossed with images of weapons, secret talismans or remaining unadorned, it contains the discarnate efficacy of the 'Emperor of the Dark Heavens'[5] commander

---

5 A title bestowed in 1304 by the Yuan dynasty emperor Chengzong.

of Heaven's Thirty-Six Celestial Armies. It also contains the efficacy of the temple's own guardian deity, the 'Black Flag General', Hei Ling Jiangjun, an autonomous commander of the temple's own local spirit armies. Tua Ya Pek's screams were thus offered as a form of reverence to higher-ranking deities, and, as a form of communication through the Emperor of the Dark Heavens embodied in their black flag informing Heaven that Tua Ya Pek was present in the human realm at that specific time and place. Formalities over, his chair was then carried to a position in front of the altar table where he accepted a cigarette in a long copper pipe which he drew on until it was burned half down, a bowl of cognac which was drunk in a gulp, and then a can of Guinness which he sipped as he regarded his devotees who were welcoming him to the mortal realm.

After numerous consultations, it was coming on 11 p.m., the air hung thick with incense, and running his fingers across his black abacus in the dim candlelight, Tua Ya Pek seemed jovial and pleased to see me. He asked me what I would like to discuss, and as I drained a can of warm Guinness, he produced his signature spine-chilling scream, thus leaving the ball firmly in my court.

"I'm going to England next Sunday. Would you give me some advice for while I'm away from Singapore?"

Tua Ya Pek spun the discs on his abacus and then picked it up and shook it to calculate the answer before returning it to the table. He then asked me if I had five coins and asked me to put them on the table. He played with the coins in his hands for a few moments, looking at them as if they were of rare beauty, then ran his hand across his abacus again and felt the discs with intense concentration.

I had been contemplating Bao Bei Ya and the development of new Underworld deities while waiting for my consultation, and he seemed to have sensed that England was not really on my mind.

"What would you like to know before you go back to England? I mean, what would you like to know about other things not related to England?"

I smiled in appreciation of his intuitive knowing. I spent a few moments organising my thoughts as consultations with Hell deities at night are somewhat unnerving, an experience shared by almost everyone I asked, and promptly decided on a direct approach to counterbalance this particular Tua Ya Pek's practice of answering questions cryptically or in riddles.

"I want to know about another Underworld deity called Bao Bei Ya. He is a new deity to be tranced in Singapore, and as far as I know, he has been venerated for less than twenty years. Why did this deity choose to wait so long before he revealed himself to humans, and to be channelled through 'tang-ki'?"

"All of the deities are actually interlinked, and each has their own department to look after. I know this deity, but we look after different departments."

"So, you don't know why it has taken him so long to be tranced by 'tang-ki'," I suggested.

"After going through many different stages in numerous courts and departments of the Underworld, he has accumulated merits. As a result, he has been promoted to the status of deity rather than being banished and becoming a ghost."

"How long has he been a deity for?"

In the hushed atmosphere of the dark consultation room, the rattle of his abacus as he shook it and then spun the discs cut shrilly through the still night air.

"How many coins did you give me?"

"Five," I replied.

"So why are there more than five coins now?"

"Because you added some coins of your own to the pile."

Each deity has items associated with them that are both represented in their anthropomorphic images and also carried when tranced through a medium, for example, Tua Ya Pek's fan and Di Ya Pek's demon-summoning plaque, and the object associated with Bao Bei Ya is a long chain of coins. The connection between the coins on the table and my questions about the Underworld God of Wealth had not escaped me, and I wondered about the coincidence, if coincidence it was, as I had never heard of a deity asking for coins in a consultation before, and he had asked for them before I had mentioned Bao Bei Ya.

"Yes, coin upon coin upon coin. Imagine for example I can promote you to be a village chief, but I can't let you ascend to the throne immediately because I have to see you can perform the job well first, so there is a probationary period. If, however, after practising you can perform the duty well, then I will let you ascend to the official throne."

"So, I understand that he has now been promoted, but why did he recently allow himself to be channelled through 'tang-ki'?"

"This is because he could not let himself be commonly known until he had officially ascended to the post that he is now assigned to."

"Does this mean that he only ascended to his official post approximately twenty years ago?"

"It is very similar to the five coins I asked you to produce. If you are able to give me five coins, I am prepared to give you another three in return. Likewise, this deity was given a chance to perform his duties, and after performing his duties for many years his performance was reviewed and then, like being given extra coins, his new rank was confirmed."

"So, you are saying that only after assuming a certain rank can a deity be tranced through a human medium?"

"That is correct."

"I understand that in the Underworld there are many ranks, for example Tua Ya Pek and Di Ya Pek both have higher ranks than Sa Ya Pek as you are first, second and third brothers respectively. What is the comparative rank of Bao Bei Ya to other Underworld deities?"

"Among these particular deities, they are all equal as there is no difference in rank between them."

"I have heard that Tua Di Ya Pek are enforcers in the Underworld, and they make sure that punishments are carried out fully. What is the role of Bao Bei Ya?"

"Do you know the Laughing Buddha, and do you know what he carries behind him? He carries a big sack. Do you know what he carries in the sack?" he asked rhetorically, and then continued.

"It is said that there are 1,000 pieces of gold. What he actually carries in his sack though are the cries of sorrow of all the commoners. So, when he goes anywhere in the mortal world, he takes away the cries, sorrows, worries and the grief, and they are frozen in his bag so that everyone is happy. Similarly, with Bao Bei Ya, people go to him to solve their money problems. He is the same as me. He comes to settle the problems of common people and takes their problems away with him."

This conversation provided several insights into the workings of the Underworld hierarchy as understood by this particular Tua Ya Pek. While the Underworld tradition, from the perspective of most practitioners, is firmly embedded in the vernacular Taoist tradition, individual temples nominally identify themselves with either the broader Buddhist or Taoist traditions, the choice commonly depending on the pantheonic attachment of their main deities. In Sanzhong Gong the primary deities are revered in both Taoism and Buddhism, and in Doumu Gong the principal deities originate from the vernacular and Taoist pantheons. Sanzhong Gong's central altar features Guan Gong[6] and Huaguang Dadi,[7] whereas Doumu Gong

---

6 In Taoism, Guan Sheng Dijun (关圣帝君), also known as Holy Emperor Lord Guan (Guan Gong), is one of the four Marshals guarding Taoism. In Buddhism, Qielan Pusa (Guan Gong) is a Bodhisattva charged with guarding the Dharma.

7 In Taoism, Huaguang Dadi is also known as Lingguan Ma Yuanshuai, one of the four

is devoted to Doumu Niang-niang and her sons, the Nine Emperor Gods (Jiuhuang Dadi). The Emperor of the Dark Heavens is venerated at both temples through their black flag, as are the Generals of the Five Directions represented in three manifestations, by their flags, within the black flag and on the tips of skewers used for ritual piercing. However, many religious concepts espoused by Tua Ya Pek clearly illustrated the Buddhist influence on Chinese vernacular religion.

For instance, the laughing Buddha (Xiao Fo) referred to at the end of our conversation is the Bodhisattva Maitreya (Mile Pusa), the Future Buddha recorded in the *Jataka* books of the *Khuddaka-Nikaya*, who is predicted to be born 5,000 years after the historical Buddha's death to teach the true Dharma. Combining Buddhist and contemporary Underworld cosmologies, Tua Ya Pek promoted the accumulation of merits both for his followers and for Underworld denizens' own self-cultivation, with Bao Bei Ya receiving deity status rather than banishment from Hell, due to gaining merits in different courts and departments of the Underworld. Outside of the Underworld tradition, comparing the roles and abilities of the Future Buddha with a recently promoted Underworld spirit would be considered inappropriate, if not bizarre. Therefore, Tua Ya Pek's affable comparison provides an insight into the elevated status afforded to Underworld deities in Singapore's present-day temple landscape, and into emic perceptions among practitioners of Tua Di Ya Pek as arbiters of religious knowledge.

The appearance of new Underworld deities is clear as a self-perpetuating mechanism: increasing the number of deities that can be channelled by existing and future generations of *tang-ki*; expanding the collective repertoire of Underworld deities' specialisations; and adding colour and variety to the festive, ritual and material culture. From a future-oriented perspective, it may be anticipated that, coinciding with societal developments imparting a negative impact on the vernacular religious tradition, an increasing diversity of Underworld deities will be venerated and channelled in the course of time. Potential candidates from Malaysia's expanding Underworld pantheon, including the 'Laughing God' and 'Bone God',[8] will be detailed in Chapter 11.

In the era of banking corporations and the mass allocation of subsidised government housing in Singapore, an Underworld God of Wealth who removes individuals' financial worries tallies with one attribute of Feuchtwang's (1991) 'imperial metaphor' as described by Charles Stafford:

---

marshals protecting Taoism. In Buddhism, Huaguang was a generic term for one of the historical Buddha's ten primary disciples (Nikaido 2015: 82–83).
8 Lo Qio Sian Pek and Pai Gu Pek.

"to connect, quite explicitly, the local world of everyday interactions, the religious world of divine interventions, and the political world of imperial (or state) control" (Stafford, 2000: 177). This provides a feasible etic explanation for the local appearance and channelling of Bao Bei Ya, which, couched in terms of technologies of religious synthesis, may be seen as a reinvention of celestial money gods, including Zhao Gongming and the Money Gods of the Five Directions (Wulu Caishen), both of these popularised in the early 2000s and performing a similar role to Bao Bei Ya in Taiwan. However, while acknowledging that the addition of a new, low-ranking Hell deity does not affect the Underworld's bureaucratic hierarchy, the popularisation of Bao Bei Ya reflects a significant reinterpretation of two aspects of Underworld cosmology.

First, prior to Tua Di Ya Pek's popularisation, common perceptions of the post-mortal journey culminated in the Tenth Court of the Underworld and the soul drinking Meng Po's 'Five Flavoured Tea of Forgetfulness' before awaiting reincarnation. In contrast, Bao Bei Ya's accumulated merits resulted in promotion and permanent residency, and many *tang-ki* now advocate that the souls of those who were previously devoted to Underworld deity worship are given the choice of reincarnating or becoming an Ah Pek in the Underworld. Tua Ya Pek noted that there is no difference in rank between the various Ah Pek, and it is now held that, having achieved this rank, by assisting the living through their *tang-ki*, their souls accumulate further post-mortal merits both in the Underworld and on Earth.

Second, and relating to the individualisation of Ah Pek when channelled, before their association with Xie Bian and Fan Wujiu, Tua Di Ya Pek were the souls of the dead policing the souls of the dead, demonic and anonymous, serving in the Underworld to accumulate enough merits to reincarnate. Now, with multiple Tua Di Ya Pek channelled from all Ten Courts of the Underworld, anonymity has been all but forsaken, each identified with a specific family name and human soul, with many Tua Di Ya Pek happy to recount details of their lives prior to becoming Hell's policemen. Prior to the modern Underworld tradition, these individual Underworld enforcers would not have been represented on temple altars, and therefore would not have received personal offerings. Instead, generic offerings of incense would have been made only within the confines of City God or Dongyue Dadi temples. Underworld enforcers have thus been reinvented, hybridisation bestowing individuality, and the transfiguration of practice allowing for plentiful offerings from their devotees, including Guinness, cognac, their favourite victuals and bespoke robes to be used or consumed through their *tang-ki*, or to be 'sent off' through ritual immolation for their use in the Underworld. The increasing popularity of the Underworld God of Wealth illustrates these developments clearly. By 2016, there were sixteen individual Bao Bei Ya, hailing from various Underworld courts, being channelled by Singapore's *tang-ki*, each sporting a singular family name, including Jiu Bao Bei Ya, Choa Bao Bei Ya, Qian Bao Bei Ya and Lim Bao Bei Ya at Xuanhuang Dian, Shenglian Gong, Longde Tang and Yunshan Dian, with each receiving personalised offerings at their temple altars.

Smoothing the journey of the foetus spirit

In addition to giving consultations, *tang-ki* also perform rituals as and when necessary to address their devotees' problems. A 'foetus assistance' ritual performed at Sanzhong Gong is of particular interest, as it contrasts both with the use of foetus ghosts enlisted into a temple's private Underworld army during Ghost Month in Malaysia and with the cosmology of and rituals for placating malicious foetus ghosts in Taiwan. The differences in interpretation will be discussed in context of transnational cultural flows in Chapter 8. Meanwhile, Sanzhong Gong's foetus assistance ritual serves to illustrate the distinction made between harmless foetus spirits as perceived in Singapore and the malicious foetus ghosts employed in Malaysia's Underworld tradition.

> *Every Thursday night at Sanzhong Gong, Tua Ya Pek is invited to possess his 'tang-ki'. The evening commenced in its usual fashion, and as chanting commenced, the 'tang-ki' began to quiver and then to sway violently back and forth in the Underworld throne. The dull thud of its legs hitting the ground each time the chair rocked resembled a metronome in its regularity, so much so that devotees kept in tempo with it creating the effect of speeding up the rhythm of their chant as the medium came increasingly closer to being possessed. As is the norm with this particular 'tang-ki', as Tua Ya Pek arrived, a piercing scream arose within him, one which gave the impression of voicing the misery and agony endured in the Underworld. Tua Ya Pek offered incense, and then the consultations began.*
>
> *A young couple had come to consult Tua Ya Pek by appointment and were therefore dealt with first. They had recently aborted an unwanted foetus and sought to hasten its reincarnation. The ritual they had requested corresponded to the long-standing conviction that if aborted or miscarried, a foetus spirit will return to the 'waiting room' in the Underworld until rebirth is possible, thus furnishing the rationale of visiting a Hell deity to ritually assist with hastening its journey through the Underworld and obtaining a prompt reincarnation.*

5.2 Tua Ya Pek at Sanzhong Gong

Behind the temple there is a small area of grassland dividing the temple from an adjacent concreted playground, and a small fold-away table was placed there, and a temporary Taoist styled altar containing a censer for incense, two candles, five pieces of fruit, three plastic cups of each tea and water, and a large bowl of uncooked rice were placed on top. Behind the altar with its back to the temple was a green chair, green symbolising the Underworld and therefore the deceased. If the ritual had been for an adult, or even a child, the individual's clothes would have been placed on the chair, but for an aborted foetus, these were replaced by a towel with the dual symbolism of a swaddling cloth and a means of absorbing foetal blood. A plastic bowl was then placed in front of the chair for the sanitary needs of the aborted foetus. In addition, articles with a symbolic connection to babies were placed on the altar table including a pair of baby shoes placed on top of boxes containing baby clothes, a bottle of milk with a pacifier (dummy) in the top, piles of sweets and biscuits and a bowl of baby food. Netherworld paraphernalia included heaps of 'Hell banknotes'⁹ to pay officials and bribe door guards in the Underworld, blank green charm papers for talisman to be drawn on, and black ink and brush for Tua Ya Pek to write with.

When the altar was completed, Tua Ya Pek stepped out of the temple to inspect it, and with a shrill scream fell to his knees before the altar. He held out his fan onto which two coins were placed, and these were used as a substitute for divination blocks as a means to divine whether or not the deities were, at this stage in the ritual, happy with the proceedings. Tua Ya Pek moved his fan allowing the coins to drop on the floor. A head and a tail would indicate a positive answer from the deities, and either two heads or two tails would indicate a negative. In the case of a negative answer, some changes to the altar would have had to be made until the deities were satisfied and a positive answer secured.

Both parents approached the altar each holding three incense sticks, and Tua Ya Pek petitioned the deities in the Underworld on their behalf. The ritual process continued as Tua Ya Pek picked up various items from the altar including sweets and baby clothes and threw them at the chair. The two coins were then cast again, but the answer negative, so Tua Ya Pek requested a bundle of lit incense and then prostrated himself on the sun scorched grass before the altar. Rethrowing the coins, a positive answer was then attained, and the parents were somberly summoned to approach the altar. At Tua Ya Pek's bidding, the baby shoes were placed on the chair by the husband who, along with his wife, was clearly in a state of distress. In his silken white robe, Tua Ya Pek, the Underworld enforcer, stood as an authority figure among the assembled company. After bending low in preparation, he straightened himself, and while pointing at a particular item on the altar with his fan, let forth a spine-chilling scream into the humid night air. Dutifully the husband picked up the item indicated with the fan and flung it at the chair. The process began quite meekly but scream after scream from the Underworld enforcer had an unnerving effect, and the items were flung at the chair with increasing violence. Once the baby items had all been thrown and assent divined by the coins, they were left strewn on the ground and the party moved inside to offer incense to the temple's Underworld deities. I did not have to wait long before the principal actors returned outside to complete the ritual.

9 Hell banknotes are offered to recently deceased ancestors, ghosts and Underworld deities and generally come in unrealistic denominations of millions of dollars in an assortment international currencies (Scott, J. L., 2007). They are considered to be real rather than merely symbolic representations of wealth after being transmuted by fire (Tong, 2004: 87).

Tua Ya Pek led the group and prostrated himself before the altar, and once again coins were cast from his fan to ascertain if the ritual could be continued. Underworld deities trance at night, and a torch had to be brought out from the temple to locate the coins which had fallen out of sight. When found they indicated an affirmative answer, and a large metal trough-shaped tray about the length and height of a child's crib was brought out and placed a few metres away from the altar on a wide grass verge separating the temple from the main road.

To delineate a new sacred space, the father was given a handful of lit incense sticks which he placed in the soil around the tray to create a ritual barrier that no spirit entity could cross. Then wads of Hell banknotes, tied with string, were piled on the ground in front of the tray, burning incense sticks and thin lit candles were inserted between the notes, and these were all placed in the centre of the tray. Alongside them was a green talisman drawn in black ink by Tua Ya Pek petitioning the Underworld deities on behalf of the parents, asking that the offerings would be accepted by the Ruler of the Underworld, Dongyue Dadi, in exchange for the soul of the aborted foetus to reincarnate sooner. The other ritual items scattered across the floor including the shoes, baby clothes, porridge, the bowl containing the porridge, the fruit, in fact everything barring the altar table and green chair were then brought and piled onto the tray. Helpers then unwrapped further packets of Hell banknotes, and these were heaped up until the other offerings were hidden buried within. The husband then accepted handfuls of Hell banknotes which he set alight and used these to ignite the contents of the tray.

In moments, the fire was burning fiercely, flames consuming all, and job accomplished, the retinue of 'tang-ki' and helpers re-entered the temple. Only the parents were left, mournfully watching in silence as the fire died down and the offerings were transformed into ash.

The act of incineration itself is a transformation process enabling material offerings "to go beyond the confines of the living world [...] replicas in the state of becoming" (Scott, J. L., 2007: 20), the burning converting offerings into usable objects in the Underworld. The offerings of money were thus transferred, through immolation, to Dongyue Dadi, and the other items for the use of the foetus until time for its rebirth.

I re-entered the temple, and after public consultations had finished, I sat facing Tua Ya Pek. I was eager to explore physiological perceptions of possessing a 'tang-ki's body from the perspective of the possessing entity, and after asking him if the evening's ritual had been successful to which he replied that the offerings had been accepted, he asked,

"What would you like to know about tonight?"

"I would like to ask you what it feels like to be in a human body? After all, in the Underworld you are spirit and have no body and now you are inside your 'tang-ki'. What does it feel like to be in somebody else's human body?"

Picking up his rattan fan he ventured "What does it feel like when I fan you?"

"It feels fresh like a cool breeze."

"Can you see the way that you feel?"

I shook my head and Tua Ya Pek fanned me again, and I tried to fathom the lesson that he was endeavouring to impart.

"Can you feel it?"

"Yes."

"Yes, of course you can feel it, but you cannot see it. My sensations translate through the same logic."

I contemplated his response and understood it to mean that while trance possession can be documented in terms of tactility and discourse on the part of the observer, after the transition from discarnate to incarnate, what he saw was not possible for me to feel, and what he felt was not necessarily the same as that which I saw. To check my understanding I enquired,

"So, when you look at me or at the other people here, do you see our spiritual essence, or do you, being a spirit, only feel our spirits the same way that I felt the cool air?"

"Because on Earth you have a physical body, so that is what I see on Earth."

"I have heard that there are many Tua Ya Pek, not just one. How old is the Tua Ya Pek I am speaking to?"

"From way below until halfway up in the sky, however far that is, that is how old I am. It is not quantitative because after you pass on, there are no more birthdays, and therefore no more ageing."

"In the Underworld, you are an enforcer of punishments, and the punishments are severe, the sacrilegious being hewn asunder in the 'Hell of Severing in Two' (Yaozhan xiao diyu), and unfilial children having their eyes plucked out in the 'Hell of Eye Gouging' (Kou yan xiao diyu). But when you come here in this 'tang-ki's body, you are humorous and benevolent, helping your devotees and giving them advice."

"As a spiritual being, I come in the spirit of helpfulness, hoping to bring good to the world, so in a way I am also cultivating myself."

The double mention of spirits coupled with the dry-throated hoarseness induced by breathing in the dense incense smoke inspired a new line of questioning.

"I would like to know more about inhabiting the medium's body, for example, your sense perceptions when drinking alcohol," I asked tentatively.

A titter of amusement among those present developed into audible giggles as Tua Ya Pek thanked me for reminding him that he hadn't drunk for a while, and that he was thirsty. He supped heartily from a fresh can of warm Guinness and pulled on a long pipe with a cigarette wedged into the end, and then issued a hellish high-pitched scream, thus testifying to his appreciation of these human delights.

"When I drink alcohol," I continued, "I know what it feels like as a human to get drunk. What does it feel like for you when you drink through the 'tang-ki's body?"

"Because I have work to do when I come to Earth, settling the problems of my devotees and people who visit the temple to consult me, I cannot get drunk! I do not feel the effects of the alcohol."

"When you say you feel thirsty, do you mean the spirit of Tua Ya Pek feels thirsty, or that the 'tang-ki's body feels thirsty?"

"I, Tua Ya Pek, the spirit, feel thirsty."

"Okay, but how can a spirit feel thirsty? A spirit has no body." I enquired.

"I am in a body!"

"Yes, good answer!" I conceded as we raised our cans and drank to each other's good health.

Underworld deities transformed: invention and reinterpretation

From this consultation, mirrored by discussions with lay informants and other channelled Tua Di Ya Pek, it is evident that, when possessing their *tang-ki*, Underworld deities perform a role reversal, from uncompromising enforcers inflicting tortures with indifference, to charming and often humorous deities solving their devotees' problems and promoting a strict code of morality, thereby entreating devotees to avoid additional suffering in their own post-mortal journeys. Translating these transformations into terms of technologies of religious synthesis, their role inversion involves modifications in both practices and meanings, transfiguring hybridisation, thus reshaping religious forms of modernity. This transformation is a tautological prerequisite of Underworld deity trance possession, as, psychologically, demonic manifestations and Hell's torments are crowd pleasers only on the silver screen. In the transformation from the dispassionate into advocates of correct moral conduct, the Underworld tradition contributes to the government's agenda by promoting the rule of law; and, in maintaining religious harmony, it assists by serving with equanimity individuals from multi-ethnic backgrounds that come to consult them.

This transformation is attributed by practitioners to their *tang-ki* becoming deity incarnate, and even though deity–devotee relationships are at their most informal in the Underworld tradition, questions pertaining to deities' sense awareness or Underworld cosmology are seldom, if ever, broached. Addressing my own reflexivity, aware of the privileged position afforded me by being granted permission by individual Tua Di Ya Pek to enquire freely about topics pertinent to my research, I realised the value of eliciting *tang-ki*'s self-perceptions and inspirational understandings while in trance possession states. In this instance, from either an etic or emic perspective, the *tang-ki*'s or Tua Ya Pek's self-commentary on physiological sense recognition during an altered state of consciousness provided valuable insights into the unvoiced subtleties of the lived religious tradition.

In contrast with practitioners present, Tua Ya Pek described sense perceptions as potentially reversed during trance possession, though that is not to say that he did not see through the *tang-ki*'s eyes, or feel through his fingers, as we both perceived the same physical materiality of people and objects. Using his fan allegorically to demonstrate the substitution of one sense organ with another, an analogy which could translate as an altered state of consciousness, he implied that what he saw in terms of, for example, a consultee's illnesses, he felt subliminally, and in cures offered in the physical shape of hand-drawn talisman containing efficacy, the efficacy could be neither seen nor felt by others in its material form. Similarly, before offering advice or making a prediction, when shaking or moving the beads on his abacus, he frequently did so with his eyes closed, calculating or receiving the solution intuitively through the sense of touch. Channelling Tua Ya Pek beneath the auspices of the black flag, practitioners' own understandings of these intuitive abilities were grounded in the Generals of the Five Directions, who, under the command of the Emperor of the Dark Heavens, gathered the information required, the abacus providing a form of intercommunication between Tua Ya Pek and these spirit armies.

In contrast to the purely physical senses, thirst is an emotion, emotion being defined as 'a thought accompanied by a physiological reaction' (Prinz, 2004; Schachter & Singer, 1962), and, during our discussion, Tua Ya Pek 'the spirit' felt thirsty. He explained that he did so due to being in a human body. This implies that when in a discarnate form Tua Di Ya Pek cannot experience emotions associated with physical cravings, and this may account for the obvious pleasure shown while imbibing alcohol, nicotine and food when channelled through a *tang-ki*. Compared to Heaven deities, who usually leave a *tang-ki*'s body when consultations are over, in the Underworld tradition *tang-ki* remain in trance states for many hours, Tua Di Ya Pek often being reluctant to leave, instead drinking and chatting with temple members long after consultations have ended. Time is not 'of the essence' in the Underworld tradition – perhaps, as Tua Ya Pek suggested, because as there are no more birthdays after death, individual souls in the Underworld do not age until reincarnation.[10] However, while the idea of age remaining fixed at the time of death corresponds with contemporary concepts of reincarnating into a new body, it does not concur with the various Buddhist and Taoist interpretations of the amount of time dedicated to post-mortal punishments in the Underworld. Among practitioners in the vernacular tradition, the most frequently mentioned period is forty-nine days, any comparative differences between Earth and Underworld time mentioned in religious texts being overlooked.[11]

Returning to the foetus assistance ritual and addition of Bao Bei Ya into the Underworld pantheon, two technologies of religious synthesis come into play. In the former, transfiguration, there is a change in religious practice without an essential alteration in meaning, and in the latter, as mentioned, there is reinvention. Prior to the Underworld tradition's popularisation, an aborted foetus would have been assumed to be free of negative karma, and, in common with Taiwan before the mid-1970s, following a miscarriage or abortion, "the parents burned incense, a Daoist master said a short prayer, and that was the end of it" (Moskowitz, 1998: 163). In contemporary vernacular religion this is no longer the case. In Taiwan, foetus ghosts are now considered malicious and are ritually appeased, at great cost, in dedicated foetus ghost temples (Moskowitz, 2001), while in Singapore, through foetus spirits' association with death, assisting their souls and those of recently deceased babies now fits resolutely within Tua Di Ya Pek's field of expertise. In regard to Bao Bei Ya and Underworld deities and wealth, Tua Di Ya Pek have been associated with gambling through the three-digit (3D) lottery since the modern Underworld tradition's inception, the history of which is recounted in Chapter 11. However, in the case of Bao Bei Ya, his relationship

---

10 This is only one Tua Ya Pek's explanation, but it coincides with practitioners' beliefs that ancestors maintain the same tastes after death as when alive, 'as if' time has stopped for them at the moment of death. This contrasts with post-mortem accounts from other cultures, where, if spirits are perceived as having an age at all, they may either continue to age or regress to a younger state.
11 The comparative passing of time between the Earth and Underworld will be revisited in Chapter 9.

with money is role specific, thereby providing devotees an Underworld equivalent of his celestial antecedents.

From an etic perspective, it is difficult to reconcile the external manifestation of the Tua Di Ya Pek tradition, including the temple-based consumption of alcohol; deities' active involvement in gambling; invocations to Underworld ghost armies to attend the altar; and Tua Di Ya Pek's roles as enforcers of Hell's post-mortal tortures with Confucian ethics and the Buddhist gaining of merits which the contemporary tradition promotes. However, in an innovative and pragmatic tradition supported by the perceived efficacy of ritual, Tua Di Ya Pek are venerated as having the necessary deific efficacy to solve devotees' problems, from changing one's luck and bestowing blessings on new businesses, to assisting foetus spirits and healing the sick. Moreover, Underworld enforcers' ability to control malevolent spirits has become a desirable and advantageous asset, associating them with graveyards and assisting the souls of the dead within them. Tangibly represented by the tombstones lining Singapore's remaining cemeteries, the individual graves are evocative of pre-Buddhist notions of the Underworld beneath Mount Tai, and the fifth-century Taoist earth prisons combining the ideas "of darkness and coldness – the darkness of entombment, the coldness of the grave, and the corpse" (Thompson, 1989: 30). The draw and attraction of graveyards to Tua Di Ya Pek is ineffable, and in the following chapter associations between Underworld deities and the graves of the dead will be explored ethnographically, drawing examples from Seventh Month cemetery rituals performed in 2017.

6

Lunar Seventh Month: the centrality of graveyards in the Underworld tradition

The Underworld tradition is intimately linked to the post-mortal journey of the soul, and to objects and places associated with the afterlife. Graveyards thus play a significant role in the tradition, as they provide a tangible link between the realms of the living and of the dead. This chapter connects the Underworld tradition directly to graveyards through Lunar Seventh Month, also known as Ghost Month, cemetery rituals. Following a historical overview of Ghost Month cosmology and the deities and taboos presently associated with it, the ethnography turns to Singapore's cemetery rituals. Part 1 describes encounters with two Underworld temples performing rituals in a cemetery plot dedicated to aborted foetuses, still-born babies and dead children, and part 2 follows Yu Feng Nan Fu Xuanshan Miao's Seventh Month rituals in their entirety. The chapter concludes with an analysis of the societal catalysts behind the increasing number of Seventh Month cemetery rituals in Singapore and discusses their role as 'everyday forms of resistance' (Scott, J. C., 1985, 1990) to contemporary land-usage legislation.

Lunar Seventh Month: Ghost Month

The antecedents of Chinese Ghost Month can be traced back to festivals in China in the era preceding the introduction of Buddhism. The Seventh Month precedes the autumn equinox, a time associated with the harvest and subsequent waning of light and physical decay, in a discussion of non-Buddhist antecedents to the Ghost Festival, and Teiser (1988) draws an analogy linking Ghost Month to the harvest and ancestral offerings. Namely, that Han dynasty emperors offering the first fruits of the harvest to their ancestors during the full moon on Seventh Month was a contributing factor in the spread of the earlier tradition. Moreover, the Taoist *Zhongyuan* festival to mark the day that the Middle Primordial, Zhongyuan Dadi,[1] descends to Earth to judge the good and evil in people's actions has been celebrated annually on the fifteenth of the Seventh Month since at least the early Tang dynasty. Taoist cosmology therefore linked the Seventh Month to judgement and death, and likely acted as an influencing factor on the development of the modern tradition. However, Buddhism provided the greatest impetus behind the continuation of Seventh Month observances in the vernacular tradition.

The Buddhist-inspired non-canonical morality tract 'The transformation text on Mulian saving his mother from the dark regions' likely had the greatest impact, as it has been the most frequently propagated by story-tellers and in theatrical performances, von Glahn also noting that such transformation texts "were widely employed by Tang [Buddhist] monks as evangelical tools" (von Glahn, 2004: 143). Based on the 'Yulanpen Sutra', in Mulian's tale, his mother, Qingti, had been reborn in the Underworld with a ravenous appetite but an inability to swallow. Thus, while Mulian made food offerings at his ancestral altar, they burst into flame as she put them into her mouth. In contemporary cosmology, this fate is shared by all ghosts in the Underworld, thus accounting for the term 'hungry ghosts' (*e gui* / 饿鬼) and the Seventh Month tradition of food offerings, as, when released from the Underworld, hungry ghosts are able to swallow. Following the Buddha's instructions, Mulian provided a feast on the fifteenth of the Seventh Month to coincide with monks emerging from their summer retreat and, as a result, Qingti escaped the tortures of the Underworld and eventually ascended to Heaven. Mulian's tale thus bridges the cultural gap between Buddhist aestheticism and Confucian filial piety, paving the way for Buddhism's further assimilation into China's vernacular religious landscape. In the 'Yulanpen Sutra', the Buddha decrees "All children can bring salvation to their parents by making offerings to monks" (Teiser, 2003: 308), thus linking the Seventh Month tradition both to filial piety and to the *sangha*[2] and securing the sutra's position in 'Buddhist historiography'; while supporting the role of ancestral offerings in the vernacular tradition ensured the continuation of Seventh Month traditions into the present day (Teiser, 1988).

Returning to the present, while the orthodox rituals remain centred on the fifteenth of the month, in the vernacular tradition, Ghost Month rituals are performed throughout the month. The likely explanation for this is that the number of temples in urban areas has far outgrown the number of ortho-

---

1 Commonly referred to as Di Guan Dadi in the vernacular tradition.
2 Community of monks.

dox ritual specialists available on a single day. In Singapore and Malaysia's Underworld tradition, the magnitude and significance of Ghost Month has been further elevated in importance, transforming it into a time of heightened ritual activity, with orthodox rituals gradually becoming eclipsed by those performed by Underworld *tang-ki*.

When the gates of the Underworld are opened

In contemporary vernacular religion, the Underworld is considered to be located in a discarnate, hierarchical and highly bureaucratic realm whose location remains elusive. Nonetheless, annually, on the first day of the Lunar Seventh Month, the gates of the Underworld are opened and the multitudinous hordes of wandering spirits, referred to euphemistically as 'good brothers' (*hao xiongdi* / 好兄弟), are, for one month, allowed to return to their origins and to wander the Earth. In the Underworld tradition these gates have been reinvented in physical locations, opening beneath Hell deity altars, through cemetery altars and by *tang-ki* in ritual spaces protected by the Underworld Generals of the Five Directions. Moreover, while it is commonly understood that the good brothers may wander, they do so under Tua Di Ya Pek's strict supervision.

Originating in the vernacular tradition, a higher-ranked Underworld deity is also charged with controlling the behaviour of released spirits and supervising their return to the Underworld. This is the 'Ghost King' Da Shi Ye, who acts as overall military commander during Seventh Month. Beneath him are his Underworld Generals with their ghost battalions, individual Tua Di Ya Pek and their private spirit armies, Ox Head and Horse Face, and Underworld scribes to record and report any crimes committed by wandering spirits. Commonly held to be a demonic incarnation of Guanyin, Da Shi Ye wields an axe or ghost-summoning plaque, is dressed in military robes or armour and wears an ornate crown on top of which stands Guanyin in her female form. A less common interpretation of Da Shi Ye's identity stems from the legend of an elderly, dying scholar who was forsaken by his descendants after they had helped themselves to their inheritances. Un-worshipped as an ancestor, he became a vengeful spirit (*guai* / 怪), eventually growing in stature to become a fearsome and destructive demon king. Guanyin was therefore sent to subdue and recruit him into the Underworld pantheon, and her depiction on his crown therefore denotes the fact that he submits only to her authority.

Da Shi Ye is necessarily merciless, one temple reporting that their Da Shi Ye statue consumes all that is left on his altar table, including, in one instance, the life of a baby placed there by its mother while worshipping other temple deities. Apart from a small number of statues which remain on Underworld altars as permanent fixtures, the majority of Da Shi Ye's images are assembled each year from paper or cardboard attached to a wooden frame because, at the close of Seventh Month, work accomplished, the deity is 'sent off' with offerings back to the Underworld. Now ubiquitous within the Underworld tradition, this ritual originated in the early twentieth century in two separate locations. One history was recorded in the 1920s *Accounts of religious groups in Minxiong village* (*Minxiong Zhuang zongjiao tuanti taizhang*) in Jiayi County, Taiwan, where Taiwan's eldest temple with Da Shi Ye in its name is located. The Taoist priest performing their *pudu* (普度) salvation ritual dreamed of Da Shi Ye requesting that his red satin image be replaced with a paper statue, and, although the exact year has not been recorded, since some point in the 1910s their Seventh Month rituals began to conclude by 'sending off' a life-sized paper image of Da Shi Ye. The second hails from Tua Pek Kong Beo in Bukit Mertajam, Penang, Malaysia, and is the most likely source of Singapore and Malaysia's present-day rituals. The temple commissioned its first paper statue of Da Shi Ye in 1920 from the Songji paper-craft shop (*Songji Zhi Zha Dian*), and the image was burned at the conclusion of its Ghost Festival. The eldest member of the festival committee suggested that paper was used to construct the statue, as wandering spirits could attach themselves to it and receive people's worship along with Da Shi Ye throughout the festival, noting that other temples in the locality adopted the tradition and, soon after, the practice spread.[3]

Seventh Month taboos have also evolved to protect the living during Seventh Month. For instance, children are encouraged to be home before sunset, and people refrain from swimming, as it is held that people who have drowned through foul-play or suicide may not enter the Underworld. Thus, after someone has drowned, unless their family engages an ordained cleric to perform a salvation ritual on their behalf, their soul remains in the water to serve out the balance of its mortal and post-mortal lifespan as a water ghost. The only way for it to break free is to drown another person, and, having obtained a substitute soul, their own soul is free to wander. Modernising this taboo, the same logic is now applied to traffic accidents, whereby another person must die in the same location to free a malevolent spirit who perished there previously. These varieties of malicious ghosts become increasingly active in Seventh Month, as they are rendered inconspicuous among the multitudes of wandering spirits released from the Underworld, and locations where there have been frequent road deaths or drownings tend to be avoided.

While these taboos are geographically widespread in the vernacular tra-

---

3 Interviewed during Seventh Month at Tua Pek Kong Beo, 14 August 2016.

dition, a distinguishing feature of Singapore and Malaysia's religious landscapes is that, while in other locations Seventh Month bodes misfortune and *tang-ki*'s activities at most temples are kept to a minimum,[4] in the Underworld tradition, Ghost Month is a time of heightened ritual activity and, indeed, celebration. It is the time when Tua Di Ya Pek become most industrious, performing rituals for the benefit of their followers' ancestors and for wandering spirits and, alongside the solemnity of cemetery rituals, to party. Examples of Ah Pek parties will be detailed in Chapters 7 and 8, in the context of Malaysia's ritual landscape where the party tradition has more fully matured.

Choa Chu Kang cemetery rituals: part 1

While there are a plethora of Seventh Month Tua Di Ya Pek-centred rituals in Malaysia, night-time visits to cemeteries during Ghost Month are a quintessentially Singaporean phenomenon, so much so that it would be fair to say that in other locations, including Taiwan, Hong Kong and in Chinese communities elsewhere in the Chinese diaspora, while based on a shared cosmology, these practices would be virtually inconceivable.

In Chinese vernacular post-mortal cosmology, one portion of an ancestral soul remains by the grave after death, the second in a spirit tablet housed in an ancestral altar and the third resides in Heaven to bestow blessings on its descendants (Harrell, 1979). In the Underworld tradition's re-elaboration of cosmology, the third portion is escorted to Hell to be judged and tortured prior to transmigration. Irrespective of which interpretation practitioners hold, the most prevalent graveyard offerings in Singapore are therefore made by individuals to collective family ancestors. Distinct from these are offerings made by Underworld temples to the ghosts of those without descendants to worship them; to the souls of the unknown whose graves are marked with numbers rather than tombstones; and to the purposely disregarded, including lost or aborted foetuses and babies that died at or soon after birth – in essence, to those who would otherwise be bereft of offerings, and who therefore suffer the most while wandering the Earth before returning to complete their post-mortal sojourn in the darkness of the Underworld.

Returning to the portion of a soul which remains by the grave after death, a singular hybridisation of cosmology has occurred in response to the introduction of the 1998 'New Burial Policy'. Implemented by the National Environmental Agency, since 1998 cadavers have been exhumed from

---

[4] Seventh Month festivals are held in both Taiwan and Hong Kong, but rituals are generally performed by orthodox clerics.

public cemeteries after fifteen years for cremation. Vernacular cosmology has evolved in response to this development, and ancestral cemetery rituals performed by Underworld temples are now held on the basis that, following exhumation, the first portion of the soul returns to the place of its original burial after cremation.

When I first conducted research in Singapore in 2010 most cemetery rituals were unofficial, clandestine and secretive. Rumours abounded of unscrupulous Underworld deities who, under the pretence of making Seventh Month offerings, actually performed rituals to capture wandering spirits to serve in their own temple's private ghost armies. This unsavoury twist to an essentially merit-making tradition provided the catalyst prompting a societal response and, in 2012, instructed by the NEA, the police clamped down on unregistered graveyard rituals. As a result, most temples now apply for an NEA permit prior to performing cemetery rituals and burn their offerings on fixed platforms in pre-allocated locations within the huge expanse of Singapore's graveyards. Rituals begin on the eve of Seventh Month and are most common on the fifteenth of the lunar month and at weekends, when, in groups most frequently led by Tua Di Ya Pek *tang-ki*, up to three thousand individuals may visit the graveyard on a single night and the graveyards themselves, as it were, come to life.

During Ghost Month in 2017 I visited the 3.18 square kilometre Choa Chu Kang Cemetery to observe night-time graveyard rituals, first on 26 August in a cemetery plot dedicated to aborted foetuses and babies, and then with a case-study temple whose preparations I recorded in detail from 25 August, and whose cemetery rituals I participated in on 2 September. I will describe the latter in full, as their repertoire contains an extensive array of elements drawn from the available Seventh Month 'ritual buffet', various combinations of which are commonly performed by other Underworld temples. The ethnography is therefore broadly representative of Singapore's Seventh Month graveyard ritual traditions. First, though, some observations of and insights gleaned from the 26 August visit.

> *I arrived at the graveyard by car at around 11 p.m. with specialist heritage hunter Raymond Goh, a researcher known as 'the island states' own "ghostbuster"'.*[5] *We noticed visiting groups concentrated in two areas: graveyard plots fenced off for exhumation, and the plots reserved for foetuses, babies and young children. We passed several groups leaving these sectors of the cemetery as we drove towards the latter where three groups were holding rituals on different sides of the 10,000 square*

---

5 BBC News Singapore, 6 April 2012, cited at www.bbc.com/news/world-asia-17594008.

metre plot. Two of the three rituals were held in subdued tones, one led by a Hao Zhu Ya (the Underworld God of Filial Piety) 'tang-ki' from 'Shengan Temple' in Jurong West, and the second by a tall Tua Ya Pek 'tang-ki' from 'Yushan Temple' in Woodlands. The third ritual at the far north end of the plot was ending as we arrived, and cutting through the silence, the unearthly scream of a Tua Ya Pek 'tang-ki' reached our ears as his followers returned to their parked vehicles and then left.

The cemetery plot itself slopes downhill from south to north and contains three permanent altars located along dark footpaths leading away from the graves into the thickets at the east and north extremities of the plot. To the east, placed on a pole a metre and a half from the ground, the first altar housed the Chinese Malay tutelary deity Tua Pek Kung, flanked by two pairs of identical Tua Di Ya Pek. All five deities were depicted two-dimensionally on the board that forms the back of the open-fronted altar and were illuminated by four red candles and a single flame from a wick floating on lamp oil in a cut-glass vase. No one there knew the age of this altar but, as the illustration depicted Di Ya Pek sitting on a can of Guinness, it is unlikely to predate the 1990s. At its centre was a small copper censer containing lit incense sticks, with opened cans of Guinness placed next to the candles for the Underworld deities to consume. Between the pairs of Tua Di Ya Pek, black painted wooden tablets were inscribed in gold reading 'Tua Ya Pek of Seventh Court' and 'Di Ya Pek of Seventh Court'. The Underworld *tang-ki* and their followers offered three incense sticks here before their own temple's rituals began, the censer in front of Tua Pek Kung serving to worship all three deities.

In the northern sector of the plot, each of the tombstones had had a plastic censer containing two red candles and incense sticks placed in front of it by the leaving group, along with an opened bottle of 'Yakult', a can of sugary drink and two straws. The tombstones each bore embossed inscriptions running from top downwards, the individual's name in the centre, their date of birth and death to the right and left (Plate 4). The candles provided sufficient illumination to read the inscriptions, one stating 'The grave of Wang Yijie', 'Born in 1990 on the fourteenth of the sixth lunar month in the year of gengwu' (庚午), 'Died in 1992 on the twenty-seventh of the third lunar month in the year of renshen' (壬申). Based on the sexagenary cycle of the stem-branch calendar, 'geng' and 'ren' each correlated to one of the five Chinese elements, and 'wu' and 'shen' to one of the twelve Chinese zodiac animals. Each of the five elements, wood, fire, earth, metal and water dominate for two consecu-

tive years creating a decennial cycle alongside the duodecennial zodiac cycle. The inscriptions therefore indicated that the child was born in the Year of the Metal Horse and died in the Year of the Water Monkey.

The second and third altars were housed side by side in red stone shelters in front of these graves. The larger was dedicated to aborted foetuses, the other to wandering spirits. The former contained a tablet reading 'foetus ghosts' which in Singapore are seen as harmless, the tablet by implication including the still-born and young children. Central within the altar, two small plastic dolls approximately twenty centimetres tall depicting a Caucasian male and female baby sat atop a wedge of decaying joss money (Figure 6.1).

To their right a single flame floated in a bowl of lamp oil, to the left a tall red candle, and set in front of the two dolls were plates piled high with offerings of biscuits, sweets, jellies, cakes and opened cartons of milk and sweet drinks recently placed there by visiting temple groups (Plate 5). The smaller altar consisted of a single tablet reading 'wu zhu gu hun' (无主孤魂), 'wandering spirits', with only a take-away meal in a polystyrene container of rice topped with fish and a red sauce, chopsticks to eat with, and a plastic cup of coffee rested in front.

The Underworld temple's altars at the upper end of the cemetery plot both featured a selection of Hell deity statues including that of the deity channelled to perform the rituals. Placed before these were cans of Guinness, a black abacus, green talisman papers, candles, and various tasty morsels. Both temples had demarcated a ritual space for their 'sending off' by positioning lit red candles and incense sticks alternately around its borders. At the front of each ritual space Hell banknotes were stacked up in the wire-framed incinerators provided by the NEA. Around these, food offerings to wandering spirits were set out on tables, and offerings of toys, sweets and colourful baubles were laid on the ground for the foetus ghosts, thus suggesting that physicality at the time of death is replicated post-mortally in spirit form.

As I mingled with both groups, members of Shengan Temple explained that they had chosen this particular cemetery plot as foetus ghosts and the spirits of still-born babies are usually forgotten, so they pray for them and provide them with sweets and toys to take back to the Underworld. They were also making offerings of joss money to their ancestors, and these had been marked with named talismans to ensure the correct ancestor received their share of the burned offering. In contrast, Yushan Temple's Tua Ya Pek rationalised their choice of cemetery plot according to Confucian ethics, thereby accounting for foetus ghosts being un-worshipped as if elder generations pay respects to their juniors,

6.1 Central to the foetus ghost's altar

6.2 Tua Ya Pek preparing to cast coins

it would equate to an inversion of the rules of filial piety, rules which out of compassion he was prepared to break.

Tua Ya Pek invited me to join in their ritual, and when he was satisfied that the ritual space was fully prepared, each participant stood behind him among the gravestones holding six lit incense sticks. In unison, we bowed before the Underworld altar table which had been placed in front of the incinerator, then to the offerings laid out on the floor for the foetus ghosts, after which coins were cast to obtain the foetus ghosts' consent before the mound of joss money was ignited. The foetus ghosts' offerings were then picked up from the ground and flung onto the pyre. In the light cast by its blaze, I asked Tua Ya Pek if their offering of Hell banknotes were for the foetus ghosts. Shaking his head sombrely, he explained that he had been summoning wandering spirits to him from across the graveyard, and when the banknotes were lit, he had released them to receive the offerings. We chatted for a while watching the offerings burn, and as I was leaving Tua Ya Pek called me back. He examined his abacus with soot-encrusted fingers and satisfied with the result thrust a large fried chicken leg mottled with ash into my hand, and insisted I eat it there and then with his blessings.

Choa Chu Kang Cemetery rituals: part 2

Preparations

Ghost Month rituals conducted in public cemeteries require advance planning. Yu Feng Nan Fu Xuanshan Miao began their preparations on Saturday, 15 July 2017, when a Tua Ya Pek from the Fourth Court of the Underworld possessed their founder and primary *tang-ki*. While he channels multiple deities, most commonly the Sixth Court Tua Ya Pek with the family name 'So', it took his assistants by surprise when he was unexpectedly possessed by the Fourth Court Tua Ya Pek. The difference was immediately apparent due to a fundamental change in the *tang-ki*'s posture, mannerisms and voice, and, after he identified himself, assistants selected the temple's finest white robes with gold fringes to dress the unexpected guest. He then informed them that the temple must perform a Seventh Month cemetery ritual this year and that he would personally direct the proceedings. As graveyard rituals now require temples to obtain permits from the secular authorities, he stipulated the time, date and location within the cemetery that he wished the rituals to be performed, pledging to return before Ghost Month to give specific instructions for the rituals, altars and offerings to be prepared.

On the following Monday, as per instruction, the temple applied to hold 'prayer activities' on 2 September from 5 p.m. to midnight at the junction of Chinese Cemetery Paths thirty-eight and twenty-one in Choa Chu Kang Chinese Cemetery. Overseen by the Ministry of the Environment and Water Resources, permits are issued by the NEA and may be applied for directly or through the relevant cemetery office. The permit was granted a month later, subject to compliance with ten stipulated conditions, two of which, C and J, few temples are able to comply with.

> C. Provide adequate number of litter bins and portable mobile toilets.
> J. No ritual / prayer shall be conducted on graves / tombstones without the consent of the next-of-kin.[6]

After the permit had been granted, the Fourth Court Tua Ya Pek returned to give instructions specifying the number of paper houses to be placed outside the temple to accommodate wandering spirits; details concerning temporary altars and offerings to Da Shi Ye, Tua Di Ya Pek and for aborted foetuses and dead babies; and the amount of Hell banknotes to be 'sent off' for each.

> *I first met the Fourth Court Tua Ya Pek on 25 September when, as promised, he returned to oversee ritual preparations for the event. After being presented with tea and Guinness, he paid respects to the temple's deities by bowing and then placing three thick incense sticks in the censers for the Jade Emperor, for Heaven deities, and for the Underworld pantheon. He then set to work writing fourteen talismans on green paper slips to be attached to a temporary external altar on which the Fourth Court's Tua Di Ya Pek statues would be placed. Writing them slowly in black ink with a shaky hand, he ordered two tables to be placed side by side outside the temple's entrance, and for the Fourth Court Tua Di Ya Pek statues to be taken from the temple's Underworld altar and one placed on each. A blue silk cloth decorated with two 'bagua' stitched in gold thread was pinned to the front of the new altar, Tua Ya Pek checking that each deity statue was in a direct line with the centre of a 'bagua'. Seven talismans were then attached to each side of the altar, seven and its multiplies being associated with 'yin' energy and Hell as forty-nine days after physiological death, souls must report to the first King of the Underworld. Flags representing the Underworld Generals of the Five Directions were then fastened to the rear of the altar, and their steeds in the form of five paper horses were placed in front, each*

---

6 Cited from the NEA certificate of approval provided by the Choa Chu Kang Cemetery office.

> with a generous bucket of feed and dried grass labelled with one the five elements from the stem-branch calendar. From left to right and corresponding to the general's flags behind, the black horse represented the north and water; white, the west and metal; yellow, the centre and earth; red, the south and fire; and green the east and wood. The buckets, food and horses would be 'sent off' with Da Shi Ye at the cemetery, but the flags, as their efficacy increases with age and worship, would remain in the temple for future use. The altar was completed with the addition of seven small cups of wine and tea for each Ah Pek, with three cups of each for the accompanying generals. Before the 'tang-ki' came out of trance, he 'opened the eyes' of each horse and placed his talisman on the front of each allowing the five Underworld generals to ride them in their discarnate form. He prepared similar talismans to be placed on the roof of each paper house, and for the censers placed on the temporary altars that he had previously instructed the temple to prepare.

The two statues themselves share an interesting back-story. Neither purchased nor replicas, they were found abandoned during the temple's first Ghost Month cemetery ritual some twenty years previously and were brought back to be worshipped on the temple's Underworld altar. Only after this Tua Ya Pek was first channelled through the *tang-ki* did the temple know which Underworld court they hailed from, though their individual family names remain a mystery. However, from the perspective of temple members familiar with their history, it seemed fitting that they should return to the cemetery from where they were retrieved, as, in a fashion, the transformation from disposed of to in-disposable, and dispossessed to possessing, signalled their acceptance of and full integration into the temple's Underworld pantheon.

> Rituals began in earnest after lunch on 2 September, the day of the graveyard ritual. The houses to accommodate the wandering spirits had arrived the day before, and a talisman had been added to each. Appropriately, there were fourteen buildings in total, seven each for male and female spirits. Standing almost three metres tall, each house had two floors with three upstairs and three downstairs bedrooms. Supported on a framework of bamboo poles, great attention had been paid to the external paper details. The naked bamboo had been decorated with pink and green paper to resemble ornate pillars, each topped with an auspicious dragon cornice, the higher pillars buttressing a sloping green- and red-tiled roof. Every room had a door and curtained windows which could be opened and closed for the spirit's convenience,

> *and a staircase leading up to a communal living area to the left of the bedrooms. Each building was able to house eight wandering spirits per room, so the temple accommodated a total of 672 souls. Arranged in a long row to the right of the temple entrance, at each end stood toilet and shower blocks for male and female spirits respectively. The entire complex was strategically placed behind the altar to Da Shi Ye, a deific presence presenting a formidable barrier between the ghost houses and temple which no malevolent spirit would venture to cross. Da Shi Ye's spiritual presence, as well as that of the temple's Heaven deities, was assured by three Taoist priests reciting a scripture generically known as the 'Tai shang qing shen ke', inviting the deities into the ritual space.*

This level of cooperation between *tang-ki* and orthodox priests is distinctive of Singapore's religious landscape and is therefore somewhat of an anomaly. In Taiwan and Hong Kong, for example, while orthodox priests perform rituals for Chinese temples, they do not, as a rule, perform liturgical rites in a shared ritual space together with possessed *tang-ki*, as the legitimacy of spirit possession is not officially recognised in orthodox Taoism. Of analytical interest, then, is why this level of cooperation has developed in Singapore, and principally so with Underworld enforcers who ordinarily receive minor if any recognition in orthodox rituals.

> *Meanwhile, eight rows of dining tables had been set up to the left of the temple's entrance for ancestral offerings. Each place setting contained an ancestral paper tablet stood upright in a wedge of gold joss money bearing the family name of ancestors which the offerings were intended to reach. For each ancestral line, a generic offering of steamed rice topped with meat, two oranges, and an auspicious 'fagao' (发糕) cake were provided by the temple, and two chop-sticks with tips facing down had been stood upright in each bowl of rice. As their tapered shape resembles incense sticks, in other circumstances, it would be ill omened to place them thus, but for ancestral offerings, the thick end of the chop-sticks rising up symbolises that the progenitor has already passed. In accord with the notion that after death individual souls maintain the same desires as in life, many families laid additional offerings pertinent to recently deceased relatives' tastes to supplement those provided by the temple including plates of roasted meats and home-made curries, packets of preferred brands of cigarettes and occasional bottles of their preferred liquors. The front table served as a temporary altar supporting a large censer flanked by two enormous lotus flowers constructed from interwoven sheets of joss papers where ancestors were worshiped by their descendants.*

The blue-faced, fanged statue of Da Shi Ye, Guanyin visibly protruding from his crown, was placed on top of an altar table literally watching over the ancestral tablets. He was constructed from cardboard attached to a bamboo frame, as, in common with other paper deities and offerings, he would be 'sent off' at the close of their cemetery rituals. After his eyes had been opened, fruit and Guinness were placed at his feet each side of a large censer sporting three green talismans. These talismans are perceived as tangible power objects, independently carrying the efficacy and authority of the deities invited into them. In the process of drawing, multiple deities may be invoked, the abstract nature of the smeared black ink painted onto the talisman slips effectively obscuring the names of the deities embodied, and the charms and weapons they wielded. As with those drawn by orthodox priests, they contained orders assigned by higher-ranking deities instructing their subordinates to perform distinct duties, thereby providing a temple's deities with a 'divine mandate'. The talismans were thus vessels embodied with the Fourth Court Tua Ya Pek's efficacy, carrying the orders and official mandate of the highest-ranking deities on the temple's Underworld altar. Both their mandate and Tua Ya Pek's efficacy would only be rescinded with the talismans' incineration.

Outside of Seventh Month, 'sending off' usually entails the immediate transfer of all material objects, including paper offerings, human proxies (*tishen* / 替身) and deity statues, as well as any discarnate forces inhabiting them, directly to a pre-selected destination in the spirit world. However, this is not the case in Ghost Month unless the 'sending off' coincides with the eve of the eighth lunar month. Therefore, the incineration of the temple's paper houses on the twelfth night of Seventh Month did not require the spirits contained within to be returned directly to the Underworld, as seventeen days remained for them to partake of offerings while wandering the Earth. Instead, the transformative power of incineration transported only the houses, money and consumables in spirit form to the Underworld for later use.

Two further interpretations of the transformation through immolation are applied to Da Shi Ye, based on dual non-competing cosmologies. The first relates to the divisible nature of the soul, thus allowing for numerous 'proxy deities', each generated by and separated from the original Da Shi Ye, and each containing limited aggregates of his total efficacy. The second is based on higher-ranking deities superintending their appointed generals as 'ancillary proxies', each deputised with the authority to perform their commander's duties. Therefore, while every temple's statue is venerated as Da Shi Ye, none is the original, their statue's efficacy deriving from one or other form of proxy implementing Da Shi Ye's will. Seventh Month cemetery rituals are performed throughout the month, and therefore, as each incineration releases the deific efficacy embodying a specific Da Shi Ye statue, the efficacy rejoins with the original and greater deity-self or, if a general, returns to command their battalions of demon soldiers under Da Shi Ye's command. After the wandering spirits return to the Underworld on the eve of the eighth lunar month, Da Shi Ye and his generals follow, before the gates of the Underworld are closed.

> *Beside Da Shi Ye was the final temporary altar where devotees placed a single incense stick on their arrival. This altar was spread on a blanket on the floor, once again containing toys, sweets, opened containers of milk and several dozen dummies (pacifiers) for aborted foetuses and stillborn babies to chomp on in their discarnate form. In contrast with Yushan Temple, so as not to break the Confucian conventions of filial piety, even though incense was offered, it was done so standing up, and without the customary bowing and paying of respects otherwise associated with the act of offering incense.*
>
> *Returning to the rituals, an altar was set up in front of the temple for the three Taoist priests who recited two further scriptures, together comprising a salvation ritual for ancestors and wandering spirits. As they recited the first of these, inside the temple, demonstrating how each Underworld court now contains multiple Tua Di Ya Pek with individual family names, the four visiting 'tang-ki' entered trance states and channelled the following deities. A Fifth Court Tua Ya Pek named Tan Tua Ya; two Fifth Court Di Ya Pek named Kang Di Ya and Fan Di Ya; and, a Seventh Court Di Ya Pek named Tan Tua Lao. Pragmatically, the increasing variety of Tua Di Ya Pek channelled has risen synchronously with the number of 'tang-ki' channelling them, the Underworld tradition's own mass-popularisation therefore furnishing an effective self-perpetuating mechanism, a catalyst itself to the hybridisation of meaning in Underworld cosmology. By providing increasing ritual spaces for Hell's previously anonymous enforcers to be channelled, individual family names and identifiable personality traits have been divulged by their 'tang-ki', and therefore, the Jade Record's model of Underworld enforcers as 'anonymous' post-mortal demonic entities has been transformed in the modern Underworld tradition.*
>
> *With five 'tang-ki' now in trance, to further prevent the possibility of attacks by malevolent spirits at the cemetery, each person attending the ritual would be provided with a red sash to be worn for protection. The 'tang-ki's first task was therefore to empower each sash with deific*

efficacy by daubing it with their blood. For this purpose, an Underworld throne and a table covered in a vermillion cloth were placed at the temple's threshold where each of the 'tang-ki' sat in turn, slashing at their tongues with daggers or porcelain shards, causing deep lacerations out of which blood flowed freely. Those present looked on nonchalantly, their faces registering varying degrees of curiosity, fascination or excitement as several hundred sashes were invested with five layers of Tua Di Ya Pek's protective efficacy. No one's expression registered surprise or aversion as in the wider 'tang-ki' tradition self-mortification is normative during major celebrations, now more so than ever as in Underworld temples blood-letting rituals have become routine.

Unperturbed by the self-mortification immediately behind them, the priests sang the concluding section of their salvation ritual, the 'Tai shang ling bao ba du wang shan shishi keyi', a scripture exhorting all spirits to learn Taoist teachings and to pay respects to their Heavenly pantheon. During the process, wielding their wooden 'five command tablets', ritual objects invested with the Jade Emperor's authority, they stamped a seal on each of the tables of ancestral offerings, while descendants continued to worship their ancestors with increasing fervour. Then chanting jubilantly, the priests flung blessed and therefore 'lucky' offerings into the crowd. First came rice, coins and sweets, and then larger offerings including oranges, and finally, several plump pineapples which members of the crowd eagerly bustled to catch. It was during this joyous melee that a quiet ritual of cosmological significance was enacted at the temple's main altar.

The temple's primary 'tang-ki' sat relaxed in a trance possession state in his throne with several assistants gathered around him, his right arm stretched across the altar table. Eight thin skewers measuring forty-five centimeters in length, each topped with the head of an Underworld general were then brought to the table and abruptly plunged into a large pear to disinfect them and keep them clean.

Then, each skewer was pushed slowly in turn through his forearm flesh, thus allowing him to assimilate the efficacy of the generals represented. When the piercings were complete, each skewer point was topped with cork to avoid injury to others, and the skewers were then bunched together criss-crossing at their centre and tied with red string to prevent the configuration from moving and ripping the 'tang-ki's skin. Colloquially, piercing the body with skewers is referred to as 'satay'.

Prior to and outside of the Underworld tradition, piercings with eight skewers are rare. If piercing is performed, the skewers would be topped with

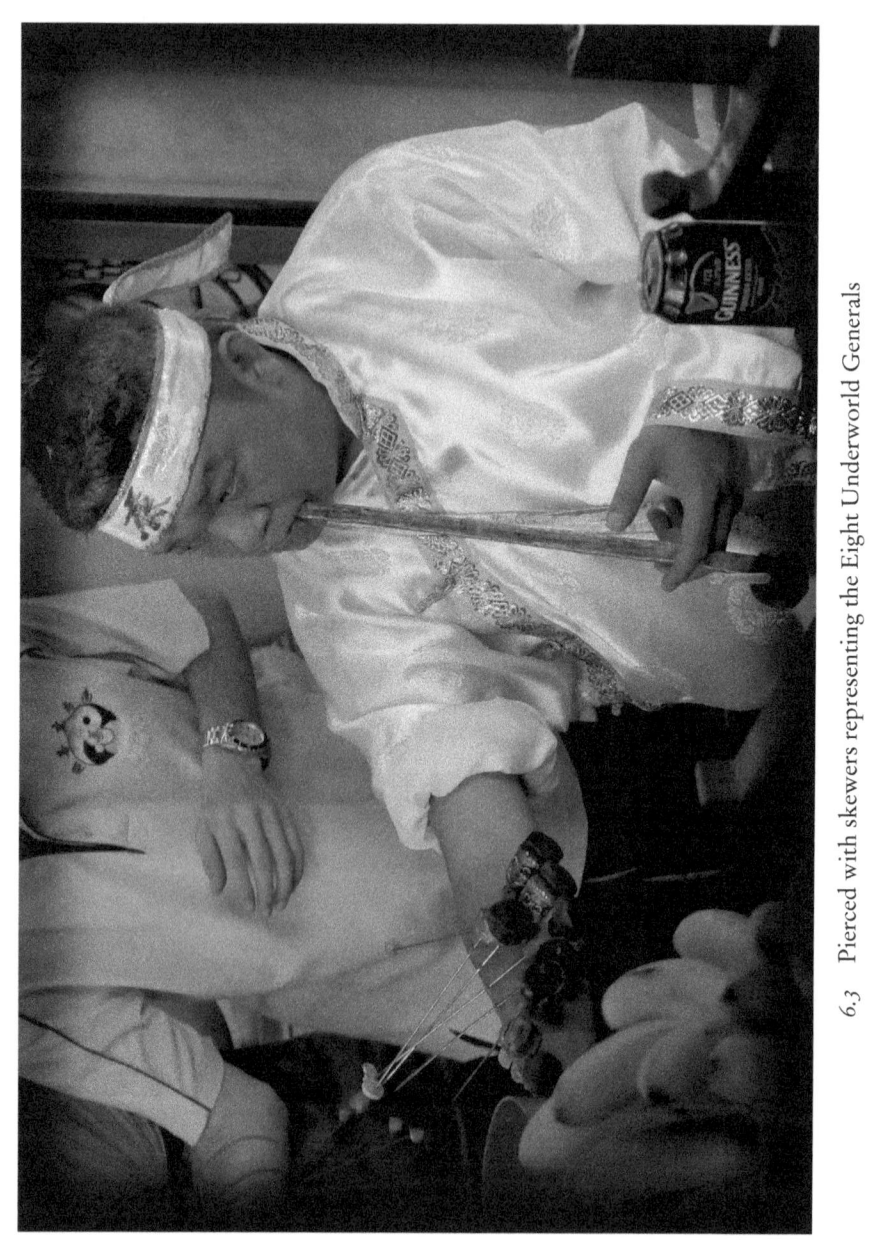

6.3 Pierced with skewers representing the Eight Underworld Generals

the heads of Heaven deities, most likely the Eight Bagua Marshals or Eight Taoist Immortals. However, while channelling Hell deities, assimilating Heavenly efficacy would be inappropriate or, in biblical terms, blasphemous. Therefore, Tua Ya Pek assimilated the powers of eight Underworld generals. The first four skewers inserted represented Generals Liu, Xie, Gan and Yang, military commanders held responsible for capturing malicious spirits and then enforcing punishments upon them. Next followed skewers topped with the heads of Generals Chun, Xia, Qiu and Dong, whose duty is to torture captured ghosts during interrogation. By amalgamating their efficacy before the graveyard ritual, this Tua Ya Pek became an intimidating threat to any evil spirits that the group might encounter.

> 'Satay' complete, the 'tang-ki' moved outside to inspect proceedings, the three scowling Di Ya Pek dragging their heavy metal chains menacingly behind them. As the Fourth Court Tua Ya Pek had ordered that they must leave the temple by 7 p.m., overseen by Tua Di Ya Pek, the paper houses and washrooms, 116 large boxes of 'Hell banknotes', twenty-four sacks of joss money folded into the shape of ancient Chinese coinage, the ancestral food offerings which had been placed together in large sacks, the Fourth Court Tua Di Ya Pek's altar, and the image of Da Shi Ye were hurriedly loaded onto trucks. The ancestral tablets had been placed inside the paper lotuses, and these, along with the temple's highest-ranking Underworld deity statues were carefully placed in two cars which would lead the convoy to the cemetery. Within an hour, the space outside the temple had been cleared, and a convoy of twenty-one vehicles including four busloads of participants pulled away from the temple.
>
> From the perspective of most present, the important rituals had already been completed at the temple: the offerings to and worshipping of ancestors and deities and the orthodox salvation rituals. The cemetery ritual itself was the pragmatic icing on the proverbial cake, a self-perpetuating mechanism incorporating all present into a participatory ritual process, thereby allowing 'communitas' to emerge, a powerful bonding experience between the individuals and possessed 'tang-ki' comprising the temple group.

'Sending off' and ritual completion

> The convoy drove into the cemetery along Chinese Cemetery Path twenty-one with occasional detours to allow other temples' vehicles to pass, and then parked close to an open space behind the intersection of

Chinese Cemetery Paths twenty-one and thirty-eight where two metal platforms had been provided by the cemetery authorities. Next to the allotted area was a burial plot for the cadavers of those whose names were unknown, the graves marked with small numbered concrete cubes in lieu of tombstones. As the vehicles containing offerings were unloaded, red candles and incense were lit and embedded in the damp soil surrounding each of these graves inviting their occupants to partake of the imminent 'sending off'.

The larger of the two platforms measured approximately fifteen by four metres and would be used for offerings to wandering spirits. First, the fourteen paper houses and washrooms were placed in a line to the rear of the platform, and then Da Shi Ye was placed in the centre atop three boxes of Hell banknotes which raised his head above all other offerings. A thick wedge of gold joss money was placed at his feet, and a folded yellow paper tablet reading 'For the male and female wandering spirits in the vicinity' was wedged upright in it by the orange-robed priest. A red plastic censer was then placed before Da Shi Ye, and three thick incense sticks placed inside by the priest. The five horses and their buckets of feed were lined up in front, and their mouths stuffed full of dried grass so that they would not enter the discarnate realms with empty stomachs. The remaining 113 boxes of Hell banknotes were piled four high in front of the houses to each side of Da Shi Ye, and these covered in loose joss money of varying denominations emptied from sacks. The final preparation was to hammer three two-metre-high joss sticks into the ground, and these were lit ceremoniously with a butane torch.

The second platform stood tangentially some ten metres apart and was caged in on three sides. This was filled with joss money that had previously been folded by temple members. The food offerings were then poured on top, the two paper lotuses containing ancestral tablets being placed carefully above side-by-side at the centre of the cage. Even though the 'sending off' was essentially pragmatic, it was emotionally charged, and performed with reverence in an atmosphere of dignified haste. Meanwhile, the Fourth Court Tua Di Ya Pek's altar had been set up in an elevated position affording the deities an uninterrupted view over the proceedings. The two stages were literally set for the ritual performance to begin.

The Underworld 'tang-ki' directing activities moved forward to position themselves between the first platform and devotees, and a hush fell as each participant was handed two lit incense sticks and directed to stand behind them. The Taoist priest closed his eyes and in a voice of great clarity, employing a small hand-bell to punctuate his speech, he recited the 'Tai yi jiu ku miao jing', a scripture intended to educate the wandering spirits in correct morality, once again exhorting them to show obeisance to the Taoist heavenly lords. As the scripture ended, the incense sticks were collected and placed in the censer in front of Da Shi Ye. Then all stood in silent awe as the joss money was ignited, licks of fire first consuming the censer, joss money and tablet, and then spreading outwards and upwards, the flames illuminating the demonic face of Da Shi Ye in a red glow, before engulfing him completely within a blanket of fire. Seconds later the heat became overpowering, and led by the 'tang-ki', the group moved across to the ancestral offerings. The same procedure was followed, and as soon as the flames had caught, prompted by the 'tang-ki', everyone hurriedly left with Tua Di Ya Pek's stern warnings of "Don't look over your shoulders" and "Do not look back"[7] still ringing in their ears.

The drive out of the cemetery took a circuitous route to avoid disturbing other temples' rituals. Including frequent detours to avoid traffic jams, the two-kilometre drive took almost an hour as the Cemetery Paths were chock-a-block with vehicles. It was 10 p.m. and rush hour in the graveyard.

The mood in the temple on our return was jubilant. The five 'tang-ki' had positioned themselves in two parallel lines at the temple's entrance, their flags held overhead forming a 'tunnel of blessings'. As each participant arrived, they were handed three lit incense sticks, and holding these as they walked through the tunnel, every Underworld deity rested their flag momentarily on each person's head, and then with whoops of encouragement, brushed their flags down devotees' backs. Even the most sombre of participants, having walked through the tunnel, entered the temple bearing a smile. Then, carrying the incense and bowing before each altar, they circled the temple's interior once, placing their incense sticks in the Jade Emperor's censer by the exit before leaving. This cunningly playful act was however essentially pragmatic, a cleansing ritual, with the Underworld deity's efficacy channelled through their flags removing any wandering or malicious spirits that had attached themselves to a living body and unwittingly been brought back to the temple.

The final ritual act was to pay respects to the Fourth Court Tua Ya Pek who had first instigated the day's rituals. He was channelled by an unfamiliar 'tang-ki' who, incense in hand and walking slowly with an

---

7 Actions which may draw a ghost's attention to a participant, who may then be followed.

arthritic gait led the temple in paying respects, all genuflecting before the Jade Emperor, the Heaven deities and the Underworld pantheon's censers. Then, he turned to face the five other Tua Di Ya Pek, gently nodding in approval signalling that the rituals he had ordered had been performed successfully, after which, the five kowtowed before him. He was then escorted back to his throne, and quietly leaving the 'tang-ki's body, the final curtain came down on the temple's Seventh Month ritual event. The five remaining 'tang-ki' shared knowing looks that revealed a sense of ritual completion, called for cognac and Guinness, and their 'Ah Pek party' began.

Conclusion

Even though in Malaysia the Underworld tradition is as prevalent as, if not more so than in Singapore, it would be rare to find these kinds of Seventh Month cemetery rituals being performed there.[8] However, Ghost Month holds an equally important position in the Malaysian Underworld tradition's ritual calendar, where a greater variety of ritual events occur, many performed on a far grander scale than Singapore's. Due to their diversity, local and transnational influences, and in some cases recently evolved organisational structure, these will be detailed according to geographical location in Chapters 8 and 9. However, before the narrative relocates to Malaysia, I will evaluate the societal implications of Singapore's graveyard rituals and the centrality of Underworld temples performing them in the context of three religious trends: extensive orthodox Taoist and *tang-ki* cooperation; Buddhist evangelism; and cemetery rituals as forms of resistance. I will show how these trends are closely linked phenomena in Singapore and highlight the socio-political catalysts behind each.

To demonstrate this, I will address two questions. First, why do Taoist priests in Singapore enjoy a closer ritual relationship with Underworld *tang-ki* than their counterparts share with *tang-ki* channelling either Heaven or Underworld deities elsewhere in the Chinese diaspora? Second, given the importance of Dizangwang in Underworld cosmology, and with an abundance of ordained Buddhist clerics available, how to account for their comparative absence in Singapore's *tang-ki* temple culture? There is no apparent scriptural answer to this conundrum.

Historically, both the Taoist and Buddhist clergy were perceived as, and employed by vernacular religionists as ritual masters, with *tang-ki* providing

---

8 One notable exception is a barefoot parade at Difang Fu in Malacca through the cemetery surrounding the temple.

personal consultations, blessings, talismanic cures and luck-changing rituals. However, in the process of its own invention, the Underworld tradition has fashioned a new culture of ritual masters, one with a highly expanded ritual repertoire – that is, the Hell deities themselves channelled through their *tang-ki*. Innovative, and in Singapore largely operating from private temples with an estimated "several hundred to a thousand spirit medium altars in private apartments in HDB" (Dean, 2018: 72), these *tang-ki* have been "free to expand into new cosmological spaces, including especially the Underworld, but also hitherto unknown cosmic realms" (Dean, 2018: 71), including Foucault's "Heterotopic spaces" (Dean, 2018: 71), heterotopias. Considering the ritual efficacy now attributed to Tua Di Ya Pek's *tang-ki*, my initial question may well be rephrased, asking instead, why do Underworld *tang-ki* who while in trance become deities incarnate, choose to acquire the ritual assistance of Taoist priests? The reframing begs a further societal explanation for the uncharacteristic and costly mass relinquishment of authority by Underworld *tang-ki*, a relinquishment which orthodox priests rely upon for their own self-perpetuation through paid participation in temples' ritual events.

Pre-1970s, Singapore's Chinese temples nominally associated themselves with either the broader Buddhist or Taoist traditions, according to the pantheon to which their primary deity belonged. While this still holds true in locations outside of Singapore, since the early 1970s this general rule has applied to only a minority of Singaporean temples containing primarily Buddhist deities. Given that societal change provides the catalysts triggering new religious developments, a socio-political explanation to all three questions can be ascertained or, more precisely, pinpointed to a footnote in an official document, namely, a footnote in the small print of Singapore's first post-independence population census in 1970, which has remained in the decennial census to date. Where citizens must register their religious affiliation, choices including 'no religion', 'Buddhism', 'Taoism', 'Islam', 'Hinduism', 'Sikhism' and 'Christianity', a footnoted caveat stipulates that Taoism includes 'Chinese traditional beliefs'. Broadly defined, Chinese traditional beliefs incorporate *tang-ki* trance possession, geomancy, the worship of local deities and those outside of orthodox pantheons, divination and the use of the annual almanac for selecting auspicious dates – in essence, all practices associated with the vernacular tradition. While this official definition has led to Chinese vernacular religionists officially identifying themselves with orthodox Taoism, in practice, the two traditions have remained cosmologically distinct. However, as the post-1970s association has served both traditions' self-interests, if one tradition goes into decline, so does the other.

This first occurred in the early 1980s, when, due to the highly competitive nature of the religious environment, fuelled by evangelism within multi-religious, multi-ethnic communities, the number of Singaporeans self-identifying with Taoism, and by default with the vernacular tradition, dropped significantly. Between 1980 and 2000 the population census indicated a decline from 38.2% to 10.8% of the population identifying themselves as Taoist, while Christianity rose from 10.9% to 16.5% and Buddhism from 33.4% to 53.6%. In essence, Taoism and the vernacular tradition lost out to Buddhist evangelism. Eng (2003, 2007) attributed this shift to a 'New Reformist Buddhism' which appealed to a highly educated youth "who fail to comprehend the cosmological whole of the Chinese religion from the ritual point of view and thus label this ritual system as irrational magical practices" (Eng, 2007: 51). Traditional religious practices, including trance possession, Eng argued, were perceived as outdated and irrelevant in the face of modernity, "an elaborate system of meaningless practices which provides no answer to questions of salvation" (Eng, 2007: 266). In contrast, New Reformist Buddhism, with a central focus on exploring the meaning of Buddhist sutras and self-development through meditation, offered a progressive approach to Buddhism, concentrating on aspects "that are considered as 'relevant', 'rational' and 'modern' and that appeal to the new generation of Chinese" (Eng, 2007: 52). According to older informants, during this same period Seventh Month cemetery rituals almost came to a halt, being replaced by Buddhist salvation rituals in monastic and temple settings. However, in light of the vernacular tradition's renewed popularity since 2000, Eng's causal analysis identifying higher education and modernity as catalysts to its decline may now be reassessed in relation to the post-2000 generation of computer-literate youth.

Among the trappings of the early twenty-first century's technological revolution came easily accessible online social media which, in Eng's hypothesis, should have appealed as 'relevant, rational and modern' to an educated youth. Instead, however, among the post-2000 generation of young Chinese enamoured by the affordances of online social media, a "'symbolic economy' of spectacular moments" (Kitiarsa, 2008: 7) emerged, and religious spectacle metamorphosed into a new commodity measured not by profits, but instead systemised and calculated in terms of view counts and 'likes'. While reformist Buddhism had catered to those who wished to study the canonical tradition, the benefits of silent meditation do not translate into attention-grabbing, online, blood-and-fire-in-your-face entertainment, an area in which Underworld *tang-ki* have excelled. Thus, internet technology, rather than re-secularising the religious landscape, resulted in the online promotion of religious spectacle freely offered by

Singapore's *tang-ki*. As these *tang-ki* increasingly moved from channelling Heaven to Underworld deities in what I have described as the 'inversion of tradition', online social media became a vehicle driving the mass popularisation of Singapore's Underworld tradition from the early 2000s onwards.

The 2010 census shows that within a decade the number of individuals self-identifying with Taoism almost doubled, from 10.8% to 18.4%. The physical and online evidence that the Underworld tradition has continued to increase in popularity since 2010 is unmistakable. The total number of Underworld temples and altars has increased dramatically; the amount of *tang-ki* channelling deities in them and the variety of Underworld deities channelled have both risen; and the overall attendance by visiting practitioners has visibly multiplied. While Underworld deities have maintained an appeal to the elder generations through association with filial piety and the ancestral cult – inherited virtues directly expressed through Seventh Month ancestral salvation cemetery rituals – the new enthusiasm is largely youth based and *tang-ki* driven. While the traverse from modernity to postmodernity remains open to academic debate, and 'postmodernity' itself is now a loaded term, I would place Tua Di Ya Pek's rapid twenty-first-century popularisation through social media as an inexorable result of what may be tentatively termed 'digitised modernity'. As a result, religious trends have reverted, the vernacular tradition led by Underworld *tang-ki* now being in ascendance, or, in digitised modernity's lexicon, Tua Di Ya Pek are now 'trending'. Their predominance in the religious landscape is clearly reflected by the sheer volume and size of Seventh Month cemetery rituals performed in 2017.

The very popularity of these rituals raises further questions. Why have cemetery rituals become increasingly important, why in these specific cemetery plots and why now? In answer, I will draw on J. C. Scott (1985, 1990) to rationalise how and why these rituals resemble 'everyday forms of resistance' against government-sanctioned urban redevelopment.

Returning to the 'Master Plan' for the Republic of Singapore, it has undergone seven reviews since it was first approved by the government in August 1958, and multiple amendments have been, and continue to be, made. The 1972 amendments allowing for the destruction of cemeteries ultimately led to the following chain of events – events which provided the societal catalyst for the transfiguring hybridisation observed in 2017's cemetery rituals.

On 18 July 2017, under the Master Plan, a 'joint statement' was made by the Singapore Ministry of National Development, the Singapore Land Authority and the NEA in a news release announcing the planned expansion of Tengah Air Base "to accommodate some of the assets and facilities from

Paya Lebar Air Base",[9] and the need to exhume 45,000 Chinese graves in Choa Chu Kang Cemetery to make space for the expansion. Unlike previous exhumations to make land available for new burials, these cemetery plots would instead disappear. Under the joint statement, both cemetery plots described in the ethnography will be replaced by new military constructions, work having already begun on the land adjacent to the 'sending off' behind Cemetery Path Twenty-one. To make space for future burials, a new 'crypt burial system' will be established. The crypt burial system will involve installing approximately 40,000 deep concrete crypts measuring 2.89 metres by 1.52 metres, the graves being only fifteen centimetres apart with a concrete division to "allow bodies to be interred in a more compact way, saving space".[10] The plan to bury cadavers in cement graves to 'save space' has proven provocative rather than conciliatory in this regard, as it is in conflict with geomantic traditions that dictate correct burial in relation to the environment that is required for the fortuitous burial of one's ancestors. Ancestors are deceased relatives. Distinguishing graveyards as "a space that is however connected with all the sites of the city [...] since each individual, each family has relatives in the cemetery" (Foucault & Miskowiec, 1986: 25), Foucault identified cemeteries as primary heterotopias, sites of representation, contestation and inversion.

The contemporary removal of graves and encroachment on Singapore's remaining cemeteries was brought very much into the media spotlight through organised resistance by the Singapore Heritage Society and the so-called "Brownies", who, since 2012, have organised multiple campaigns to save historic tombs in Bukit Brown Cemetery from damage by a major road construction project. In contrast, at the time of writing, there has been no structured resistance to the Tengah Air Base expansion plans. However, substantiating Kenneth Dean's claims that "The flattening and homogenization of space through capitalist urban renewal in Singapore has somehow enabled spirit mediums to access heterotopic spaces" (Dean, 2018: 71), the *tang-ki* that I interviewed or accompanied to Choa Chu Kang Cemetery all confirmed that their atypical choice of cemetery plots had been influenced by the impending destruction of the graves located in them. In opposition to the planned desecration, these rituals share commonalities with Scott's 'everyday forms of resistance', "where daily exercise of power sharply limits the options available" (Scott, 1990: 91) and where "Acts of power from below, even when they are protests – implicitly or explicitly – will largely observe

---

9 Channel NewsAsia, www.channelnewsasia.com/news/singapore/government-to-exhume-over-80-000-graves-acquire-land-to-make-way-9041536.
10 Straits Times, 22 June 2016, www.straitstimes.com/singapore/cemetery-to-be-redeveloped-again.

the 'rules' even if their objective is to undermine them" (Scott, 1990: 93). The *tang-ki*'s confirmations of intent underline the causal interrelationships between land legislation and government-enforced exhumations, and the Underworld tradition's ritual use of cemeteries as sites of resistance.

Foucault's second principle of heterotopias "is that a society, as its history unfolds, can make an existing heterotopia function in a very different fashion" (Foucault & Miskowiec, 1986: 25). When a change in function transpires, it is accompanied by a corresponding change in practice and meaning, which, in terms of technologies of religious synthesis, means that transfiguring hybridisation will occur. The twenty-first-century transfiguration of forms of practice includes burning offerings in pre-allocated incinerators, the shifting focus from ancestral graves to those in areas soon to be reallocated for military use and Underworld deities overseeing the rituals. While the essential purpose of providing wandering spirits and ancestors with money, clothes and food through burning offerings has remained consistent, there has been an accompanying change in meaning, hybridisation, with daily Seventh Month rituals performed for foetus ghosts and anonymous cadavers rather than in ancestral plots as in previous years. However, these particular ritual forms and forms of resistance by Underworld *tang-ki* are distinct to Singapore. Crossing the Johor Strait into Malaysia, its Underworld tradition has evolved in reaction to a very different set of societal catalysts.

Therefore, having set a baseline of comparison incorporating the primary attributes and singularities of the Underworld tradition's material and ritual culture and interpretation of post-mortal cosmology in Singapore, the narrative will now move to Malaysia. Portraying an Underworld tradition even more *tang-ki*-centric than Singapore's, the following chapter will focus on an Underworld temple at the centre of a Chinese community located in Klang, Selangor State, Malaysia. In contrast to Singapore, Malaysia's Underworld tradition has emerged and flourished among an ethnic Chinese minority living in a Muslim-dominated state. Chapter 7's analysis will therefore focus on how Malaysia's Underworld tradition is playing an integral role in ethno-religious community formation, and, in the process reinforcing a strong sense of ethnic Chinese identity. The comparison between Singapore and Malaysia's Seventh Month ritual traditions and interpretations of post-mortal cosmology will then be completed in Chapters 8 and 9.

Part III
The Underworld tradition in Malaysia

7

Malaysia and the party spirit: *guanxi* and the creation of 'intentional' communities

In both Malaysia and Singapore, the Underworld tradition's mass popularisation has been brought about by differing combinations of societal catalysts, thereby producing both unities in and diversities between the two Underworld traditions. Both have involved the same inversion of Heaven to Hell deity worship, visually characterised by a predominantly shared material culture constructed around the veneration of Tua Di Ya Pek. However, expedited by a limited land and population demographic, Singapore's bureaucratic ability to exercise power, coupled with its promotion of ethnic and religious harmony, has in effect prevented religious groups from appreciably influencing the secular landscape. Singapore's Underworld tradition is therefore a refined and polished consequence of societal catalysts, but incapable of producing significant societal change outside of its own ritual sphere.

In comparison, the geographical spread of Malaysia's ethnic Chinese population is dispersed across a total area approximately four-hundred and sixty times that of Singapore's. Moreover, moving further from the urban metropolises of Kuala Lumpur and its satellites, Johor Bahru in the south and George Town to the north, the state's ability to exert authority over temples, their activities and sphere of influence diminishes exponentially. In Malaysia's townships the Underworld tradition has thus brought about significant changes in the secular landscape, most notably in the production of new ethno-religious communities based around Underworld temples, their *tang-ki*, festivals and the promotion of ethical codes based on the 'Jade Record' but largely reinterpreted in line with prevailing socio-political issues. This chapter therefore introduces Malaysia's Underworld temples as focal points of evolving ethno-religious communities and as hosts of large-scale and fully evolved Ah Pek parties in which inversions of authority in the Heaven–human–Underworld hierarchy are ongoing.

Malaysia's Datuk Gong also continue to play an independent religious role in secular society and, unlike Singapore's evicted and relocated Datuk Gong rehoused in Chinese temples, their altars remain present in construction sites, shopping malls and hotels, playing a similar tutelary role as Tua Pek Kung in Singapore or Tudi Gong in Taiwan. Many Malaysian temples include external altars to house them, though these are now most prolific in Underworld temples. This affiliation of Islamic saints from the Sufi tradition disinherited by the dominant Sunni branch of Islam may be seen as a pragmatic, self-perpetuating mechanism on the part of their Chinese and Malay *tang-ki* to ensure the survival of the broader Datuk Gong tradition. In comparison to Singapore, where their rank is perceived as lower than that of Chinese Underworld deities, in Malaysia their status has been elevated in many local vernacular pantheons (Plate 6).

A further inversion of religious authority has recently occurred. Within the internal logic of the vernacular tradition, temples in which deities have been worshipped the longest are generally perceived as the most efficacious, and therefore draw the largest numbers of visitors and commonly play a parental role in expanding temple networks. However, in Malaysia, successful Underworld temples are replacing older temples as focal points of ritual practice and community formation. Epitomising this phenomenon is Yinfu Tan, a new Underworld temple located in the outskirts of Klang in Selangor State.

Yinfu Tan: history and recreation of the Underworld as a ritual space

The ground floor of Yinfu Tan houses a model recreation of the Ten Courts of the Underworld[1] and a selection of its sub-hells. While broadly reflecting the Underworld's structure as described in the 'Jade Record', the recreation also illustrates the transfiguring hybridisation of practices and cosmology which are becoming increasingly common in the Malaysian tradition. Doubling as a ritual party space for the channelling, worship and use of Hell deities, and as a visual representation of post-mortal cosmology, the recreation illustrates how medieval understandings of karmic retribution have been modernised in line with contemporary Malaysian morality vis-à-vis ethnic

---

1 Three-dimensional Underworld recreations have become increasingly common, an early example being at the Temple of the Eastern Peak in Beijing (1322). More recent portrayals include Haw Pah Villa (originally Tiger Balm Gardens) in Singapore (1937); Wang Sean Suk Hell Garden in Chonburi province, Thailand (late twentieth century); and in the Chin Swee Caves, Pahang, Malaysia (1975).

power imbalances, corruption and environmental destruction. Therefore, after describing the temple's own creation myth I will return to the historical narrative, drawing comparisons between the causal nexuses connecting individual and bureaucratic transgressions and post-mortal punishments in the 'Jade Record' and those described and depicted in Yinfu Tan's Underworld.

The development of Yinfu Tan's sphere of influence has been rapid and, guided by Di Ya Pek as channelled through his *tang-ki*, Ah Boon, the temple illustrates new potentials made possible by the escalating dominance of Underworld temples in contemporary Malaysia. The present-day temple complex is sandwiched between two narrow lanes of ramshackle bungalows and industrial warehouses on land progressively purchased since 2009. At the top of the lane stands Sanbao Gong, a temple dedicated to Heaven deities which predates Yinfu Tan by approximately fifty years and provides the backdrop to Yinfu Tan's own creation narrative.

The ability to channel deities runs in Ah Boon's family – a trait often referred to as having a 'tang-ki bone'[2] – his maternal grandmother, paternal uncle and mother all being *tang-ki* before him. His grandmother was the resident *tang-ki* at Sanbao Gong prior to its redevelopment, when it was still a large, one-roomed wooden structure where she channelled the deity Zheng He, the deified Ming dynasty admiral and navigator who led expeditionary voyages charting the waters and cultures from Asia to East Africa. She had also brought two small Tua Di Ya Pek statues from Fujian Province to Sanbao Gong, and these were originally housed in a rickety, floor-level wooden shrine in front of the temple.

After Ah Boon's grandmother passed away, Sanbao Gong's manager dreamed of Di Ya Pek visiting his temple. Soon after, in January 2006, while walking home with his mother after dark, Ah Boon, who at the time did not practise any form of religion, saw an image of Di Ya Pek standing in front of his wooden shrine smoking opium. The figure, which Ah Boon recalls as being a little over a metre tall, solid in form and dressed in black robes, remained silent. On seeing it, his mother rushed into Sanbao Gong, returning with incense, and both offered incense to the apparition, after which the figure disappeared.

Two months later, the same Di Ya Pek visited Ah Boon in a lucid dream and, even though he felt 'as if' awake, he was unable to react, as Di Ya Pek systematically applied increasing pressure to his head, pinning him down as he lay rigid on the bed. After waking up he felt drained of energy, a

---

2 Also 'spirit bone'. One interpretation is that unborn children grow as flowering plants in the Heavenly Garden, and thirty-six bones link to form a bridge severed at birth between the soul of a person and the mortal realm. However, for the *tang-ki*, the spirit bone remains to serve as a bridge between realms (Chan, 2006).

condition which remained undiagnosed by physicians and lasted until May, when, as he walked past the same shrine, Di Ya Pek immobilised him and then forced his way into Ah Boon's body. Before losing consciousness of his surroundings, Ah Boon recalls feeling cold and dizzy, and then seeing Di Ya Pek's shadow, accompanied by two faceless assistants, moving towards him, and Di Ya Pek penetrating his skin and taking control of his body. This was the first time that Ah Boon had experienced trance possession and, while maintaining vague recollections of his soul being led towards the gates of the Underworld, he remains unaware of actual events while in the trance state.

When someone unexpectedly enters a trance state in ritual settings, those present commonly strip the person to the waist and stay with them to ensure that they do not accidentally come to harm. On this occasion this was accomplished by Sanbao Gong's elderly caretakers, and soon a group of village residents congregated who later informed Ah Boon of what had transpired. During this involuntary trance possession Di Ya Pek declared that he wanted his statue to be put inside a candlelit temple and to be offered incense and joss money. When asked which Di Ya Pek he was, bringing observers' attention to the Tua Di Ya Pek statues, he replied that his original soul was that of Fan Wujiu and that he served in the Fourth Court of the Underworld. As the statues originated in Fujian, the burial place of Xie Bian and Fan Wujiu, the claim was considered reasonable. Before pronouncing what was seen at the time as a bemusing prophecy, given the financial circumstances and remote location of the village, he first informed the residents that he wished to help them. When questioned why he had chosen Ah Boon, he replied that not only was he the son of a *tang-ki*[3] but, suiting his purposes, Ah Boon had been born under the stars of Lunar Seventh Month. Di Ya Pek then prophesised: "Within eight years, in place of the small wooden shrine in which my statue is housed, a palace will be built in which a community of devotees will gather to understand the Underworld, and which will attract visitors from far and wide." Di Ya Pek then left Ah Boon, but thereafter possessed his new *tang-ki* on a weekly basis.

The Di Ya Pek channelled in 2006 was foreboding, frequently using broken glass to release the *tang-ki*'s blood, observers recalling that the throne itself often became red with his blood. When questioned about the severity of the self-mortification imposed on his *tang-ki*, Di Ya Pek replied that in the Underworld he oversaw the 'Blood Pool Pond', thus accounting for his blood-lust when channelled. Interestingly, the 'Blood Pool Hell' predates the lives of Fan Wujiu and Xie Bian by many centuries, being a twelfth-century Chinese addition to the Buddhist canon from the 'Blood

---

3 Understood to mean that Ah Boon had inherited a '*tang-ki* bone'.

Pool Sutra of the Correct Teaching of the Great Canon as Preached by the Buddha' (*Foshuo Dazang zhengjiao xuepen jing*).[4] At a later date, Di Ya Pek informed me that he had taken over responsibility for the 'Blood Pool Hell' from an earlier, pre-Ming dynasty Underworld enforcer.

Illustrating human control over a deity's conduct through contractual means, towards the end of 2006, prompted by the intensity of self-mortification, Ah Boon's mother petitioned Di Ya Pek to change his ways. Placing a sheet of joss paper on the altar, Di Ya Pek agreed, but on the condition that Ah Boon serve him for a total of eight years. Therefore, after writing her name alongside that of Di Ya Pek, at his request she sealed the agreement with her finger-print daubed in Ah Boon's blood, the paper thereby becoming a contractual agreement between her family and the Underworld enforcer. Once he was bound by the terms of the contract, the self-mortification ceased and, in his increasingly amiable guise, Di Ya Pek first became popular in the local community and, as word of his efficacy spread, among those from further afield.

Ah Boon continued channelling Di Ya Pek at Sanbao Gong until a small piece of land had been purchased a few minutes' walk further from the main road, and in early 2009 the original Yinfu Tan was built there to house the Tua Di Ya Pek statues. The interior of the temple was painted black, and Ah Boon rendered images in fluorescent acrylics of Ox Head and Horse Face above the central altar. These were flanked by Biancheng Wang, the king of the Sixth Court, to their right, and to the left by the Judge of Commissioning Destiny, Siming Panguan, the chief judge of the Underworld in many Song dynasty Taoist narratives (Choi, 2017).

Several months later Di Ya Pek instructed the temple to purchase an adjacent plot of land on which the present-day temple is built, and prophesied that someone would soon agree to finance the construction of a new, palatial temple complete with a model reconstruction of the Underworld. Due to the terms of the contract with Ah Boon's family, he wanted the project completed within five years, a timeframe which, given the size of the undertaking, seemed implausible. A chain of events then occurred leading to Di Ya Pek meeting Yinfu Tan's future sponsor, Dato[5] Zeng, a businessman based 1,600 kilometres away in Sabah, East Malaysia. The events which followed greatly reinforced Di Ya Pek's perceived efficacy and prophetic exactitude.

Dato Zeng's mother-in-law had bought a house close to Subang Airport in

---

[4] Based on the earlier 'Yulanpen Sutra' describing Mulian saving his mother from Hell (Grant & Idema, 2011).
[5] Malaysia consists of thirteen states and three federal territories. 'Dato' is an honorary title in Malaysia, presented by the state where the ceremonial head of state is also a hereditary sultan.

Kuala Lumpur some years before, and had been troubled by wandering spirits in and around the house. Local religious specialists had failed to remove them and, having heard of Yinfu Tan's reputation for performing exorcisms, she came to consult Di Ya Pek, who resolved to assist. Ah Boon therefore visited their house and met Dato Zeng, who, not being religious minded, retired upstairs before Di Ya Pek was channelled to perform the exorcism.

In Singapore, exorcised spirits are commonly imprisoned in miniature coffins constructed from exhumed coffin wood, and in Malaysia, inside small, cardboard, gendered human effigies. Both the coffins and effigies are then sealed with a green talisman and chained to an Underworld altar until the spirits are released in Seventh Month. At Yinfu Tan, given Di Ya Pek's penchant for Guinness, a new tradition has evolved whereby exorcised spirits are imprisoned in empty Guinness bottles stoppered with joss paper and sealed with Di Ya Pek's talisman.

The spirits having been bottled, before de-trancing, Di Ya Pek asked to speak to Dato Zeng about his two businesses, a chain of shopping malls and a travel agency. He had been trying to get his parent company listed on the Kuala Lumpur Stock Exchange for over three years but, even with his political connections, the application process was still ongoing. Di Ya Pek first described the Dato's predicament with great accuracy and then suggested that, with his deific intervention, the applications would all be passed within a week. In return for his assistance Di Ya Pek asked for 300,000 Malaysian ringgits to build a new temple. Surprised by Di Ya Pek's knowledge, and sceptical of the likelihood of deific intervention influencing Malaysia's financial institutions, the Dato agreed. The rest, as they say, is history. The new temple was started in 2012, its outer shell built within six months and the interior, complete with its three-dimensional recreation of Hell, finished by mid-2013.

The temple is an imposing two-floored structure. The ground floor contains Di Ya Pek's interpretation of the Underworld and the upper story consists of a flat roof, central to which is a palatial altar room for Heaven deities, flanked by two separate octangular altar rooms for Tua Di Ya Pek's worship and use. The ground floor's layout includes two long corridors, one on each side, running the depth of the temple and linked by a central connecting corridor, the three forming the shape of an 'H'. On one side of the connecting corridor is Di Ya Pek's own multifunctional chamber containing his altar and a banquet table, and on the other are two smaller rooms containing multiple Underworld altars, all cloaked in darkness. Upstairs, the Jade Emperor and Xiwangmu the 'Queen Mother of the West'[6] reside side

---

6 Textual references to Xiwangmu date back to Zhuangzi in the fourth century.

by side on the Heaven altar. This in itself is an atypical configuration. Of note is that, outside of dedicated Jade Emperor temples, the Jade Emperor is represented by a temple's primary censer placed outside its main entrance. Yinfu Tan has both, the inclusion of the Jade Emperor on the central altar symbolically raising the temple's status in Klang's temple landscape. Adding weight to Di Ya Pek's elevated status, located each side of the main Heaven altar are stairs spiralling down into the darkness of Di Ya Pek's own chamber and the Underworld recreation beyond. There, in its far corner, locked within a medieval-style, iron-barred prison cell replete with mannequins shackled and chained to the floor and walls, a crate of Guinness bottles containing exorcised spirits is stored until Tua Ya Pek's birthday, when they are released.

Description and analysis of Yinfu Tan's recreation of the Underworld

In Yinfu Tan's model recreation, every king stands solemnly in judgement behind a table covered in red cloth with an assortment of gold utensils and their name chop. The desks are sheltered by a pavilion, with two stone pillars supporting a curved, red- and green-tiled roof attached to the wall behind.

The Ten Courts are represented along the walls of the two parallel corridors, accompanied by written descriptions of each court explaining who will be punished there, by which method and for what crimes. The courts are interspersed with scenes of the tortures perpetrated in a selection of the Underworld's sub-hells. On a practical level, this leaves room for a *tang-ki*, their entourage, throne and a temporary altar, thereby allowing visiting Tua Di Ya Pek *tang-ki* to enter a trance state in front of the Underworld court in which their master[7] serves. There are no windows in the Underworld recreation to facilitate the circulation of the dank, incense-infused air, no overhead lighting, and the lurid fluorescence illuminating the 'hellscapes' is too dim to penetrate the darkness of the black-walled corridors, thereby creating a prevailing sense of actually walking through a hellish subterranean chamber.

Accompanying each hellscape, embossed in gold lettering, are details of the crimes punished there, most being duplicated with minor variations in multiple courts to stress their present-day relevance. The tortures presented in vivid three-dimensional detail reinforce, through repetition, the tradition's dominant phantasmagorias of Hell. For example, the 'Hell of Sword Trees' (*Jian shu diyu*), the 'Hell of Severing in Two' and the 'Hell of Boiling Oil' (*You guo diyu*) are familiar to most practitioners in both Singapore and Malaysia. The simplification of cosmology is pragmatic, allowing

---

7 *Tang-ki* refer to the deities they channel as their 'master' or 'boss'.

7.1 The Third Court of King Songdi

practitioners to recall a more unified purgatorial system than would be possible if the 'Jade Record' were represented in its full complexity. Moreover, while the temple's reinterpretation of the 'Jade Record' mirrors their own contemporary sense of morality, more significantly, it reveals the prevalence of actual crimes and injustices perpetrated by or exacted on members of the community. The Underworld recreation may be not only therefore read as a commentary of the temple's moral outlook but also analysed as a reflection of wider social, environmental, judicial and political problems encountered by Malaysia's ethnic Chinese minority.

In the following description of the Underworld courts I will first summarise crimes and punishments emphasised in Maspero's (1932) translation of the 'Jade Record' and then compare these to those highlighted by Yinfu Tan. While there are clearly similarities, the comparison illustrates the modernisation of moral causality in Malaysia's post-mortal cosmology, comparable representations being widely depicted in temple decorations or elucidated upon by Underworld *tang-ki* elsewhere in Malaysia.

In the 'Jade Record's' First Court, those whose merits equal their demerits are sent to the Tenth Court for reincarnation, the remainder being taken to the 'Terrace of the Mirror of the Wicked' (*Nie jingtai*), where they see reflected the victims of their wrongdoings before being sent for punishments in the remaining courts. A worse fate awaits suicides, they being first returned to Earth as hungry ghosts to live out their allotted years, predetermined at time of birth by the Lords of the Northern and Southern Dipper, after which they are sent to the Ninth Court's 'City of the Dead-by-Accident' (*Wangsi Cheng*), where they are destined to suffer Hell's torments indefinitely. In Yinfu Tan's First Court the model includes the king, two scribes with pens and a chained prisoner who is kneeling, their reflection clearly visible in the 'Mirror of the Wicked' placed in front of the king's desk. Here, in accord with the 'Jade Record', and in contrast with Singapore, where it is commonly held that all crimes will be punished, it is proclaimed that 'If one's merits equal one's demerits, the prisoner may go straight to the Tenth Court to await reincarnation'.

The process of karmic retribution then begins in earnest in the Second Court, where the king, Chujiang Wang,[8] orders punishments. In the 'Jade Record' he sentences dishonest matchmakers, fraudsters, incompetent physicians and those who have maimed or injured humans or animals to be brutalised in the sixteen sub-hells under his jurisdiction. Maspero mentions starvation, being chopped to pieces and fed to wild animals, or slowly roasted while chained to a red-hot pillar. In Yinfu Tan's depiction the Second

---

8 'Wang' meaning 'king'.

Court contains a scribe and a demon striking a chained prisoner while an Ah Pek looks on nonchalantly and those who have killed, injured or robbed others are sentenced there by the king. Noting that today many people use threats to force others into submission, the temple interprets injuring and robbing politically, warning that people who abuse bureaucratic authority to cold-heartedly bully or threaten others will be punished in the court's sub-hells. Also singled out are con-artists who cheat others out of their wealth, especially those who cheat the elderly, a crime described as the most heinous, blood-sucking example of robbery. The guilty are punished in the 'Hell of Pus and Blood' (*Nong xie diyu*). Imposing a timeframe reminiscent of the second-century 'Sutra on the Eighteen Hells' (*Fo Shuo shiba ni li jing*), the punishments in all of Yinfu Tan's sub-hells can last hundreds or thousands of years. The temple warns that the degree of suffering increases in each of the sixteen sub-hells. Linked successively, the torture seems endless.

In the 'Jade Record', the Third Court's sub-hells are reserved for unjust officials, those who have not respected their superiors, cheats, forgers, slanderers, those who have escaped from justice, women who deprived their husbands in the bed chamber and the unfilial who have sold the land on which their ancestors were buried. Sentenced by Songdi Wang, the guilty face bodily mutilations, being buried in mounds of flesh-eating creatures or being flayed without mercy. In Yinfu Tan's reinterpretation, crimes committed as a result of devious thoughts, deluded resentments and ignorance are judged, but with no gender bias or mention of bed chambers. The temple's primary emphasis is once again on government officials who are disloyal, receive bribes or do not fulfill their responsibilities to look after the populace. The temple's secondary focus is on those who help others to terminate marital contracts, commit perjury or defame others. 'Today,' the temple notes, 'freedom of speech has reached unrestrained levels, giving rise to misfortunes caused by defamation and public criticism both in print and on social media.'

In the Fourth Court, Wuguan Wang passes judgement on the mean minded, the tight-fisted rich, defrauders, dishonest traders, those who steal from temples and physicians who, although capable, do not provide cures to those requiring them. The culpable are variously crushed or buried alive, placed kneeling or sitting on sharpened bamboo poles or made to drink quicklime, which causes an exothermic reaction, thus boiling the body from within. In addition, the location of what Maspero calls "The Lake of Fetid-Blood" (Maspero, 1932: 365), now known as the 'Blood Pond Hell', is a sub-hell of this court. In both orthodox traditions the 'Blood Pond Hell' remains an exclusive domain for women. The 'Blood Bowl Sutra of the Correct Teaching of the Great Canon as Preached by the Buddha' (*Foshuo*

Dazang zhengjiao xuepen jing) expounds that it is for women "Who every month leak menses or in childbirth release blood which seeps down and pollutes the earth gods" (Grant & Idema, 2011: 25), and who then wash their bloodied clothes in the river from where water is drawn to make offerings of tea to Heaven deities, thus rendering them impure. Analogously, in orthodox Taoism, the twelfth-century 'True scripture of the Heavenly Worthy of Primordial Beginnings who saves Beings from the Blood Pond' (*Yuanshi tianzun jidu xiehu zhengjing*) describes menstrual and childbirth blood as polluting water sources so that "People, without knowledge and awareness, draw water for drink and food and offer it as sacrifice to the spirits" (Lee, 2003: 22), thus offending the Three Taoist Luminaries. Women are therefore punished in both orthodox traditions with the same post-mortal fate. In contrast, in the vernacular tradition, the reified meaning attached to this sub-hell is gender inclusive. At Yinfu Tan it is a place of torment for the disrespectful, those who have evaded paying taxes or rent, shown a lack of filial piety or demonstrated disloyalty to superiors. In another of the Fourth Court's sub-hells, the 'Hell of Lifting Sharp Rocks' (*Ding shi li feng xiao diyu*), those damaging the environment are punished. Addressing contemporary ecological anxieties, environmental destruction is punished in three of Yinfu Tan's courts, numbers four, six and seven, the Fourth Court judging those who have cut down an excessive number of trees for profit. Deforestation is a major public concern in Malaysia, the World Wildlife Fund Malaysia noting that "In the 20 years from 1983 to 2003, there was a reduction of about 4.9 million hectare of forest cover in Malaysia".[9] Between 2000 and 2012 Malaysia had the world's highest rate of deforestation,[10] the *Telegraph* headlining "Malaysia destroying its forests three times faster than all Asia combined".[11]

In the 'Jade Record', the Fifth Court is ruled over by King Yama, Yanluo Wang, and reserved for perpetrators of what were perceived as more serious transgressions of morality. Further demonstrating the influence of monastic Buddhism, in addition to the punishment of murderers, also punished here are hunting, fishing and the butchering of animals, the destruction of religious texts, the breaking of religious vows and prostitution. As such, King Yama pronounces judgement on those who have broken three of the Five Precepts: to abstain from killing living beings, sexual misconduct and lying. In contrast, Yinfu Tan's Fifth Court is for those who have killed or

---

9 www.wwf.org.my/about_wwf/what_we_do/forests_main/.
10 https://news.mongabay.com/2013/11/malaysia-has-the-worlds-highest-deforestation-rate-reveals-google-forest-map/.
11 *Telegraph*, www.telegraph.co.uk/news/earth/earthnews/8295896/Malaysia-destroying-its-forests-three-times-faster-than-all-Asia-combined.html.

plotted another's death for personal gain, caused grievous injury to another, accepted bribes to the detriment of the weak or profited from lending money with exorbitant interest rates. All these actions are interpreted as bullying, and, as in the Second Court, those who have bullied the weak are punished in a sub-hell, in this instance the 'Hell of Flying Knives and Burning Stones' (*Fei dao huo shi diyu*). In total, Yinfu Tan mentions five sub-hells spread through the Underworld where various forms of governmental, personal and online bullying are punished. While gang-related extortion is not uncommon, informants from ethnic Chinese and Indian minorities commonly expressed resentment towards what they perceived as government-sanctioned bullying, imposed bureaucratically through the NEP and NDP in the education, business and employment sectors. The repeated emphasis on bullying the weak suggests that both extortion and officially sanctioned discrimination are now primary social concerns within Malaysia's ethnic minority communities.

In the Sixth Court, Biancheng Wang punishes prisoners for religious sacrilege: verbally disrespecting deities; destroying their statues for profit; printing deity names on material goods for non-religious use; and for owning obscene books. That two Underworld courts are dedicated to the abuse of religious objects and perceived sexual deviancy suggests that both were prevalent at the time of the 'Jade Record's' composition. The Sixth Court's punishments are varied and severe, and Giles's (1926) translation of the sixteen sub-hells illustrates that the highly selective choice of punishments now promoted is likely based on their visual impact. After all, given the cinematic realism of contemporary media, kneeling 'on iron shot', 'noisome smells', being 'butted by oxen' or 'nipped by locusts' have lost the emotional impact originally intended. In the modern tradition only the fifteenth sub-hell of the 'Jade Record', the 'Hell of Severing in Two', is now commonly portrayed. In the temple's depiction the prisoner is lying belly-down on a raised bed of hot coals illuminated from beneath by orange and red lights, his back arched and his tortured face looking up at visitors as they pass. A thick blade drenched in a ghostly green glow, tipped at one end with a maliciously fierce dragon's head, is being manipulated from the other end by a Hell demon. As the demon pushes down on the blade's long handle, the prisoner's body is slowly severed asunder, the model being frozen in the moment that the blade has cleaved through the flesh and muscle, just before breaking through the spine (Plate 7).

At Yinfu Tan, entrance to this sub-hell has dual causalities, one environmental and the other religious, as both are considered equally disrespectful to Heaven and Earth. The first addresses the over-logging of forests and contamination of water sources, issues brought into the public domain due to the scale of pollution caused annually by deforestation fires to

1 Yu Feng Nan Fu Xuanshan Miao

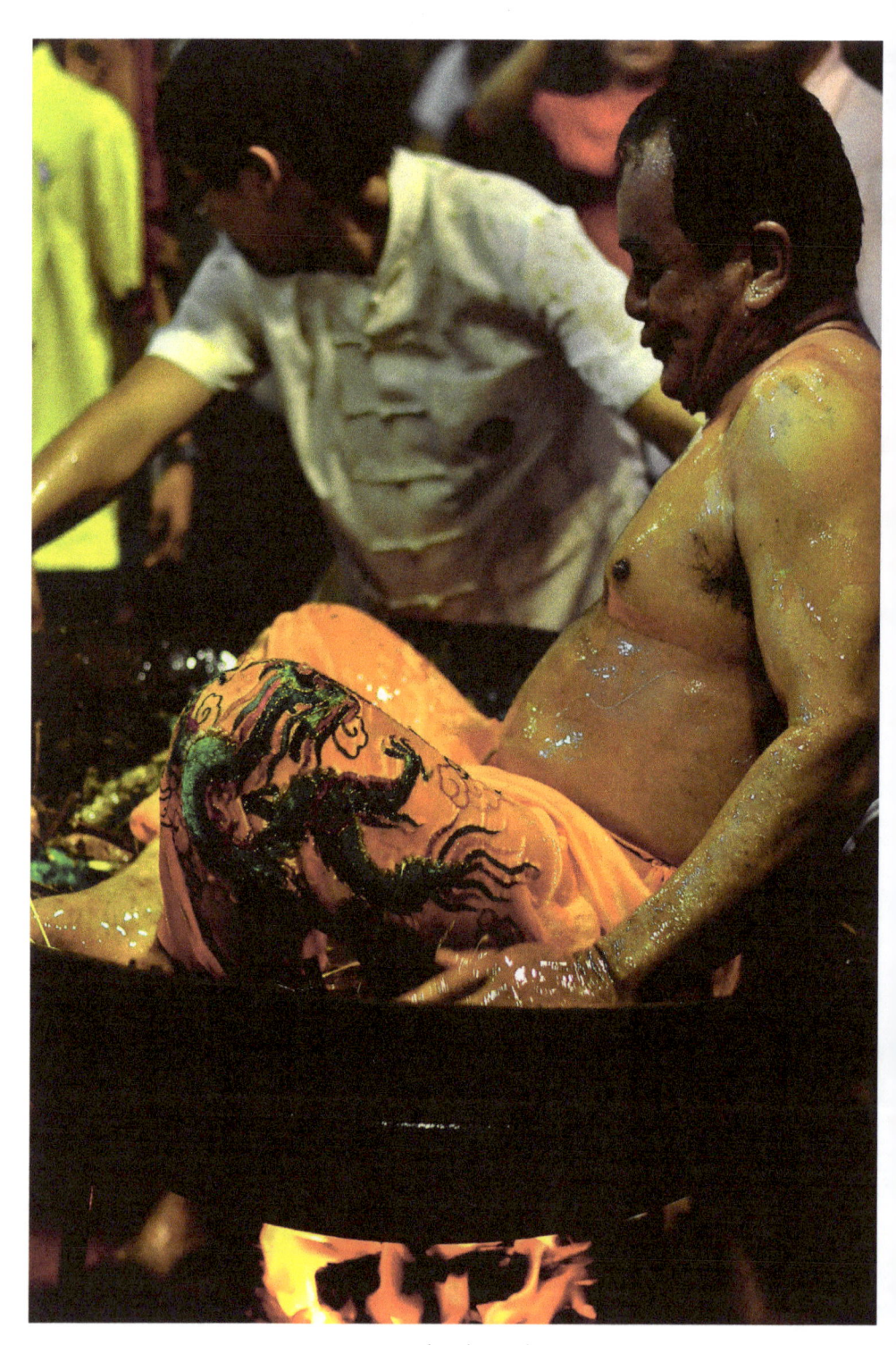

2   Oil wok ritual

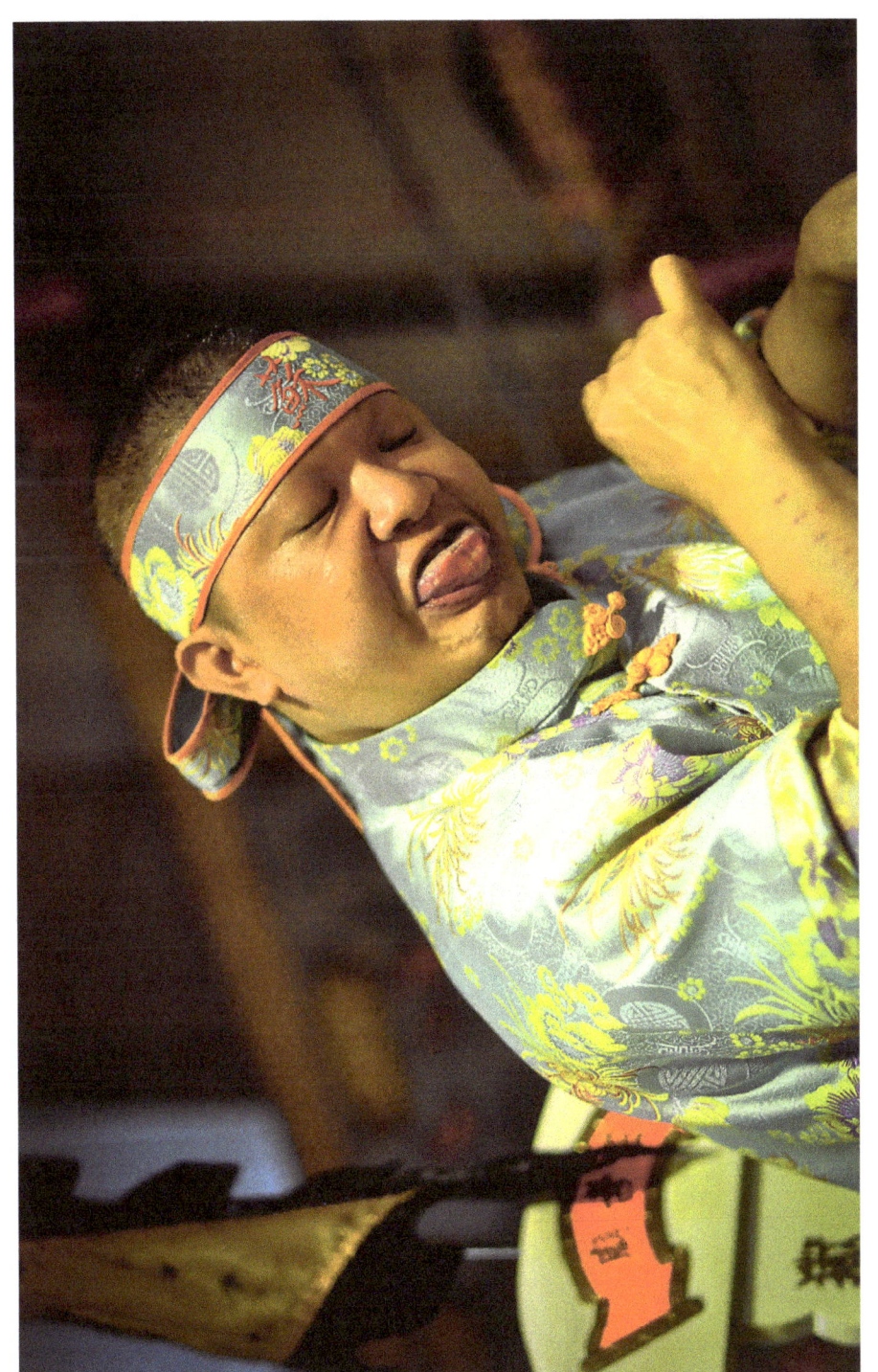

3 Tua Ya Pek splices his tongue

4 Cemetery plot for foetuses, babies and young children

5   Offerings before the foetus ghost's altar

6 Guan Gong paying respects to a Datuk Gong, Malaysia

7 The 'Hell of Severing in Two'

8 Ah Boon resting in Di Ya Pek's altar room

9 Di Ya Pek and *luk thep* dolls

10 Dasheng Gong Chenghuang Dian's Underworld altar

11 One pair of Tua Di Ya Pek at the conference

12 My coffin ritual at Brickfields Chenghuangmiao

13 Miniature coffins frequently found on Singapore's Underworld altars

14 Anxi Chenghuangmiao's Tua Di Ya Pek (top) compared to their common depiction in Singapore and Malaysia (bottom)

15 Inviting the temple's deities at Anxi Chenghuangmiao

16 Feeding Tua Ya Pek opium at Penang's City God Temple

clear land for East Malaysia's and Indonesia's palm-oil and pulp-and-paper industries. In 2015 a Forbes Asia headline read "Indonesia's forest fires choke Malaysia, Singapore"[12] and the BBC similarly reported that "Forest fires saw a thick haze blanket parts of South East Asia for months".[13] The second focuses on imitating religious specialists to defraud people of their possessions, thus addressing both *tang-ki* incapable of entering trance possession and those impersonating priests, monks and nuns to offer religious services for profit. Those who have blasphemed deities are also punished in 'Hell of Severing in Two'. Whereas in the 'Jade Record' all who have taken "Holy names in vain" (Giles, 1926: 401) are severed, Yinfu Tan adds the caveat that 'We cannot all believe in deities, or in the same deities, but as Chinese we should not blaspheme any'. This reflects the prevalent interpretation of post-mortal cosmology in Malaysia's Underworld tradition[14] – an interpretation diametrically opposed to Singapore's post-mortal ethnic inclusivity – namely, that entry into Chinese Hell, rather than being dependent on actions or beliefs, is determined by blood; in other words, on patrilineal descent.

Moving on, in the 'Jade Record' those who have violated graves, those who have indulged in or promoted cannibalism and those who have sold their affianced into slavery are sentenced in the Seventh Court by the demoted Lord of Mount Tai, Taishan Wang, whose absolute sovereignty over of the world of the dead was ended by the Celestial Masters. In the absence of cannibalism or slavery, at Yinfu Tan rumour-mongers, extortionists, thieves, alcoholics, drug addicts and those who have created discord among family members without regret are sentenced to torture in the 'Hell of Tongue Removal and Cheek Piercing' (*Ba she chuan sai xiao diyu*). Alongside this multiplicity of debauchery, remaining staunchly focused on the environment, the temple also brings attention to the use of fire or explosives to clear land in forested or mountainous areas, as, in the process, millions of animals are killed. Perpetrators are sent to the 'Hell of Boiling Oil' (*You guo diyu*) and, noting that hikers enjoy a barbeque, the temple warns that if a forest fire is started due to carelessness, those responsible will be repeatedly fried, brought back to consciousness and refried in the same sub-hell.

With the ancestral cult and Confucian filial piety central to the vernacular tradition, filial piety includes the correct worship of and offerings made to one's – or, in the case of married women their husband's – patrilineal

---

12 Cited at: www.forbes.com/sites/mclifford/2015/09/10/indonesias-forest-fires-choke-malaysia-singapore-burning-land-just-for-fun/#1fc38c5e4ec8
13 Cited at: www.bbc.com/news/business-35109393
14 Some Malaysian Buddhists not involved in Underworld tradition may share the Singaporean view.

forefathers. Among the living, filial piety goes beyond mere obedience, entailing on children to not cause their parents either anxiety or sorrow. In the 'Jade Record', failure to meet all of these responsibilities is punished in the Eighth Court, overseen by Dushi Wang, penalties including having one's tongue torn out, having nails driven into one's head, being crushed and mutilated by the wheels of chariots or being submerged in pits of excrement. Yinfu Tan's Eighth Court also judges the unfilial, and, inverting the Confucian rules of 'Five cardinal human relationships' (*wulun* / 五倫), explicitly identifies and punishes those who have mistreated their children or stepchildren. Klang is the former capital of Selangor, a state which has experienced among the highest cases of child abuse in Malaysia, with stepchildren more frequently abused than biological kin (Noremy *et al.*, 2012). Also punished are fraudsters who scheme and steal money from others through deception, whether in writing, face-to-face or online. Fraud is punished in three of Yinfu Tan's Underworld courts, exposing scams as an increasingly serious social problem. *TIME* magazine has described Malaysia as "A global hub for internet scams preying on the lovelorn" and attributes this to "Lax student visa regulations and a high-tech banking system",[15] thus allowing Nigerian and Ghanaian scammers to set up base there. Other major scams receiving media coverage include Malaysia travel scratch cards, travel package scams, property sales scams and banking and investment scams. In 2017 Channel Newsasia reported on "1,883 cases of investment scams between 2015 and Apr 2017, resulting in losses of up to US$89 million".[16]

Returning to the 'Jade Record', beyond killing one's own parents, the ultimate unfilial act is suicide, and this is punished in Pingdeng Wang's Ninth Court in the 'City of the Dead-by-Accident'. Unlike other sub-hells, there is no escape, the unfilial reliving their own suicide indefinitely and thereby foregoing eventual reincarnation. In addition, the 'City of the Dead-by-Accident' plays host to souls sentenced to permanent death for crimes committed in the Underworld, the post-mortal execution transforming the soul into a shadow soul (*jian* / 魘) to be tortured indefinitely. The Court's other sub-hells accommodate abortionists, producers of pornography and their customers, who are sentenced to pulverisation in a grain-mill, or to have their heads stewed or brains removed and replaced with a hedgehog. Similarly, at Yinfu Tan, the Ninth Court is reserved for the most serious crimes, including murdering one's own parents. However, greater emphasis is placed on robbing, raping or killing with unfettered

---

15 *TIME*, 9 July 2014, http://time.com/2968765/malaysia-is-becoming-a-global-hub-for-internet-scams-preying-on-the-lovelorn/.
16 www.channelnewsasia.com/news/asiapacific/thousands-of-get-rich-quick-dreams-dashed-by-scammers-in-8915880.

anger, as neither abortion nor pornography is now perceived as a serious crime. Yinfu Tan's Tenth Court closely matches the 'Jade Record' as detailed in Chapter 3.

Tua Di Ya Pek and the party spirit: the creation of community

In earlier chapters ethnographic emphasis has been placed on individual rituals accompanied by conversations with deities. However, in order to demonstrate differences in the ambiance of temple settings generated by the contrasting environments afforded by Singapore's urban redevelopment in a rich, Chinese-majority city-state with a comparatively less developed and unregulated ethnic Chinese minority in an urban township, this sub-chapter will instead focus on communal rituals and community events. My intention is to convey how an emotional attachment to Yinfu Tan's Di Ya Pek, underpinned by reciprocity and debt, has contributed to the generation of a close-knit ethno-religious community.

Recognition of this temple's spiritual efficacy and the increasing prestige of its *tang-ki* are a result of, and have resulted in, the temple's spreading fame and increasing sphere of influence. By 2015, *tang-ki* from many of Klang's temples, and increasingly so those based further afield in central and southern Malaysia, have chosen to channel deities there, thus forming one of several overlapping ritual networks of primarily independent Underworld temples. Lacking a single controlling or parent temple, many of the visiting temples play a similarly central role in community formation in their own localities.

In contrast to Singapore, where a temple's anniversary is commonly its primary ritual event, necessarily so as a temple's funds for the coming year are largely raised in auctions during their closing banquets, a wide variety of festivals take precedence in Malaysia. At Yinfu Tan, ritual precedence is given to Di Ya Pek's birthday, and *tang-ki* from Yinfu Tan's informal ritual network, accompanied by their followers, flock there to pay their respects and to participate in the three days of festivities. Following an ethnographic description of the celebrations between 6 and 8 July 2015, the role of an Underworld temple playing host to and unifying a broader secular community will be discussed.

Di Ya Pek's party: day one

Rituals began in the late afternoon, before the public arrived. After assembling a spectacular, three-tiered paper palace for the Jade Emperor's pleasure during the festival, three orthodox priests chanted a variation of the 'Five Cinnabar Spells' scripture (*Wu Dan Zhou*), inviting the Jade Emperor and informing him of the temple's proposed activities. Unlike in Singapore, where Taoist priests work alongside *tang-ki* at temple festivals, no *tang-ki* in trance states were present, and the orthodox ritual presence was kept to a minimum. The priests would participate only twice more towards the end of the third evening: once to report the temple's rituals to Heaven deities and again to 'send off' the Jade Emperor at the festival's close. All other rituals were overseen or performed by Di Ya Pek, sometimes with the assistance of *tang-ki* channelling Underworld and Heaven deities from the Buddhist, Taoist and local vernacular pantheons.

> *By early evening, the temple was thronging with around eight-hundred people who had come to participate in Ah Pek's birthday celebrations. Most were gathered in an open unpaved space separated from the temple by a narrow lane, sitting in groups at large round tables enjoying the lavish buffet dinner and drinks donated to and redistributed by the temple. At each table were clusters of friends or families spanning several generations, and every group seemed familiar with those sat at the tables around them. It was clearly a community event, with many of east Klang's ethnic Chinese population enjoying the festivities. A large stage complete with lasers and speaker stacks had been set up at the end of the open space furthest from the temple for a 'getai' (歌台) variety performance featuring song and dance later in the evening. Separating the public from the stage was an area cordoned off with red string and containing two long tables. The table to the left was fronted by red plastic chairs to allow wandering spirits to sit and enjoy the entertainment, and the other was reserved for Di Ya Pek and his invited guests.*
>
> *I asked after Ah Boon and was told that he had been looking for me as he was preparing to enter trance and as was his custom, he was first taking a meditative repose on the cushioned platform in front of his Underworld altar (Plate 8). Once rested, he invited me to enter the small altar room across the corridor with him, and a heavy black curtain was pulled across the entrance behind us. He sat in darkness at a small desk with a supply of joss and talisman papers, incense, candles, and an abacus facing the altar. Only a metre across, the altar was tri-level, with Tudi Gong as the highest-ranking deity placed in the top centre. Although a low-ranking deity, as Tudi Gong's palace is first port of call in the post-mortal journey of the soul, and as individual Tudi Gong cross out the newly deceased's name from the 'Register of Births and Deaths' ('Shensi bu'), they command a comparatively privileged position the Underworld tradition. The second level was occupied by small Thai figures including a black and gold Thai Buddha and robed Theravada*

monks. On the lowest level flanking a small censer, Di Ya Pek's statue was placed to the right and Tua Ya Pek's to the left, their customary positions inversed to show Di Ya Pek as senior in this particular temple's hierarchy.

I stood next to Ah Boon while a select group of his inner circle quietly chanted an invocation, though without the percussion ubiquitous to Singapore. Ah Boon's eyes closed, and he gradually swooned into a trance state, the quietude abruptly shattered as his fists slammed down repeatedly on the desk as Di Ya Pek arrived. After being dressed in his black robes he relaxed back into his throne, was handed a pipe which he sucked on greedily, and then turned his attention to a senior devotee and myself. Wishing him a happy birthday, we drank to his lasting health many times from small glasses of cognac and water which were instantly refilled. I mused over drinking to the good health of a person already long deceased, but as toasting to 'another great year in Hell' would have been inappropriate, I conformed with others' birthday greetings. After all, as there are no more birthdays, or as Di Ya Pek later stressed, birthday parties in the Underworld, he had channelled through Ah Boon to celebrate his birthday with his followers and godchildren in Klang. Our drinking companion had brought with him an exquisitely carved and painted statue of Di Ya Pek that he had purchased in Anxi along with two jade rings for his wife and himself, and between several more pipes and further toasts, Ah Pek 'opened the eyes' of all three objects. Illustrating the dominance of Di Ya Pek over all other deities at Yinfu Tan, these objects were later placed on the temple's Heaven altar in front of the Jade Emperor's statue to absorb the temple's spiritual efficacy before being taken home. I reflected that while Dizangwang, Bao Gong and city gods may be placed on Underworld altars, placing Di Ya Pek on a Heaven altar is essentially taboo, and that Yinfu Tan was likely establishing another local precedent.[17] In Singapore where this particular ritual propriety has remained unchanged, Underworld deities are not placed on Heaven deities' altars.

Meanwhile, Di Ya Pek's arrival was interpreted by visiting 'tang-ki' as time for them to enter trance, and walking out into the connecting corridors, I was met with the sight of approximately fifteen 'tang-ki' simultaneously channelling deities from different Underworld courts. Some were accompanied by percussionists, and all with devotees chanting invocations, the 'tang-ki' concurrently displaying frenzied bodily

---

17 Others include Guinness bottles for exorcised spirits, 3D Underworld reconstructions and Hell deities dancing.

and facial contortions as each entered different stages of or attained complete trance possession states. A cacophony of sounds echoed between the walls: drums, cymbals, chants, commands, the rattling of multiple abacuses, yells, screams, and the crack of whips displacing the billowing incense smoke, all reverberating through a seemingly subterranean man-made simulation of Hell. As each 'tang-ki' became possessed, their helpers paid obeisance and then dressed them in appropriate identifying robes, and handed them their whips, weapons and flags. I noted that this degree of inter-temple cooperation and mass synchronised channelling is no longer uncommon in Malaysia and is distinctive of central and southern Malaysia's Underworld tradition. The magnitude of their Underworld festivals and ritual events is therefore unrivalled in either Singapore or in northern Malaysia.

Di Ya Pek had returned to sit at his own lavish altar, the room richly decorated with depictions of Underworld torments and life-sized statues of Hell's lower-ranking denizens, all dimly illuminated in garish shades of red, blue and green emanating from fluorescent light tubes set into the floor. As visiting 'tang-ki' made their way to pay respects to Di Ya Pek, and indeed throughout the entire three-day party, each visiting Underworld 'tang-ki' was trailed by assistants, one carrying a tray of cognac and water, another a crate of Guinness, and a third with a rack of pre-prepared opium-laced cigarettes.

Upstairs, at temporary altars set up in the open space on the first floor of the temple, Heaven deities were also being channelled including red and green Fazhu Gong;[18] Sun Wu Kong; Jigong; Lotus Flower San Taizi and Nezha;[19] and, a charismatic local Datuk known as Datuk Green. Similarly making their way to pay obeisance in Di Ya Pek's chamber, they waited in line and exchanged niceties and toasts with various Tua Di Ya Pek, Heaven and Hell deities bowing to each other as pantheonic equals. On entering the Underworld altar room, all 'tang-ki' offered incense to Di Ya Pek, many kneeling with a flourish to do so, and then drank toasts to him with cognac, whisky or Guinness[20] before leaving the room. Reinforcing my impressions from previous ritual events, the equality shown between Underworld and Heaven deities, and the latter's deference to Di Ya Pek both confirmed the changing power balance between the two pantheons in contemporary Malaysia.

---

18 Deified post-mortally, Fazhu Gong is personified in green, red or black, representing him as a student, as a warrior and as a Taoist priest.
19 The Third Prince before and after promotion as described in the Ming dynasty novel *The Investiture of the Gods*.
20 Datuk Gong toast without alcohol, due to their Islamic origins.

Formalities over, our group moved to the upper floor of the temple where a table bedecked with offerings had been placed outside Di Ya Pek's octagonal altar room, central to which were three large roast pigs, these surrounded by platters piled high with roasted fowl, cooked fish, desserts, and bottles of alcohol. A throne had been placed at the head of the table, and here devotees, godchildren and the general public who had not paid respects to Di Ya Pek at his Underworld altar queued up to do so.

First however a celebratory ritual act was performed: making the initial cut into the largest and centrally placed pig thereby bestowing Di Ya Pek's blessing on it before being chopped and distributed among the guests. Di Ya Pek hovered over the carcass with a sharpened meat cleaver while sniffing it gleefully to absorb its spiritual essence, and then summoned the head of the temple's committee, senior temple members and myself to place our hands over his, and together we enthusiastically thrust the cleaver through the porcine flesh. The variety performances had already begun, and as the cleaver sank through the animal's back and the assembled crowd of around one hundred yelled "Heng Ah! Hong Ah! Huat Ah!" (prosperity, prosperity, prosperity / 兴啊, 旺啊, 发啊), the words were hardly audible above the amplified 'throb-throb-throb' of the music below. The 'tang-ki' channelling the Underworld Tiger General,[21] his face and hands blackened with ash and paint then mounted the tables of offerings to enjoy their scent before ripping chunks of meat from the sacrificial pigs with his teeth. Amplified further, the digitally produced rhythm from the stage some fifty metres away became overpowering, and the pressure of the sound waves could be noticeably felt on one's skin. Meaningful conversation now impossible, Di Ya Pek decided to dance,[22] twirling merrily with devotees, local residents and with other Underworld deities.

From the vantage point of the upper floor's balcony, I reflected that these kinds of communal participation allowing for informal and spontaneous interactions with Hell deities have become the norm in Malaysia's Underworld tradition, as has their sharing of alcohol and food. This has culminated in the creation of all-inclusive temple environments catering to the whims and tastes of the wider community, 'tang-ki' and laymen alike. In contrast, while Singapore's Ah Pek parties are informal events, they remain largely exclusive, the deities sharing food and alcohol

---

21 A deity unique to the local Underworld pantheon.
22 According to informants, he was the first Ah Pek to dance at parties, and the trend is now spreading in Malaysia.

primarily among themselves, thus creating an air of exclusivity which distances them hierarchically from the devotees present.

From the balustraded balcony, I surveyed and instinctively analysed the temple's wider community drawn together by the worship of Underworld deities who, it was held, would inflict the severest of tortures on their devotees' souls after death. What, I wondered, in light of this, was the societal glue binding the temple's community together? A community hailing from an eclectic mix of professions spanning the social and economic spectrum and comprising all age groups from young children to the eldest pensioners. Familiar with community members from past events, and well acquainted with the trials and tribulations of the temple's regular devotees, observing the multiplicity of social interactions below, I began to comprehend the extent that 'guanxi' (关系) played in cementing interpersonal relationships within the temple's community. 'Guanxi', a powerful force in Chinese culture based on reciprocal favours whereby each member of the community could call on another for assistance, acquiring a reciprocal debt in the process, thereby producing a self-perpetuating system of favours granted, favours reciprocated, and favours owed.

A systematic and culturally ingrained system, *guanxi* is a compelling force resembling the 'you scratch my back and I scratch yours' mentality found elsewhere, but in which debts may be carried over by successive generations of individuals, families, businesses, temples and local communities. *Guanxi* is intentional, as it "Must be consciously produced, cultivated, and maintained over time" (Gold, Guthrie & Wank, 2002: 6). In Malaysia's religious landscape, and epitomised by Underworld *tang-ki* temples such as Yinfu Tan, temples consciously enhance this process by acting as social intermediaries in the production of reciprocal debt, thereby accelerating local community cohesion. Beyond the contractual relationships between deities and devotees negotiated through divination blocks or a *tang-ki*, a secondary web of reciprocal interpersonal relationships thus permeates a temple's secular community and, when required, outsiders are assimilated into a temple's larger communal *guanxi* network through adoption as a deity's godchildren through their *tang-ki*. At Yinfu Tan, Di Ya Pek frequently adopts multiple godchildren of all ages, thereby granting them access to the temple's *guanxi* network, and during the three-day celebration numerous individuals approached Di Ya Pek for this purpose.

Days two and three

The remaining two days resembled the first, in that there were multiple *tang-ki* in trance at any given time while the party continued. The key rituals included the ceremonial crossing of a *pingan* (peace) bridge (平安桥) on day two, a ritual undertaken to remove negative energies influencing participants' lives, and the sending off of the Jade Emperor's palace on the final day. However, in terms of time and energy spent, the primary activities included the consumption of alcohol and subsequent bonding between *tang-ki*; between *tang-ki* and their devotees; and, both unifying the local secular and religious communities while expanding the temple's ritual network, Di Ya Pek bonded with all those present.

Turning then to the ceremonial crossing of the Peace bridge, it was reasoned that, with so many deities present through their *tang-ki*, further layers of ritual protection were superfluous. By 8 p.m. the courtyard in front of the original Yinfu Tan was thronging with those waiting for the bridge to be opened. Following established tradition, people would cross in groups according to their Chinese zodiac sign, and there was a buzz of excitement as devotees gathered around Underworld *tang-ki* based on compatible birth years. When crossing the bridge, each person carried three incense sticks, gold joss money as an offering to the Jade Emperor, and a small cardboard male or female effigy, the same as conventionally used to trap exorcised spirits. In bridge crossings, the effigy is a paper representation of oneself, a proxy self, absorbing one's bad luck when carried over the bridge and, in doing so, taking on one's identity in '*qi*' form. This embodiment of '*qi*' is a form of spiritual deception, as, following the transference of one's '*qi*' into it, any wandering spirit with malevolent intent towards an individual would later follow their proxy self into the flames during the Jade Emperor's sending off, and thus be removed from the human realm.

> *The final evening began with the ritual 'sending off' of the Jade Emperor's palace. Resembling a traditional 'tour of the borders', the palace was carried in three sections to the back gate of the temple where three Taoist priests, the 'tang-ki' and devotees assembled. The priests led the way out of the temple's gate and past Sanbao Gong to the main road where a small altar had been erected. However, amid the mass of 'tang-ki' and followers, the priests soon merged into the background allowing Di Ya Pek to assume his role as master of rituals at the head of the procession.*
>
> *Led by Di Ya Pek, the procession turned right along a muddy lane running adjacent to the temple at the end of which a space had been*

prepared for the sending off. A circular wall had been constructed of wedges of joss money inside of which the Jade Emperor's palace was reconstructed. The gap between the palace and outer wall was piled high with joss money folded to resemble ancient coinage with the gold joss papers and effigies from the Peace bridge crossing placed on top. To complete the configuration, the Generals of the Five Directions represented by their paper steeds were placed within the circle to prevent wandering spirits from grabbing the money once ignited. Flouting Confucian decorum in the performance of rites (li / 礼), and in contrast to his Singaporean peers, Di Ya Pek then addressed the Jade Emperor directly and cast divination blocks to ascertain if the offerings were acceptable. All attendees carried three incense sticks, and when a positive answer was received, Di Ya Pek instructed these to be placed inside the palace, the sending off ignited from the palace's interior.

The flames caught quickly, and within a minute the palace crumpled into the surrounding fire. As the flames leapt up, the 'tang-ki' joyously circled the growing inferno, military deities pointing their weapons towards the pyre, and others waving their flags in front of them either as benediction or to protect themselves from the growing heat. Once the palace had been reduced to embers, ritual over, the crowd promptly dispersed, and with the exception of Di Ya Pek, who was carried aloft by four bearers in his palanquin, devotees walked back to the stage opposite the temple to enjoy the remaining entertainments.

As the party continued outside, in the Heaven deity's altar room, Di Ya Pek relaxed in a throne beside the Jade Emperor's altar, casually smoking and drinking cognac, while 'tang-ki' channelling both Heaven and Underworld deities approached him to pay their parting respects. Some bowed low and others offered incense, and all drank to Di Ya Pek's prosperity 'as if' the Jade Emperor's statue was not present.

The significance of this ritual display of inversion in the Heaven–Underworld hierarchy becomes apparent in a comparative context. In Singapore, Underworld enforcers do not approach the highest-ranking Heaven deities directly, as they are considered to be of too low a rank. However, Singapore's *tang-ki* require the Jade Emperor's endorsement to channel deities, and this is given in one of two Jade Emperor temples. Therefore, *tang-ki* channelling Underworld deities do not enter these temples themselves, instead kneeling at the entrance to cast divination blocks, and their assistants entering the temple to acquire the Jade Emperor's stamp on their flags and certificates. Furthermore, great show is made by *tang-ki* of bowing to and obeying higher-ranked deities. In contrast, ritual displays disregarding Confucian decorum and ignoring deific rank have become increasingly common in Malaysia.

> On returning to the party, as Di Ya Pek and an entourage of visiting Ah Peks walked past me towards the main stage, an unfamiliar 'tang-ki' thrust a cold beer into my hand and invited me to follow.
> Di Ya Pek was once again in the mood for dancing, and, bathed in the stroboscopic diamond-white glare of stage lighting, he grabbed my arm, raised his own beer in a toast, and then danced me round and round with increasing rapidity until he collapsed laughing into a chair at the table reserved for wandering spirits, and then beckoned me to sit by him. The mini-skirted performer was singing a techno rendition of 'Gangnam Style' and pulling the heavy steel chain from around his neck, Di Ya Pek draped it over my shoulders advising that it was for added spiritual protection at this particular table. More Underworld deities from various courts joined us, and after many more drinks had been served, she sang 'Happy Birthday' Marilyn Munroe to J. F. Kennedy style for Di Ya Pek, and he jovially invited her to come down from the stage to dance with me. I politely declined suggesting that as it was his birthday, it would be more appropriate if they danced together, and with a whirl, to a chorus of 'Happy Birthday' and 'Huat Ah', they were off. The party ended some time later around 3 a.m., on an upbeat note. After a great deal of dancing and twirling on the part of the singers and assembled Tua Di Ya Pek, the female star of the show, now dressed in a red and black tinsel thong, matching brassiere and ankle-high boots, took the microphone and asked everyone to raise their glasses to toast Di Ya Pek. She then handed the microphone to Di Ya Pek who passed it directly to me, and after loud and animated "Heng Ah! Hong Ah! Huat Ah!", each word of which was echoed in turn with marvellous enthusiasm by the assembled crowd of deities and devotees alike, Di Ya Pek returned to his altar room, de-tranced, and Ah Boon, in his quiet and sober manner retired to bed.

Discussion

By the time of the 'Jade Record', Underworld cosmology had coalesced into an accessible and established vernacular form in congruence with Buddhist afterlife doctrines, the family cult of ancestral veneration and the principal teachings of Confucian ethics. Resonating with multiple socio-religious elements which together constituted the greater part of pre-modern Chinese thought, the Underworld's fundamental structure,

7.2 Tua Di Ya Pek dancing

as illustrated in Yinfu Tan's recreation has remained consistent into the present.

Goh (2009) proposed that transfiguration brought about by political, economic and cultural forces may radically reshape the "Materiality of everyday life and existential order that lies at the basis of Chinese religious beliefs and practices" (Goh, 2009: 113). The ethnography illustrates this in the recent transfiguration of behavioural norms, conveyed through the reconfiguration of pantheonic hierarchies largely expressed in new, intoxicant-based ritual practices, both factors conflicting with the Buddhist and Confucian morality which the 'Jade Record' inherently promotes. The transfiguration has been accompanied by hybridisations of Underworld cosmology, the first emphasising that one's post-mortal fate is based on blood rather than on moral transgressions, and the second reinventing the causal relationships between moral transgressions and post-mortal fate. While the first is specific to practitioners within Malaysia's Underworld tradition, the latter, in highlighting the contemporary issues of corruption, fraud and environmental damage, is broadly representative of shifting values throughout Malaysia's ethnic Chinese communities.

In contrast to Singapore, where Tua Di Ya Pek teach that everyone must visit the Underworld to suffer for their iniquities, more commonly in Malaysia, in addition to blood-line exclusivity, and matching the 'Jade Record', it is maintained that if one's merits equal one's demerits, punishments may be avoided. These opposing stances mirror social reality in the two locations. Singapore's multicultural society is constitutionally rooted in ethnic equality and meritocracy, corruption is minimal, and, for those caught committing a crime, sentences are notoriously harsh. In Malaysia the opposite is true, with the ethnic inequality enshrined in the constitution manifesting in the preferential treatment of *bumiputras*, and corruption perceived as rife in the social domain. Low-level corruption infiltrates everyday life and carrying two wallets is not uncommon, so that if one is stopped by the police for a minor offence the wallet containing less money can be produced to pay a discreet 'on the spot' fine. However, corruption permeates up to the highest levels of bureaucracy as is shown by the much-publicised case of Malaysian Prime Minister Najib Razak, chairman of the board of advisors to the 1Malaysia Development Berhad (1MDB). The 1MDB fund was established when Najib Razak took office and was intended to finance projects considered to be of national importance. However, this was not to be. The *Routledge Handbook of corruption in Asia* reports that "US$700 million found its way into the personal accounts of the Prime Minister [...] The Attorney General, who had been appointed after the Prime Minister dismissed his predecessor, found no wrong doing" (Scott & Gong 2016), and the *Guardian* headlined "More than $1bn deposited in Malaysian prime minister's account".[23] As societal catalysts trigger religious change, the resulting transfiguration seen in the inversions in the Heaven–Underworld hierarchy may therefore be analysed in ethnopolitical and socio-religious terms: ethnopolitical as reflecting an underlying aspiration for bureaucratic accountability, the realisation of which would involve an equalisation of power relations at a societal and therefore ethnic level; socio-religious as an indication of Underworld temples' and their *tang-ki*'s growing importance in the creation and maintenance of ethnic Chinese communities vis-à-vis older Heaven deity temples.

Moving on, outside of orthodox Buddhist circles, there is nothing untoward about the moderate consumption of alcohol as demonstrated by the offering of tea and alcohol to ancestors and deities on home and temple altars. Furthermore, as far back as practitioners can remember, most Tua Di Ya Pek *tang-ki* in Malaysia have consumed both alcohol and opium during trance possession, and in Singapore the ritual consumption of alcohol is now equally prevalent. I have previously speculated that the rapid popularisation of Singapore's Underworld tradition among younger generations may have been hastened by increasing limitations on personal freedoms. Developing this line of thought, temple-based alcohol consumption may be linked in part to social discontent, this specific indication of nonconformity being exacerbated by the Liquor Control (Supply and Consumption) Act of 2015 prohibiting the sale or consumption of alcohol in public places from 10.30 p.m. to 7 a.m.[24] While this Act coincided with and is therefore a probable catalyst of the recent popularisation of Singapore's Ah Pek parties, the increasing centrality of alcohol in the Singaporean tradition among younger temple members that are now, or who are preparing to become, *tang-ki* resembles Scott's everyday forms of resistance, in this instance against an officially sanctioned morality seen as constraining these individuals' social self-determination. In contrast, among the same ethnic and generational demographic in Malaysia, the consumption of alcohol in Underworld temples stands in opposition to Islamic sobriety, not as a form of resistance but, rather, marking difference as an unashamed ritualistic and communal statement of ethno-religious self-identity.

Another key difference between the two religious landscapes is the magnitude of and the effort invested in the preparation and managing of Malaysia's community-based events and, significantly, their all-inclusive nature. In

---

23 *Guardian*, 1 March 2016, www.theguardian.com/world/2016/mar/01/more-than-1bn-deposited-malaysian-prime-minister-account-najib-razak.

24 Licensed businesses may open later according to individual licences, but these are mostly prohibitively expensive. However, private temples are not public places.

comparison to Singapore's Ah Pek parties, which are *tang-ki* rather than community oriented and in a fledgling state of development, I would describe Yinfu Tan's event, with its buffets, live entertainment, redistribution of food and alcohol among the public and frequent community-wide human–deity social interactions, as an example of a fully matured tradition. Every adult who approached an Underworld *tang-ki* was offered a glass of cognac or whisky diluted with water, thereby instigating deity–human interactions in paying mutual respects to each other in a toast. Both cause and effect, this levelling of comparative rank illustrates Malaysia's changing human–deity relations: namely, a human demotion vis-à-vis previously unworshipped Underworld enforcers who are now highly sought after and deeply venerated, accompanied by an elevation in human status vis-à-vis Heaven deities who were previously socially detached from practitioners.

The transfiguration of religious antecedents illustrated by the inversions of authority in the Heaven–human–Underworld hierarchy, and in the mass consumption of intoxicants, are interrelated, as both have contributed to the production of what may be described as an 'intentional community' (Kamau, 2001). In light of the open use of narcotics and mass consumption of alcohol, the way in which inversions in the Underworld–Heaven hierarchy were expressed by Heaven deities' ritual participation in the Underworld recreation, and through their public deference to Di Ya Pek illustrates a relinquishment of both moral and actual authority from the Heaven to the Underworld pantheon. In addition, reflecting the comparative status of the ethnic Chinese in a majority Malay state, the renegotiation of authority was extended to Datuk Gong, who communicated on an equal footing with all Chinese deities. Both of these precedents are becoming the norm in central and southern Malaysia. The wider analytical significance of these inversions lies in their mirroring social reality, as in Singapore, where an ethnic Chinese majority strictly governs the state, Heaven deities have maintained their authority and Underworld deities hold a higher perceived rank than Datuk Gong and, in practice, when channelled through *tang-ki*, exert their dominance over them.

Returning then to the production of community, I would describe Yinfu Tan's as 'intentional' on two grounds. First, due to enlarging the community's *guanxi* network through ritual adoptions of godchildren; and second, after its creation had been prophesised by Di Ya Pek, its construction as 'a palace in which a community of devotees will gather' has gradually been brought to fruition under the temple's guidance. Kamau (2001) identifies intentional communities as those where "Relationships may ignore or cut across the distinctions of normal society, which are now irrelevant" (Kamau, 2001: 24), just as they do in *guanxi* networks. In the process, strong emotional bonds are created which Kamau equates with Turner's *communitas* (Kamau, 2001: 24). In an analysis of church communities, Bradshaw describes *communitas* as "A sacred bond that emerges as people gather to worship in communion with one another. They submit to unifying symbols, through the leadership of a ritual specialist, and transcend the structures that normally characterize human communities [...] Communities, however, do not transform themselves into *communitas*; instead, people experience it within the context of community" (Bradshaw, 2002: 220). At Yinfu Tan, the unifying symbols are the Underworld recreation and the deities channelled there, the primary religious specialists are Tua Di Ya Pek as channelled by Ah Boon and the structures transcended are power relationships in the conventional Heaven–human–Underworld hierarchy. During the three days of festivities, *communitas*, which was largely alcohol driven, was experienced *en masse* as Di Ya Pek toasted, joked and danced with his guests. The combination of all-inclusivity; alcohol as a catalyst to human–deity social and emotional bonding; the elevated status of Tua Di Ya Pek; and changing perceptions of morality among Malaysia's ethnic Chinese, catalysed by ongoing societal issues, have transformed the possibility of a socially diverse intentional community united through Underworld veneration into an actuality. The self-perpetuating mechanisms underpinning its continuation are Di Ya Pek's adoption of multiple godchildren, thereby facilitating the ongoing expansion of the temple's secular *guanxi* network.

In contrast, with Chinese constituting Singapore's ethnic majority, a majority not only living in a highly regulated religious landscape but lacking equivalent societal catalysts including social, economic and political marginalisation, it would be extremely improbable for any single Underworld temple to evolve as the focal point of a similarly large and analytically significant ethno-religious community. Meanwhile, the trend of Underworld temples serving as the foci of community formation is growing in Malaysia; a further example of an intentional community forming around the mass channelling of Underworld deities will be explored in context of Seventh Month rituals in Chapter 8.

8

Seventh Month rituals in southern Malaysia: salvation rituals and Ah Pek parties

Introduction

Chapter 7 focused on the influence of ethnic minority status on the creation of community in Malaysia's Underworld tradition, and the purpose of this chapter is to expand on this theory and to further illustrate significant differences between the Underworld traditions in Singapore and Malaysia. While offerings to ancestors and wandering spirits are integral to Seventh Month rituals in both locations, the ethnographic section of this chapter illustrates an Underworld Ghost Month calendar that is more *tang-ki* and community based and less cemetery centric than Singapore's. In Malaysia, the primary ritual activities serve to promote the Tua Di Ya Pek tradition and inter-temple cooperation, bringing together and expanding their associated lay communities while generating good fortune and karmic merits for the living. The activities highlight the ongoing invention of tradition and appropriation of authority from the orthodox traditions; transnational cultural flows from Thailand; the relative importance of City Gods and their temples; and, linked to this, the symbolic importance of and tangible emphasis on Fujian's Anxi Chenghuangmiao.

Researched in multiple locations, the ethnography is spread across two chapters, the narrative moving geographically from south Malaysia in this chapter, to central Malaysia in the next.[1]

Employing Weller's (1987) term 'unities and diversities', my argument is that the analytical process of isolating diversities without an accompanying

---

1 The rationale behind dividing the ethnography is based not only on geographical location, but due to this chapter's events being exclusive to the Lunar Seventh Month, while the rituals described in Chapter 9, while performed in Seventh Month, may also be performed by various temples at other times coinciding with auspicious dates and deities' birthdays.

historical sociology sheds little light on the interrelationship between the development of religious traditions and the broader socio-political landscape. Therefore, of key import is drawing correlations between societal catalysts in Malaysia and specific reactions to them manifested in the religious landscape as new diversities. Reformulating this statement as a question, I would ask, what can we learn of significant value from the diversities illustrated in the four Malaysia-based ethnographies? Therefore, while outlining the diversities, the societal catalysts that generated them will be analysed in a comparative context within each ethnography.

Starting with two events in Muar, the royal capital of Johor State, the first encompasses the final two days of Muar City God Temple's (Xinjiawang Chenghuangmiao) elaborate Seventh Month 'salvation rituals' (*pudu* and *chaodu*) for ancestors and wandering spirits on 15–16 August 2016. Their event incorporates the most common elements of Ghost Month ceremonies found at other temples and is therefore generally illustrative of Seventh Month events throughout Malaysia's Underworld tradition. The description of the temple's material and ritual culture is supplemented by information from interviews with the temple's founder / *tang-ki*, Mr Lin Yayuan. The second event is an annual Tua Di Ya Pek conference originating at Muar City God Temple in 2013, but now hosted by a different temple annually, 2015's conference being held at Dasheng City God Temple, Muar Dasheng Gong Chenghuang Dian. As Muar City God Temple was the first City God temple in Malaysia to be formally recognised by Anxi Chenghuangmiao and is ritually linked through the 'division of incense'[2] (*fenxiang* / 分香) from the 'parent temple' and replica statues, both events were attended by the cultural advisor and the former manager of Anxi Chenghuangmiao, Mr Chen Qixin and Mr Hu Jingze. The significance of their presence will be discussed further in Chapter 10.

Seventh Month at Muar City God Temple

Muar City God Temple is an exquisitely decorated, multi-storeyed temple where Buddhist and Taoist deities from the celestial and Underworld pantheons are venerated in well-defined areas in the ascending levels of the temple. As the blueprint of the temple's construction is loosely based on the multi-level design of Anxi Chenghuangmiao, I will first describe some key features of the temple's layout.

Approaching the temple from the front, behind a five-metre-tall copper

---

[2] A portion of incense containing the identity and efficacy of the original deity in lieu of a deity statue.

censer dedicated to the Jade Emperor three stone steps lead up to the temple's main entrance. The first room is divided into three sections of equal depth, the room's two layers being linked by a stone staircase whose fifteen steps span the width of the building, with six pillars supporting the roof. At the foot of the stairs, as if guarding the altar beyond, are life-sized statues of Tua Di Ya Pek. Their tongues are sticky with accumulated layers of opium, and the pedestals they stand on are littered with offerings of cans of Guinness, packets of cigarettes and several large ashtrays. Devotees commonly light cigarettes for the deities, either holding them up to the deities' mouths or leaving them alight in the ashtrays below for them to enjoy.

Ascending to the City God's altar, visitors pass two pillars engraved with gold calligraphy, one reading 'The first Chenghuang in Fujian to be bestowed with the emperor's robe and crown' (*'Chong xi pao guan Bamin di yi'*), and the other, 'There is only one Chenghuang to be awarded this honourable title in five counties' (*'Bao feng bojue wu yi wushuang'*). The honour refers to titles bestowed upon Anxi Chenghuangmiao's City God, allowing him to be dressed in robes decorated with imperial five-clawed dragons. As Giddens and Giddens note, "A dragon with five toes was the official symbol of the emperor of China [...] Anyone other than the emperor using the five-claw motif was put to death" (Giddens & Giddens, 2005: 48). According to Anxi Chenghuangmiao's representatives, during the Song dynasty, Anxi's Chenghuang was posthumously bestowed with a gold crown and jade seal and conferred with an earlship for his theophany which protected the residents of Quanzhou's five counties from disasters. He was later granted permission to wear the imperial dragon for having successfully cured a chronic disease of the Qing dynasty Empress Dowager Cixi. With these honours and title, he is thus the highest-ranked City God in Fujian Province. Being buried above Anxi Chenghuangmiao has therefore contributed to the elevated status of Xie Bian and Fan Wujiu, although cosmologically they are of equal rank to other Tua Di Ya Pek from other Underworld courts. This distinction is well known among practitioners, and both complements and reinforces a widely spread conviction that Xie Bian and Fan Wujiu are the Underworld's *original* Tua Di Ya Pek.

The altar itself is unconventional, resembling an earl's bedchamber, with the central doors incorporating a large circular window behind which Chenghuang sits in ceremonial robes, with statues of his wife and children in side chambers. A large copper censer is placed in front of the City God, and this contains the incense obtained from Anxi Chenghuangmiao in 1987, two years after the temple was first established. As such, the statue contains the same deific essence as Anxi's City God.

The highest level of the temple houses an altar for the replica statues of

Anxi's City God and his wife provided by the committee of the new Anxi Dongyue Si Chenghuangmiao,[3] their 'eyes opened' in Anxi Chenghuangmiao on 11 July 1999. The altar is presented as an open Chinese pavilion with an ornate roof and red silk curtains tied back to reveal the deities, and is flanked by further Tua Di Ya Pek statues. The altar room contains four pillars supporting the roof, two with green- and red-tiled dragons wrapped around them with their heads and upper torsos visible and their tails vanishing through the floor, and two with the dragons' tails coiling up towards the ceiling and their midriffs dissolving into the floor.

On either side of Chenghuang's altar a fenced yellow pathway leads to a viewing platform three floors above a multi-functional altar room containing three larger-than-life gold statues depicting the historical Buddha flanked by two radiant Guanyin. The tables before them are bedecked with flowers, and during Seventh Month multiple female Guanyin *tang-ki* bestow blessings on devotees as they kneel in prayer.

The final altar room is located on the temple's ground floor, where, enclosed with thick glass because this area is considered to hold the power or '*qi*' of the temple, the four dragon pillars descend from the ceiling. The dragon's tails wrap elegantly down two diagonally positioned pillars with their hind claws close to the ceiling, the other pillars supporting two magnificent dragon heads meeting jowl by jowl in the centre of the enclosed space. Behind them on the far wall is the temple's most sacred object, the Bodhisattva Dizangwang, not in statue form but as a natural object formed from natural clay with mineral inclusions and seemingly growing out of the floor. The image has a fascinating back story.

The original temple was founded in 1985 and dedicated to a local Chenghuang and to Tua Di Ya Pek. Mr Lin channelled Di Ya Pek there, who informed his devotees that he wanted Dizangwang to be worshipped alongside him and, still in a trance state, painted Dizangwang's image on a large piece of hardboard. This was rested against the temple's back wall, a censer placed in front, and Dizangwang became integrated into the temple's primary pantheon. Hidden from view behind the board a natural mound began to grow, and when the board was removed a year later it resembled a seated deity image which was then worshipped as Dizangwang. Over the years the mound continued to grow, both in size and in similarity to Dizangwang. When the resemblance became undeniable, Di Ya Pek informed his followers that the mound was no longer a representation of Dizangwang, but rather, his physical embodiment (*huashen* / 化身), and must be worshipped and treated as such. Once the new temple was completed in 2005, as Dizangwang

---

3 Detailed in Chapter 10.

was held to safeguard the temple's land spirits (*diling* / 地灵), his *huashen* was moved into his present-day position behind the four magnificently carved dragon pillars. Di Ya Pek then painted in vague details defining the deity's facial features, robe line and feet, and a red sash, garlands of flowers and a long necklace of wooden beads were hung around its neck.

There is no equivalent senior ranking Chinese deity worshipped in natural form in Singapore, neither is there likely to be. In contemporary Singapore, with very few exceptions, the most notable being at the grave of Datuk Syed Abdul Rahman on Kusu Island, even Datuk Gong are rarely venerated in non-anthropomorphic form. In contrast, while a minority of Datuk Gong are venerated in both anthropomorphic and natural form in Malaysia, most are worshipped by Malay and Chinese religionists in their original organic forms. The continuation of this custom lends legitimacy to the highly venerated figure now worshipped as Dizangwang's physical embodiment. In this instance, the absence of societal catalysts to change, specifically, Singapore's urban renewal and Sinification of Datuk Gong, has rendered the recognition and worship of Dizangwang in a semi-anthropomorphic natural form acceptable and, with Di Ya Pek's endorsement, legitimate.

> *I first saw this Bodhisattva channelled by the temple's 'tang-ki' on 15 August 2016. After entering a trance state, the 'tang-ki' was dressed in Dizangwang's flowing orange robes, red gown and crown, and entered the glass room where he performed a slow dance while holding two paper fans, one black, the other white, representing the opposing forces of 'yin' and 'yang'. Weaving between the dragons, each of them was touched with both fans, the performance culminating with his bringing the two fans together in a combining of energies thus filling the narrow gap between the two dragon's heads. The ritual is known as jiachi (加持), and its purpose is to add power and strength to the land spirits protecting the ground on which the temple is built. Dizangwang then picked up a large crystal ball, and much in the same manner as taijiquan (太极拳) masters manipulating their own invisible 'qi' energy, circulated the crystal between his hands as his arms effortlessly glided in gentle circular movements. Dressed in white with golden crowns, and each carrying a single lotus flower, the Guanyin 'tang-ki' entered and after reflecting the temple's own hierarchy by paying obeisance to Dizangwang,[4] danced facing him, their lithe bodies following the movement of the crystal ball which he manipulated. On many Underworld altars Dizangwang holds the highest rank, and due to his vow in the 'Sutra of the Fundamental*

---

[4] In Buddhism they hold equal ranks among the 'Eight Great Bodhisattvas'.

8.1 Dizangwang's 'huashen'

Vows of the Bodhisattva Kṣitigarbha' ('Dizang pusa benyuan jing') not to achieve Buddhahood until the halls of the Underworld are empty of human souls, is intimately connected with the Underworld tradition. After the dance was completed, Dizangwang returned to his dragon throne and his crown was removed. After paying respects to the temple's dragons he closed his eyes, and after a moment of silence the 'tang-ki' slapped his palms on the table before him as the deity left, and then collapsed unconscious into Dizangwang's throne.

Separated from the temple by a wide flagstone path, the ritual area for the Seventh Month *pudu* and *chaodu* salvation rituals ran parallel to the temple. These two terms are often used interchangeably, as most Seventh Month rituals involve both, though the prevalent perception among practitioners is that *pudu* refers to Taoist salvation rituals for *guhun* (孤魂) "orphaned or desolate souls" (Boltz, 2008: 794), while *chaodu* is performed for ancestors and has Buddhist origins. Incorporating both traditions, Muar City God Temple set up Buddhist and Taoist altars for the orthodox chanting of scriptures, though, as in Klang, the primary focus of the ritual events was on the temple's *tang-ki* channelling Di Ya Pek and Dizangwang and, on the final day, on Tua Di Ya Pek, with a visiting *tang-ki* channelling Tua Ya Pek.

The ritual space was divided into three sections, the largest being in the centre containing ancestral tablets and a palace for their residence, with a small section parallel to the temple's entrance for Da Shi Ye and boxes of joss money for the sending off, and the smallest tented area at the far end set aside for the temple's Underworld spirit armies. Between the temple and ritual site stood a wooden boat which would be sent off with the ancestral tablets, joss money and Da Shi Ye to mark the closure of the temple's festival. Many features of the festival match those at Yu Feng Nan Fu Xuanshan Miao described in Chapter 6, as they are ubiquitous to the Seventh Month tradition in both locations. Therefore, I will focus on the differences that are distinct to, and thus provide insights into, the Malaysian Underworld tradition.

First was the prominence of the Buddhist altar facing the tables of offerings. This area was approximately ten metres deep and closed in on three sides by golden silk drapes hanging down in waves from the centre of the roof and falling into pleats at floor level. The altar was similarly decorated in gold silk and fitted with loud speakers used in the early afternoon when Buddhist clerics came to chant. Only one deity was present, Dizangwang, depicted on a floor-to-ceiling length cloth scroll as sitting on a lotus throne floating in the ocean under azure blue skies. While Dizangwang is associated with Hell in both Underworld traditions, rendering this distinctive is the inclusion of a purely Buddhist altar and chanting at a City God-cum-Underworld temple's ritual event. The incorporation of the Buddhist clergy is common in Chinese temples throughout Malaysia. Therefore, while the importance of Dizangwang to this particular temple explains to some extent the orthodox Buddhist presence, it cannot account for the far wider trend across Malaysia.

I previously discussed the influence of the decennial census in Singapore as creating a predominantly Taoist self-identity among practitioners, especially so in *tang-ki* temples, that is to say, in the vast majority of Singapore's temples where Underworld deities are channelled. Also in Malaysia, the official categorisation of religion has influenced vernacular religionists' self-identification, but with Buddhism. In Malaysia's first two post-independence censuses, compiled pre-1980, the categories available included Islam, Hindu, Christian, Buddhist, no religion and others, with neither Taoism nor traditional Chinese beliefs officially recognised. In 1980 a new category of 'Confucian/Taoist and Tribal/Folk Religion' was added which, by implication, placed Confucianism, Taoism and the vernacular tradition on a par with religions practised among Malaysia's non-Islamic indigenous tribes. 'Confucianism/Taoism/Other Traditional Chinese Religion' was only recognised as an independent category after 1990. Buddhism had thus been firmly linked to a Chinese ethnic identity in Malaysia, much in the same way as traditional Chinese religious practices had been linked to Taoism in Singapore. This was reflected in the 2000 census data, with 19.2% of religionists self-identifying with Buddhism, as compared to 2.6% with 'Confucianism/Taoism/Other Traditional Chinese Religion'. To further complicate the issue, the categories were altered again in 2010, with 'Tribal' religions being reincorporated into the same category as non-Buddhist Chinese religions, and the percentage of adherents identifying with Taoism and Chinese traditional religion dropping significantly, to 1.3%. While these figures do not reflect the lived reality of practitioners, with most explaining that they are both Buddhist and Taoist, due to Buddhism's official endorsement, the inclusion of Buddhist chanting lends a similar legitimacy to temple events as the inclusion of orthodox Taoist rituals in Singapore's temple landscape.

Another significant difference between the Underworld traditions is the worship in Malaysia of minor land deities, Diji Gong, a deified variation of Diji Zhu, the spirit of the original owners or landlords of a tract of land.[5] Accounting for the difference, in Singapore, where most temples occupy land previously owned by the British authorities or by European entrepreneurs, the original landlords have neither been recognised as Diji Zhu nor deified as Diji Gong. In contrast, Ming dynasty Chinese settlers in Malaysia

---

[5] In both locations annual offerings are made at Chinese New Year to Diji Zhu by most households that follow the vernacular tradition.

often resided on or purchased unoccupied land which has commonly been passed down through the generations or sold to other Chinese residents. It is the worship of these deceased landowners, deified as Diji Gong, that is distinct to the Malaysian vernacular tradition. Illustrating Diji Gong's local standing, at Muar's event a line of paper shops were placed adjacent to families' ancestral tablets and offerings were placed there for generic Diji Gong representing all past owners of the land. These included landlords of hardware, electrical, computer, cell phone, furniture, clothing, fruit, grocery and shoe stores, pharmacies and supermarkets. The temple owner explained that their presence serves two purposes. First, when land changed hands in the past there may have been unresolved disputes or unfair purchases that led to bad karma being accumulated around the property, especially so where land disputes lasted beyond the landowner's death and were inherited by their descendants. As all of the past landowners were represented, making offerings to the Diji Gong reduced animosity between them, thereby restoring karmic balance to the contemporary world. Second, when the present owners of businesses make offerings, it informs the associated Diji Gong of who is now using the land, and in return for offerings they bestow blessings on current owners' businesses.

Moving on, the most striking divergence in the material culture, and one pointing towards the influence of Thai vernacular religion on Malaysia's Underworld tradition, was located in the tented area with its back to the primary ritual space. Constructed from black canvas and illuminated with green fluorescent lighting, the tent was fully enclosed to house the temple's Underworld spirit army. Inside were ten round tables, each surrounded by plastic chairs on which a wedge of joss money and a talisman drawn in black ink had been placed. The table settings were basic: a single bowl of rice with black chop-sticks and an empty bowl and glass accompanied by four cooked dishes and a plentiful supply of opened Guinness bottles. Standing out among these, the central table is of key interest. Placed on thick piles of joss money which served to raise the height of five chairs by about thirty centimetres sat half-metre tall, ultra-realistic plastic dolls portraying young Caucasian children with fixed expressions and lifeless, baby-blue eyes. Raised so as to see the offerings in front of them, two were female, the first dressed in a pink T-shirt with a line drawing of a zebra and bright pink leggings, her long, matted pony tails tied with pink ribbons. The second wore white plastic trainers, a navy-blue skirt and lilac blouse with a matching lace hat. Both were dirty, as if they had been dragged along the floor or through muddy puddles, as were the three male dolls beside them. One of these had straight blond hair and the other two wavy brown hair, all three sporting baseball caps and 'onesies', one displaying Mickey Mouse, another a cute yellow cat and the last announcing

'A Good Day' in blue lettering on a while background. The contrast between their childlike innocence and unkempt appearances added to their sinister demeanour. They were contemporary Thai *luk thep* (child-spirit) dolls, their dirty hands and faces suggesting that they had been previously discarded and then recycled for their current purpose: to accommodate the spirits of malicious foetus ghosts enlisted into the temple's spirit army.

Modern-day *luk thep* dolls are based on an earlier tradition of *kuman thong* first mentioned in the Thai epic '*Khun Chang Khun Phaen*' (Baker and Pusuk, 2010), "Where the necromantic power of the roasted foetus – the *kuman thong* – enhances Khun Phaen's own power" (Johnson, 2016: 446). Traditionally, the spirits were obtained "Through a grisly ritual involving grilling human foetuses and entombing them in a clay jar" (Ancuta, 2014: 213), others being baked and covered in gold leaf for temple-based worship. In the twenty-first century the tradition has evolved in Thailand, the visually gruesome foetuses being replaced with lifelike and lovable Caucasian dolls. "The modern way tends to be to hide both the contents and the concept of Kuman Thong behind the representation of a cute child to make it more palatable to the general populace [...] Many devotees have reported that they still work in the same way though, it is merely masking their true nature for the sake of the taste of the bearer" (Jenx, 2016: 63). *TIME* magazine recently reported: "The phenomenon of Thailand's *luk thep* dolls reached viral status in January 2016, when Thai Smile Airways started to allow passengers to purchase seats and meals for their realistic dolls. *Luk thep*, which translates to *child angel* [...] have become an intriguing part of Thai culture to the outside world".[6]

Their appropriation into Underworld temple culture is a reinvention both of the traditional exegesis of vulnerable foetus spirits commonly assisted in their post-mortal journeys in Singapore, and of the related 1980s reinvention of foetus spirits in Taiwan as vindictive foetus ghosts (*ying ling*) who must be placated to prevent them bringing misfortune to their would-be parents. The inclusion of *luk thep* dolls combining the *kuman thong*'s powerful, malicious and enraged foetus ghosts into a temple's private Underworld spirit army as vindictive foetus ghosts therefore represents a major deviation from the norms of Chinese vernacular religion both within and external to the Underworld tradition. The commonality between the Thai vernacular and Chinese Malaysian Underworld traditions is that, in both, foetus ghosts' power is manipulated to achieve their new masters' ends. Societal catalysts pertaining to their incorporation include Malaysia's sizeable Thai population and its proximity to Thailand.

6 *TIME* magazine, http://time.com/4353544/thailand-luk-thep-doll/.

Outside of Seventh Month, the temple's dolls are stored in a child's coffin in an alcove beneath the altar to the Underworld generals. On the 29th of the sixth lunar month the coffin is brought out and opened and, while those present offer incense, Di Ya Pek invites the foetus ghosts and Underworld soldiers to partake in the feast and offerings which will begin at 11 p.m. on the following day, Seventh Month Eve, when the Gates of the Underworld are opened. On the final day of the festival, Tua Di Ya Pek inspected every part of the ritual area, burning green talismans to further protect the ritual space and paying respects to deities as appropriate. In stark contrast both cosmologically and visually to Dizangwang's golden altar at the far end of their ritual space, the *luk thep* dolls housing the foetus ghosts also commanded singularly tender consideration from the *tang-ki*.

On entering their tent, which also contained ritual objects including an altar, censers and casino chips, cards and *mah-jong* (麻將) gaming tables for the soldiers' entertainment, both *tang-ki* paid unrivalled attention to the dolls, patting their heads affectionately and revisiting their table several times to confirm that the foetus ghosts they contained were happy with their substitute bodies and the sugary offerings provided (Plate 9). After the festival, a similar ritual to that of the 29th was performed on the final day of Ghost Month, with Di Ya Pek instructing and overseeing the foetus ghosts and soldiers' return to the Underworld, after which the coffin was closed and replaced in the alcove beneath the Underworld general's altar.

The conclusion of the combined salvation rituals was performed by the two *tang-ki* in the absence of orthodox clerics, who had performed their rituals earlier in the day. Having offered incense to the temple's deities and those at the temporary Seventh Month altars, Tua Di Ya Pek entered the canopied area containing the tables of ancestral offerings. Together, followed by those whose families were represented, they walked along every row, Di Ya Pek blessing the offerings with his plaque and Tua Ya Pek with his fan. They then sat side by side behind an empty yellow table placed beside the ancestral Palace with their pipes, Di Ya Pek supping Guinness and Tua Ya Pek sipping from a bottle of Martell Cordon Bleu. Their devotees then collected their ancestral tablets and formed into groups according to the Chinese zodiac sign of the eldest patrilineal family member present. Each family then approached Tua Di Ya Pek, who blessed the ancestral tablets presented to them and then the devotees themselves. Prior to the popularisation of the Underworld tradition, and elsewhere in the present-day Chinese diaspora, the notion of having one's ancestors blessed by Hell deities would be inconceivable.

Before moving on to describe the Tua Di Ya Pek 'conference', as the conference began at Muar City God Temple as a new tradition in 2013, I will first discuss its origins and the ritual significance of Chenghuang's robes to the perpetuation of the tradition. The initial idea came from Di Ya Pek, who wanted to expand Chenghuang culture and the temple's ritual network, the temple's *tang-ki* describing the conference as 'inviting Tua Di Ya Pek to a party'. Having hosted the conference for three years, Di Ya Pek decided it was time to pass the metaphoric baton on to other temples. The actual baton passed is a set of robes and head-dress belonging to their Chenghuang replica statue, thus symbolically legitimising future conferences with the authority and titles of Anxi Chenghuangmiao's City God. At the time of my visit their own City God was dressed in a replica set of clothing, the original clothes being still with Dasheng City God Temple, as the two temples were waiting for an auspicious day after Seventh Month for them to be exchanged. Their own City God replica from Anxi came naked, which is in itself unusual, as most replicas come dressed in the same clothes as their 'parent' deity. Curiously, their replica's clothes were commissioned by a Jigong temple in Singapore, manufactured in China from a photograph of Anxi's City God, and brought back to Singapore to be auctioned at their annual anniversary banquet. That a Malaysian temple should outbid Singaporean rivals reflects the reality of Malaysia's City God temples playing a progressively more active role in their Underworld tradition than their Singaporean counterparts, an increase which corelates with Anxi Chenghuangmiao's expanding field of influence in Malaysia.

Dasheng City God Temple: Tua Di Ya Pek conference, 7 August 2016

Held annually on the first weekend of Seventh Month, the Tua Di Ya Pek conference, formally titled 'Anxi City God's cultural exchange' ('*Qingxi Chenghuang Xianyou Bozhu wenhua zhi ye*') and promoted by the host temple as 'Ten Courts Tua Di Ya Pek cultural exchange' ('*Shi Dian Da Er Ye Bo*[7] *wenhua jiaoliu hui*'), brings together one pair of Tua Di Ya Pek from each Underworld court. Surpassing Yin Fu Tan in terms of the number of Underworld deities simultaneously channelled, it is the most formal and meticulously organised Ah Pek party in the Underworld tradition. The *tang-ki* present hailed from a total of fifteen participating temples, thirteen from small townships in Johor State and one from each of Selangor State and Kuala Lumpur. The sixteenth temple, Anxi Chenghuangmiao, was represented not by its *tang-ki* but by two of its executives, whose presence lent further legitimacy to the event.

Once again illustrating the role of Underworld temples in community

---

7 Da Er Ye Bo is the Mandarin pronunciation of Tua Di Ya Pek.

formation, Dasheng City God Temple's own community congregated to welcome visiting temples, to provide entertainment and to cook and refill the buffet dinner provided for all. In the late afternoon the fourteen visiting *tang-ki* temples arrived in convoys of one to three buses carrying assistants, paraphernalia and followers from their own temple communities. The total number of participants numbered around one thousand. The commonalities binding this temporary and intentional community together were ethnicity and Tua Di Ya Pek veneration. As ritual reciprocity between *tang-ki* is the norm, members of the thirteen temple communities from Johor State were already familiar with one another and may be seen as a distinct extended ethno-religious community in its own right.

As each temple arrived, participants offered incense communally at five censers: outside the temple's entrance to the Jade Emperor, in the temple's front altar room dedicated to an eclectic ensemble of Heaven deities, before the Underworld altar and, finally, at external altars to local Diji Gong and Datuk Gong. According to the temple's owner, when the Underworld temple had first relocated from a rubber plantation to is present location in 1990, local residents were unaccustomed to Hell deity worship, so the Heaven altar room had been added. However, by 1999 the Underworld deities had become the most frequently consulted through their *tang-ki*, and the most often worshipped, petitioned and consulted with divination blocks in their statue form.

The two colours most often associated with the Underworld are black and green as seen replicated in the material culture by talisman drawn in black ink on green paper slips, Tua Di Ya Pek's black abacuses, the green bamboo leaves decorating Tua Ya Pek's robes and so forth. The walls of the Underworld altar room were therefore painted green, and the room contained a five-levelled altar with a black leather-topped table placed in front, on which many opium-laced cigarettes were drying on trays for the Tua Di Ya Pek's use.

The space to the left of the altar served to house the temple's Tua Di Ya Pek's wardrobe. Several sets of black and white robes hanging from crucifix-shaped stands, and an assortment of black, white and gold hats complete with tangled black hair stood upright above the robes on racks attached to the wall. The room was bathed in green fluorescent light, the darkest point being the altar itself, where the whites of the largest deity statues' eyes on its highest level, including Dongyue Dadi, Chenghuang, Bao Gong and Tua Di Ya Pek, shone with green incandesce, reflecting the ambient light. On the second level, smaller statues of Tua Di Ya Pek took central place, with Zhong Kui the 'Ghost Catcher' to their right and the Underworld God of Filial Piety Hao Zhu Ya to their left. On the middle layer were three further pairs

8.2 Tua Di Ya Pek's wardrobe

of Tua Di Ya Pek accompanied by Ox Head and Horse Face. Beneath them was a deep granite shelf for the imposing Underworld censer, with seven small cups containing alcohol, offerings of bottled Guinness and cigarettes, and Tua Di Ya Pek's flags supported in wedges of Hell banknotes (Plate 10). In an alcove beneath the shelf were statues of five Underworld generals and five ghosts that serve the temple's Tua Di Ya Pek. Once incense had been offered to all the temple's deities, each *tang-ki*'s assistants then went to set up individual altars on square yellow tables where Tua Di Ya Pek would be channelled after dark.

A fourth ritual area surrounded by a white picket fence was sectioned off for the host temple's Underworld Generals of the Five Directions, each represented by a flag and plaque standing upright in a red earthen censer and sheltered by a waxed paper umbrella. These were strategically placed on the floor in a semi-circle, effectively separating the edge of the temple's grounds from the road and neighbouring buildings. In front of each censer were offerings of tea, wine, rice and joss money, and each umbrella was reinforced with Tua Ya Pek's efficacy manifested through his talisman. Facing the flag of the Underworld General of the Central Camp was a sixth censer with offerings of tea and alcohol, behind which remained the charred ashes of Hell banknotes burned on Ghost Month Eve.

When the Gates of the Underworld open, there is no definitive answer as to where the spirits emerge into the human realm, though there is a widespread consensus that the locations include graveyards and the space below Underworld altars guarded by Tua Di Ya Pek and their Underworld minions. The final item added to the General's configuration was Di Ya Pek's spirit-catching chain, in this instance laid on the ground between the joss money and central censer in the shape of a door. On Seventh Month Eve, Di Ya Pek performed an 'eye opening' ritual to 'open the eyes' of the door, rendering it spiritually active, the configuration therefore functioning as a heavily guarded portal between the temple and the Underworld. The spirits of those who had been born, resided or passed away in the locality were invited to re-enter the neighbourhood through it after the Gates of the Underworld had been opened. The positioning of the five flags intentionally formed a restrictive barrier to direct the wandering and ancestral spirits towards the temple and to the plentiful offerings that had been provided for them.

Soon after darkness had fallen, over a period of about five minutes, the twenty 'tang-ki', stripped to the waist in front of their own altar tables entered trance states. After each of the Underworld enforcers arrived, they were dressed in their robes, several of the Di Ya Pek having their faces painted black, and were then handed long wooden pipes with opium cigarettes wedged into the bowls, along with their first drinks. Their attention was variously turned to consulting their abacuses, smoking their pipes, writing talismans, and blessing devotees with their fans or with exhaled opium smoke carrying their efficacy.

The entire community then gathered, and everyone was handed three incense sticks to pay respects to a tablet representing Anxi's City God which culminated in bowing three times, the entire community moving in unison. Then, to the accompaniment of 'the flag song' ('Da qi ge'), a joyous composition composed in 1966 by Zeng Zhongying for the film 'The Snake Beauty' ('She meiren') and performed by a local youth orchestra on traditional Chinese instruments, the twenty Tua Di Ya Pek mingled with the assembled crowd of visitors, many of whom carried babies or young children that the Underworld enforcers affectionately cooed over or jested with and then blessed.

The actual conference area was covered in red and white tarpaulin, with a long strip of red carpet starting at each end of the 'tang-ki's temporary altars and leading into the luxuriously furnished ritual space. An hour after dark the Underworld deities lined up in front of the conference area, each holding a fistful of incense sticks and bowing three times in front of the City God's censer before entering bare footed along the red carpet. Tua Ya Pek walked in with tongues lolling, and Di Ya Pek with their ghost-catching chains dragging beside them. Each deity was flanked by helpers holding brightly coloured hanging banners proclaiming the name of the temple they came from, with each pair of Tua Di Ya Pek and the Underworld courts in which they served being ceremoniously announced over the loud-speaker system in resemblance of a royal parade. At the threshold, their incense sticks were taken and placed in the City God's censer, after which the deities struck martial postures and variously flourished their fans or demon-expelling plaques before entering.

Ten executive desks covered in red velvet, one for each Underworld Court, were set up in a 'U' formation around a central table and the City God's censer. The central table contained place settings for visiting deities, and at its centre the character 'shou' (壽), meaning 'longevity', was formed from uncooked rice, the empty spaces between the lines filled with purple-wrapped chocolates with the effect of making the Chinese character stand out. At the table's far end, closest to Anxi City God's temporary altar, paper depictions of the Gods of Prosperity, Status, and Longevity, their 'eyes opened', faced towards the entrance, and behind them stood a tablet representing all deities protecting the ritual space.

After the twenty 'tang-ki' had entered, Chenghuang's robes from Muar City God Temple, enclosed in a gilt-framed, glass-fronted box, were taken from the temple's Underworld altar room, placed on a wooden tray with offerings of wine and tea, and ceremoniously carried to the rhythmic accompaniment of drums and gongs into the conference area. A second tray containing a copy of Anxi City God's ornamental jade seal (yu yin / 玉印) topped with an intricately carved lion's head followed behind. The ten pairs of Tua Di Ya Pek had by this time settled at their desks (Plate 11) but stood up as a sign of respect and watched appreciatively as both items invested with the authority of Anxi's City God were carried past them. The robes were then placed in the centre of the top level of the City God's altar and the jade seal was placed one level below.

Formalities over, Tua Di Ya Pek were served with three small plates of delicacies to accompany their Guinness and chatted among themselves and with their assistants serving them tea, opium and cognac. It was intriguing to watch the burly tattooed 'tang-ki' nodding in jovial approval while eating the morsels, handling them deftly with thin wooden chop-sticks, their delicacy contrasting with their forceful demeanour and previous martial postures. Several of the 'tang-ki' unaccustomed to eating while in trance states chose instead to absorb the spiritual essence of the food, 'tasting' the food by putting their noses close to it and inhaling deeply.

The casual atmosphere that prevailed allowed me to chat with each of the Tua Di Ya Pek individually, and beyond pleasantries, my questions revolved around two primary topics: the purpose and ethics of opium smoking, and, the nature of the Underworld that they hailed from. As there was general agreement on both subjects, the following discussion with one pair of Tua Di Ya Pek is broadly representative of the views and interpretations advocated.

I had been invited to join a pair of Tua Di Ya Pek and sat facing them across their desk. Tua Ya Pek had furnished me with a tall can of Guinness, his mouth remaining open when not talking, his tongue protruding lazily over his bottom lip, and his white robes parted at the collars revealing as small section of a magnificent tattoo of a dragon emerging between swirling clouds. His hat was unusually large, perhaps two-thirds of a metre tall with black ribbed edges holding the four sides together as it curved back from its base which was decorated in gold and inset with semi-precious stones. Constructed from tanned hide with the words 'one glimpse, great felicity' running from top down in broad black characters, it complimented this Tua Ya Pek's larger-than-life *personality.* By his side sat a short, stocky, serious-faced Di Ya Pek absolutely absorbed in smoking his pipe which was forearm length and held nimbly in what resembled a pugilist's fist. The thick covering of opium on the cigarette bubbled furiously as the tobacco burned down, and by applying spittle and adjusting his inhalations he made it burn evenly. His plates of delicacies remained untouched on the table, and his free hand rested against the corner of a metal-framed black abacus. Tua Ya Pek fed his last remaining delicacy to an assistant who knelt down as Tua Ya Pek placed it in his mouth with chop-sticks before returning his attention to me. A pipe was passed to him and dutifully lit, and after inhaling deeply, he held it out across the table to me. Recognising this as a test of character rather than an invitation, I paid my respects to them both by raising my Guinness can once to each and drinking to their good health. Having never touched or consumed opium myself, I began by asking them whether, as Hell deities, opium affected them differently to the way in which it would a living person.

"Differently," Di Ya Pek answered in a clear voice tinged with enthusiasm. "Opium is my power, alcohol is my energy. My power and energy combine together, and the insights in my mind's eye become much clearer, and this increases my power to help others and cure them. It doesn't make me sleepy or drained as it would do to people."

Tua Ya Pek was nodding in sagely agreement as he continued to smoke, and added, "The more opium I smoke, the more awake I become."

"That's right," continued Di Ya Pek. "And the more awake we become, the more easily we can float between dimensions to find answers to people's problems. That is why I say that opium is my power, as it stimulates my abilities, and alcohol my energy as it gives me my strength. Let's drink first, then we can discuss more."

Not being fond of warm Guinness, I asked if there was an alternative, orders were given, and a few moments later, Tua Ya Pek's assistant handed me a chilled bottle of a local beer.

After some friendly banter concerning my poor taste in alcohol and suggestions of Guinness being the drink of the gods, I suggested, "At Heaven temples, most visitors are older people," and opening my arms to bring attention to the crowd gathered for the conference continued, "but Tua Di Ya Pek gatherings always attract younger generations, more so than the elderly. Do you think that opium, alcohol and tobacco act like magnets, inducing the younger generations to visit or become devotees at Underworld temples?"

"Yes, that is why so many young people come – they like to drink with us," Tua Ya Pek replied. "Many youngsters, after drinking with us in the temple, say they would rather come to the temple and drink than go to clubs and discos. Isn't it better to drink in a temple than in a club with gangsters and all other kinds of temptations?"

"Of course," I replied, "but isn't there an irony in preaching morality and post-mortal retribution for sins while drinking and smoking opium? I mean, if your followers smoke opium and regularly consume copious amounts of alcohol, won't they be severely punished in the Underworld after death?"

Di Ya Pek turned to me, only the whites of his eyes visible beneath half-closed eyelids, "They understand," he said, "that when I return to the Underworld, I will take all the opium and alcohol with me because it is I, Di Ya Pek, who is smoking opium and drinking, and not the human 'tang-ki'."

I considered the chain of crimes perpetrated to make their opium consumption possible, and the demand–supply causality, and rephrased my question accordingly. "Even so," I suggested, "someone must break the law to grow the opium, others to harvest it, gangsters to smuggle it, and dealers to sell it. There are thousands of Tua Di Ya Pek in Malaysia consuming opium, creating a demand that motivates others to break the law for profit. Applying the laws of cause and effect – karmic retribution – won't you and they be punished for this?"

I had expected the question to produce a debate, or at least some deliberation, but instead received an immediate answer from both.

"We are already dead," they concurred, "so we can't be punished again!"

"Yes," I replied, "but what about all the living involved in getting the opium to you?"

Tua Ya Pek leaned so far over the desk that all I could see were the whites of his eyes, and in a quiet voice replied, "I will tell you a secret. Tua Di Ya Pek are not involved in all of this. Temples grow their own opium on small plots of land, and each temple only harvests enough for their own deity's needs. There is no money involved, and no sin, as our devotees are serving us by following our orders."[8]

As Tua Ya Pek relaxed back into his chair, I asked both deities what would happen to me in the Underworld if I smoked opium. Di Ya Pek consulted his abacus while Tua Ya Pek cooled himself with his rattan fan. Shaking his head very slowly and lifting his shoulders in puzzlement, Di Ya Pek replied that each religion had an individual Hell, and

---

8 While generally true, this is not the case for all temples.

> that he could only see into his own. I had heard from various informants that some Chinese had converted to Christianity to avoid post-mortal punishments, but reluctant to ask questions about a religion that Di Ya Pek was self-admittedly unable to answer, instead asked about the post-mortal fate of the irreligious.
>
> "Tell me then, which Underworld or Hell do people with no religion, or, freethinkers who reject religious beliefs but follow their own spiritual path go to after death?"
>
> As Di Ya Pek answered and Tua Ya Pek nodded in agreement, my curiosity regarding Chinese Christians from the perspective of Malaysian Tua Di Ya Pek was satisfied.
>
> "It depends on your blood – Caucasian, Indian, Chinese and so on, they all go to their own Underworld. It is not religion dependent."

The conversation provided new insights into opium use, and a reconfirmation of inconsistencies between the two Underworld traditions in connection with the ethnic make-up of the Chinese Underworld mentioned in Chapters 4 and 7. In discussions with other Tua Di Ya Pek at the conference, and later with numerous *tang-ki* in Kuala Lumpur and Penang, these interpretations were closely replicated. While in Singapore Tua Di Ya Pek's Underworld is perceived as an inevitability and, as such, is ethnically all-inclusive, in Malaysia admission is dependent on a patrilineal Chinese ancestry. This variance in post-mortal cosmology is analytically significant, as Tua Di Ya Pek in both locations were conceptually describing the same Underworld.

> *Returning to the conference, most of the delicacies had been consumed, and large Cuban cigars had been handed out. Some Tua Di Ya Pek were clearly enjoying the new indulgence, others wrinkling their noses and returning to their opium cigarettes in long bamboo pipes. Meanwhile, much to visitors' delight, entertainments continued outside of the ritual square while the Underworld deities continued their business, individual deities paying respects to others at their desks. Soon after, ceremonies over, the Tua Di Ya Pek and their assistants lined up for group photographs with members of the host temple,[9] and then returned to their individual altar tables where the 'tang-ki' de-tranced.*

---

9 In response to questions, *tang-ki* noted that while material objects have changed over time, their essential functions remain consistent and are therefore recognisable. For instance, buses substituting for horse-drawn carriages, electric lights for lanterns, drawings for photographs and so forth.

Conclusions

These two Seventh Month events have shed light on important differences between the Underworld traditions in the two locations. The list is extensive and includes the underlying Buddhist influence in Malaysia; the appropriation of elements from Thai vernacular religion leading to new ritual practices based around combining *kuman thong* and *luk thep* cosmology, and the subsequent invention of a distinctly Chinese Malaysian variation of malicious foetus ghosts; the worship of Diji Gong and their inclusion in salvation rituals to benefit local communities; the continuation and comparative non-Sinification of the animistic Datuk Gong tradition and their *tang-ki*'s affiliation with Underworld temples; the prominence of and the rationalisation behind Underworld *tang-ki*'s opium consumption; Underworld temples, in these specific instances City God temples, providing a central focus around which ethnic Chinese communities have evolved; and the comparative importance attributed to Anxi Chenghuangmiao in southern and central Malaysia's Underworld tradition.

Societal factors that have triggered these changes have been suggested from the influence of Malaysia's census categorisations in promoting Buddhism; population demographics and proximity accounting for transnational cultural flows from Thailand; the influence of immigration patterns and past land ownership on Diji Gong veneration; and Anxi Chenghuangmiao's active expansion of its ritual network through sponsoring events promoting its own City God's tradition. Crucially, and influencing the entire temple landscape, is the socio-political marginalisation of non-Malays, thereby providing a powerful catalyst to temple-based community formation as a means of self-perpetuating a Chinese ethnocultural identity. Given that Underworld temples now provide the primary locus of ethno-religious community formation, of key analytical interest is the degree of influence that legislation and affirmative action through the NEP and NDP has had in the production of a bloodline cosmology rendering Malaysian perceptions of the Underworld as an exclusively Chinese domain.

I will therefore utilise the dichotomy in post-mortal interpretations as a starting point to analyse broader societal developments which may have triggered this divergence in cosmology.

Looking first at political catalysts to the multi-ethnic character of Singapore's post-mortal cosmology, the following analogy unfolds. The state's sensitivity to and emphasis on "Multiracialism (and multilingualism, multiculturalism, and multireligiosity)" (Kong & Yeoh, 2003: 4) in formulating ethnic integration policies has led to the allocation of HDB housing and admission to educational institutions being proportional to the numeric population of each ethnic group on a national level. The Singaporean interpretation of post-mortal cosmology ostensibly evokes the same principles of equality, thus mirroring contemporary socio-political realities.

Applying the same analogy to Malaysia, the ancestral bloodline cosmology reflects the post-independence restrictions placed on and exclusion of ethnic Chinese in multiple arenas of the socio-political domain. Following independence, while the Singaporean agenda was fuelled by the intention of promoting a primary Singaporean national identity from its ethnic and cultural diversity, Malaysia's Independence Constitution stipulated the ideological demotion of Chinese ethnicity, whereby "The Constitution defines a Malay as a Muslim, a Malay speaker, and a follower of Malay custom" (Freedman, 2001: 417).

The NEP of 1971 which followed was calculated to redistribute the wealth and political influence of the ethnic Chinese minority by placing significant restrictions on non-Malays in the fields of higher education, public sector employment and shareholder ownership in Malaysian companies. Language too became a political weapon under the NEP, and the mandatory use of the Malay language in secondary and university education, combined with preferential admissions for Malays, further isolated ethnic Chinese from the mainstream polity (Carstens, 2005). While in Singapore "A system of multilingual education that is a part of a broader government strategy of multiculturalism and multiracialism, which [...] served the purpose of building a new national identity" (Hill & Lian, 1995: i) was in place, across the border, due to new linguistic regulations, the degrees of those who had graduated from private Chinese secondary schools were no longer recognised in Malaysia, and, finances allowing, students were forced to continue their studies abroad. Similarly, "Malaysian Chinese graduates of Malaysian public high schools, encountering the pro-Malaysian admission policies of Malaysian universities, likewise left the country in increasing numbers" (Carstens, 2005: 160).

Consistent with the theory of self-perpetuating mechanisms evolving as reactions to social adversity, the state-sanctioned prejudice provided the societal catalysts required to stimulate heightened cohesion among Malaysia's ethnic Chinese population. Having been marginalised on ethno-religious and linguistic grounds, temples adorned with Chinese calligraphy and religious iconography provided the ideal locus for fostering an ethnic Chinese self-identity through community formation. Moreover, Underworld temples offered an additional means of ethno-religious opposition, with their *tang-ki* sharing copious amounts of alcohol with practitioners in the midst of a Muslim-majority state. Therefore, utilising the same analogy of local cosmology mirroring political realities, I propose that ethnic exclusion largely accounts for the ethnic exclusivity promoted in Malaysia's Underworld tradition.

In the following chapter the ethnography will move north, to central Malaysia, and further demonstrate the reinvention of Thai rituals and their subsequent appropriation into Malaysia's Underworld tradition. Beginning with luck-promoting 'coffin rituals' in Brickfields City God Temple in Kuala Lumpur and describing the rituals from the perspectives of both observer and participant, the narrative will then return to Yin Fu Tan's Underworld recreation and the releasing of exorcised spirits on Tua Ya Pek's birthday. The chapter will conclude with in-depth discussions that followed their release, in which Di Ya Pek describes the relative nature of post-mortal time and provides an alternative 'historical' interpretation of the Chinese Underworld's creation and transformation.

9

Seventh Month rituals in central Malaysia: coffin rituals and the releasing of exorcised spirits

Coffin rituals at Brickfields Chenghuangmiao, Kuala Lumpur, 30–31 August 2017

Located at the far end of an unassuming alley, the temple complex is hidden from sight behind other low-rise buildings. Entering through two industrial, iron-barred gates, only after turning into a narrow, unroofed corridor separating their Datuk Gong altars, Jade Emperor's censer and altar tablet for wandering spirits from the main temple does the compound's layout of ritual areas become apparent. The main altar room is divided into four sections, with two altars at the front dedicated to Heaven deities, that on the left to Guanyin and Guan Gong in his Buddhist incarnation as Qielan Pusa, the protector of the Buddhist teachings, and that on the right to deities from the vernacular and Taoist pantheons including Jigong, Tudi Gong and Taoist Marshals. Facing the *tang-ki*'s desks in the centre is the temple's main tri-level floor-to-ceiling Underworld altar. The most senior deity, Dizangwang, is placed at the centre of the highest level, bathed in red light beneath a lotus flower painted on the domed ceiling, and flanked by Dongyue Dadi and Yanluo Wang. A solitary life-sized statue of their City God occupies the middle level, three metres above the floor-level altar spread out below. This houses the lower-ranking deities, who are distributed across the width of the temple, with Da Shi Ye in an elevated central position flanked by Tua Di Ya Pek, Sa Ya Pek (Third Brother) and the Underworld God of Filial Piety Hao Zhu Ya. Five Underworld ghosts are placed in front of them, alongside plentiful offerings of Guinness for all. The two rear corners are dedicated to Ox Head and Horse Face and contain multiple images of each. The temple's central space contains five large desks for the *tang-ki*, each accompanied by a child's coffin on which the *tang-ki* sit to channel Underworld deities and to give public consultations. A total of fifteen *tang-ki* channel Underworld deities at this temple, the most frequently tranced being Tua Ya Pek from the Fourth, Fifth, Sixth and Seventh courts, Di Ya Pek from the Seventh and Eighth courts, Hao Zhu Ya and Da Shi Ye.

Exiting the main temple, at the far end of the corridor and adjoined to the temple's outer wall is a covered area containing altars for twelve Taisui and a local Datuk Gong. In front of these is the external ritual space, the floor tiled and containing two full-sized coffins placed on portable mortuary tables so that they can be easily rolled into place for rituals. Facing the coffins across the corridor is the stone tablet to wandering spirits, with a matching stone censer beside which, and furthest from the iron gates, is a round, brick, open-topped incinerator for paper offerings. Beyond the ritual space, a large quadrangle opens up with cooking and washroom facilities for the temple's community.

The following narrative is reproduced from recordings and notes taken on the ninth night and in the early hours of the tenth day of Ghost Month 2017. While this temple's coffin rituals are not exclusive to the Seventh Month, they are considered to be most efficacious if performed during this period. The rituals were performed by Tua Ya Pek from the Fifth, Sixth and Seventh courts, rendered distinguishable by their green, white and cream-coloured attire, and, dressed in black, a Seventh Court Di Ya Pek.

Around midnight, led by the Sixth Court's Tua Ya Pek, the four Hell deities left the temple with their flags draped over their shoulders and walked in single file along the narrow corridor separating the temple from the wasteland beyond, and eagerly approached the coffins to inspect them. The larger coffin was then rolled into the centre of the ritual space which was bathed in darkness, and a stone censer was placed at its foot opposite the wandering spirits' altar. A thick joss stick was then added, and a red candle lit either side provided the main illumination for the coffin rituals, diffused light only filtering into the edges of the ritual space from the courtyard beyond. The coffin's lid was covered in a black cloth decorated with a single embroidered character running its length, 'shou' (寿), meaning longevity. The Fifth Court Tua Ya Pek dropped a four-metre length of heavy iron chain on the ground at the foot of the coffin, and, taking hold of one end, laid it in a straight line extending from the coffin towards the wandering spirits' altar. Passing about fifty centimetres to the left of the censer, the chain's far end reached the edge of the tiled floor which demarcated the ritual area's border. Di Ya Pek laid a second chain parallel to the first, the gap between them perhaps a metre across and representing the Blood River which separates the

Underworld from the world of the living. Metal steps were then placed each side at the foot of the raised coffin by Tua Di Ya Pek's assistants forming a bridge allowing the Blood River to be symbolically crossed.

Di Ya Pek then approached the coffin and flinging strips of 'path money'[1] ('lu qian' / 路钱) in the air for wandering spirits, with the authority invested in and efficacy manifested through his flag began blessing the coffin. Using the flag's staff, he drew four 'qi' talismans, the first at the foot of the coffin facing the wandering spirits' altar, then moving clockwise on its other three sides. Then, ascending the steps to the right of the coffin he climbed on top and crouching added a fifth talisman to the coffin's lid. The other three deities looked on casually while smoking opium cigarettes wedged into their long pipes, and then each in turn performed the same ritual benediction of the coffin and surrounding ritual space.

Once this process had been completed, assistants were beckoned to remove the coffin's lid so that the inside could be empowered and blessed. The coffin's interior was luxuriously cushioned, with layers of compacted joss money accumulated from previous rituals lining its base and two faded green talismans drawn in black ink standing out against its cream lining. The four 'tang-ki' circled the open coffin several times throwing more slips of path money over it as they hit the coffin's exterior with their flags. Their attention was then turned to the coffin's interior where each 'tang-ki' wrote a 'qi' talisman with their flag, after which, a single green talisman was freshly drawn, set alight, and used to write a final talisman in fire as it burned over the head of the coffin, its spent ash being allowed to fall silently inside. Meanwhile, those who would be undertaking the coffin ritual had been given a wedge of silver joss money (xiaoyin / 小银) to hold,[2] and were separated by gender into two lines to the right of the coffin, each individual looking on in various states of interest or trepidation.

There was a momentary stillness as the first person was called to approach the right side of the coffin. He bowed slightly, as a sign of respect to the Underworld deities, and turned to face the coffin, standing straight backed as Di Ya Pek placed his flag on his head and then brushed it downwards on all sides of the man's body as a form of 'qi' cleansing, and then wrote a talisman with the tip of his rolled-up flag a few centimetres from the participant's back. At the Sixth Court's Tua

---

1 Representing low-value coins in the spirit realms.
2 Gold joss money is offered to Heaven deities, and Hell banknotes for the recently deceased and the Underworld minions.

Ya Pek's invitation, clutching the wedge of joss money in his right hand, he then ascended the three metal steps next to the coffin and carefully climbed inside, standing momentarily before lying down and disappearing from view to all except those standing immediately beside the coffin. The heavy coffin lid was then carried over, and the man sealed inside. The Sixth Court Tua Ya Pek then circled the coffin once again hitting its sides with his flag, and then ascending from the right side, he strode around on top of the sturdy lid, crouching to wave his flag before writing three 'qi' talismans over the occupant's head, torso and feet before descending to run his flag over the coffin's exterior, and striking the top and sides of the coffin again with his flag staff. Each of the three remaining Hell deities then ascended the stairs in turn and repeated the same ritual form. When this had been completed to their satisfaction, the lid was removed, and the Fifth Court Tua Ya Pek placed his flag over the man's face and lifting a corner gently blew opium smoke under it. Then, after sliding his flag across the man's face towards himself, Tua Ya Pek tapped the far end of the coffin indicating that the ritual was over. The man then removed the joss money from his chest, sat up and clambered out, descending the stairs to the coffin's left where he was told not to cross back to the other side of the coffin or pass the chains until all the rituals had been completed. Two Tua Ya Pek then pulled in the chains, in effect moving their far ends around twenty centimetres closer to the coffin, thus decreasing their length and forming two small bundles of chain at the coffin's foot. The next person was then called, and soon I was standing at the front of the queue.

Before proceeding, I was asked to remove all objects from my pockets before presenting myself barefoot before Di Ya Pek. Even though his flag did not touch me, I was aware of a tingling sensation as he wrote a talisman behind my back, and then the Sixth Court Tua Ya Pek led me to the steps ascending to the coffin. Singularly focused on my every sensation, it felt as if time were slowing as I ascended and then stepped carefully into the coffin. The layer of joss papers in its base felt silken to the touch, and, lowering myself down I noted that some were aged by time. The well-padded space was horizontally cramped, so I stretched my body, but no matter how I manoeuvred, I could feel the pressure of all four sides of the coffin's lined interior pushing against me. Lying down, the view from and sensations felt inside coffin were very different from my prior observations and my own expectations. Looking up, the darkness was more acute, and while three of the Ah Pek peered down into the coffin, the distinct odour of opium followed their every movement. I had placed the wedge of joss paper over my 'dantian'

(丹田)[3] *and the seventh court Tua Ya Pek pointed to it with his flag, and then at a higher spot on my chest, and as my elbows were tightly wedged between the coffin's sides, twisting my wrists I carefully slid the money towards the spot indicated with my fingertips. The Fifth Court Tua Ya Pek then counted out four pieces of joss paper, four being synonymous with death,[4] and placing them over my eyes, in a gentle voice intoned "Sleep". I heard a grating noise as the coffin lid was slid into place, and a dull thud as it dropped, sealing me off from external stimuli. Enclosed in the constricted space in complete darkness, unable to see and afraid to move unless it caused either set of joss papers to move, my other senses instantaneously heightened. I was acutely aware that the air inside the coffin had rapidly become stagnant, foetid with the odours of stale incense and opium smoke, and dry sweat emanating from the decaying joss papers and every other surface of this living grave. The coffin's walls and lining blocked outside chatter from the temple, though in the few moments of silence available, sleep eluded me. I then recognised the tapping on the coffin's sides as the muted sound of Ah Pek's flag striking it, then a brief claustrophobic silence was followed by the unmistakable tread of feet above me as Ah Pek wandered back and forth on the coffin's lid (Plate 12). I had crossed an imagined boundary when passing over the chain and stepping into the coffin, the Blood River, the steps flanking the coffin representing the Naihe Bridge, and in doing so, had figuratively crossed from the world of the living into the Underworld, and was, at least symbolically, dead. The footsteps on the coffin instigated a cold sweat, and metaphorically deceased, I reflexively interpreted the sound as someone literally walking across and then stamping on my grave. While this process was repeated by the other 'tang-ki', I formed a firm conviction that after death, I did not wish to be buried. My reverie was disturbed by the repeated tolling of the temple's bell, and then by the soft draught of temple air as the coffin's lid was lifted. The straight edges of the joss papers covering my eyes were in an instant replaced by the soft blanketed texture of Tua Ya Pek's flag brushing against my face, the musty air by the heady aroma of opium, and the silence with his murmured blessing barely audible over the hubbub of noise in and around the ritual space. The flag was then withdrawn disappearing over the head of the coffin and clutching the wedge of joss paper in one hand, I sat up to reorient myself before*

---

3 Located approximately three finger widths below the navel, this is considered to be the generating and collection point of one's '*qi*'.
4 Based on homonyms, 'four' and 'death' are both pronounced '*si*', the former in a sharp falling tone, and the latter in a dropping and rising tone.

emblematically re-crossing the Blood River back into the land of the living. After Di Ya Pek's name had been stamped in black ink on my shirt just beneath the neckline, the coffin ritual was over, only the burning of the joss money I had held as an offering to the Underworld deities remaining to do. The two chains were once again shortened by bringing the ends closer to the coffin, an action repeated after each person's coffin ritual, meaning that after the last person exited the coffin, the chains had been fully retracted into two piles, and access to the Blood River and therefore to the Underworld removed.

After the night's coffin rituals had been completed, the black cloth was replaced on the coffin's lid, and the four Tua Di Ya Pek circled it in a clockwise direction striking it with their flags before writing 'qi' talismans on the foot of the coffin. Then, after snuffing out the two red candles by the censer, they flung handfuls of path money into the air which were left strewn over the ritual space for wandering spirits present. All participants then lit three incense sticks and following Tua Di Ya Pek's cue, dropped to their knees to pay respects to wandering spirits who, given that it was Seventh Month, were there in abundance. As the incense smouldered, the three Tua Ya Pek stood up and showered us with joss money and while it was still falling, Di Ya Pek, with his back to the tablet bestowed blessings on each of us. As a final benediction, channelling Underworld efficacy through their flags, the three Tua Ya Pek rested them on each participant's head as with mixed emotions we knelt there in silence to receive their blessings.

Our last ritual act was individually igniting the joss money which had been carried into the coffin, thus transferring it to the discarnate realms for the four Tua Di Ya Pek's later use. Meanwhile, the four were paying respects at the Jade Emperor's censer, and alerted of their departure by the scraping of chains dragged along the concrete floor, I followed them into their altar room.

Perched on his coffin-throne, the gold-robed Tua Ya Pek from the Seventh Court puffed nonchalantly on an opium cigarette while an assistant opened a fresh can of Guinness and handed it to him. Toying with the can and blurring the accustomed boundaries between the observer and the observed, he examined me with a probing gaze, his facial expression fluctuating between curiosity and fascination. While the stub of the opium cigarette was removed from his pipe with tweezers and another inserted, he beckoned me to drink with him. Pushing a freshly opened Guinness towards me, in a high-pitched voice hard to reconcile with his wide frame, regal green cloak and masculine demeanour, he asked if I would prefer to share his pipe. Expressing my preference for beer, and now in an informal consultation with him, I was keen to elicit Tua Ya Pek's perceptions of the coffin ritual.

"What is the power that improves one's luck? Does it arise from Tua Di Ya Pek's blessings, or from Heaven deities that govern one's fate?" I asked.

"It is the power from the Underworld."

"With whose authority?" I enquired, to which he replied idiomatically "Heaven's secrets cannot be revealed" (Tianji buke xielou / 天机不可泄漏), a common response to questions thought to be inappropriate. I therefore moved on to discuss Tua Ya Pek's insights into the coffin ritual itself. I had assumed that the coffin's symbolism was literal, the figurative death and revitalisation of one's ego 'sans' previously attached negative karma, so pursued this line of enquiry.

"Why," I asked, "use a coffin for a luck-promoting ritual?"

"Coffin in Chinese is 'guancai' (棺材), and we associate the sounds with 'shengguan facia' (升官发财), 'shengguan' meaning 'to be raised up', you know, 'to get promotion' and 'facia', 'to become wealthy'." Tua Ya Pek paused to consult his abacus. Then turning to face me, neck craned slightly back, he gently exhaled a warm cloud of opium smoke which glided overhead, a perfumed aroma remaining in its wake, and continued, punctuating each remark with a slight nod or tangential glance which I reciprocated to signal comprehension. "The process is like dying and reincarnating. First you step into the coffin and stand upright, but while lying down you enter a transformative state, and once the joss paper has been placed over your chest and eyes, it is presumed that you are already dead. Like a reincarnation, when you again stand tall to leave the coffin, you feel different, as negative influences have already been removed from your path."

"I didn't feel noticeably dead while I was lying inside the coffin," I retorted, immediately realising the paradoxical nature of my reply.

Tua Ya Pek's solemn expression broke into a broad knowing smile. "Of course not, a thick wedge of silver money was placed on your chest!" I looked at him quizzically, my gaze following his hand as it moved slowly towards me and settled gently over my solar plexus. "Here," he continued, retracting his arm, "is where your soul enters before birth, and where it will leave from when you die, that is why it was protected. You have entered the Underworld realm of the dead but were unaware as your life soul (ling hun) remained in your body."[5]

---

5 This is the temple's own interpretation. In orthodox Taoism, the soul of the 'spiritually uncultivated' will leave through the *huiyin xue* (会阴穴), a point between the reproductive

The next day I returned to interview the temple's owner, Zhang Songba, to ascertain the history of the temple and of the coffin rituals performed there. He founded the temple in 1995 and Tua Di Ya Pek have been channelled there since 1996, Mr Zhang noting that at that time there were very few *tang-ki* in Kuala Lumpur trancing Underworld deities. Proud that his was one of the first temples where they could do so, he lamented that, even now, Underworld deities are more prevalent in Penang than in Kuala Lumpur. This, he suggested, is because Penang's City God temple is the eldest in Malaysia, even though their Chenghuang is not from Anxi. "Ours is from Anxi," he explained, and, reminiscing, remarked in rising tones of incredulity, "There were many temples in China before Mao, then none, then more again, but *now* they charge an *entrance fee*!"

The luck-promoting coffin rituals are a recent addition to the temple's repertoire, Mr Zhang offering two interconnected explanations for their presence. He first saw a coffin ritual being performed in 2010 by Buddhist monks in Bangkok, in which nine ornamental coffins were used, and soon discovered that Theravada coffin rituals were not uncommon in Thailand. Justin McDaniel (2014) describes these as 'born again' Buddhist rituals which, while lacking the intoxicant-fuelled night-time intensity of Chinese Underworld rituals, have similarities in symbolism and purpose. In terms of difference, the coffins used in Thai rituals are decorated with multiple images of the Buddha, they have no lid and the rituals are performed in the daytime "to rid participants of bad karma and help reconcile them to the inevitability of death".[6] Illustrating their popularity, at Wat Ta Kien in the Bangkok suburb of Nonthaburi, coffin rituals are held as many as twelve times a day for groups of up to twenty people, with a larger coffin on offer to fit an entire family. The following description of Wat Ta Kien's rituals is similar to McDaniel's, and to those in multiple online sources: "After reciting prayers, participants line up in front of their casket. Once the order is given by a microphone-wielding monk, each person lies down in his or her coffin. Bright pink sheets are draped over the coffin and then removed to symbolise death and rebirth in a ritual that lasts barely a minute."[7] McDaniel adds that Ekachai Uekrongtham's popular 2008 film *The Coffin*, in conjunction with stories of individuals winning the Thai lottery soon after participating, have

---

system and anus, and for those who have cultivated themselves the soul will exit from the *bai hui xue* (百会穴), located on the crown of the head. These two acupuncture points are regarded as important gateways of life and longevity representing, the extreme ends of the *ren mai* (任脉) and *du mai* (督脉) meridians.

6 Mail Online, 18 January 2016. Cited on 2 February 2017, www.dailymail.co.uk/wires/afp/article-3404479/Devotees-cleansed-bad-luck-Thai-resurrection-temple.html.
7 Ibid.

made Thai coffin rituals increasingly popular. After returning to Malaysia, Mr Zhang discussed coffin rituals with his *tang-ki*, leading to the following chain of events.

In 2013, during their annual Seventh Month parade, a high-ranking police officer complained to Di Ya Pek that even though he had been coming to the temple for many years the winning lottery numbers offered to him had never been correct. Di Ya Pek replied that he would win a hefty prize the next day, which he did, promptly returning to the temple to make a donation. In the consultation that followed Di Ya Pek suggested that, rather than a financial donation, what he really wanted was a small coffin to replace his throne in the altar room, a secure coffin which he could also use to trap exorcised spirits which had brought bad luck to his devotees. After it was purchased and seen by other visitors, further coffins were donated to the temple's various Tua Di Ya Pek in place of customary food, alcohol and cash offerings. After a coffin had been provided for each *tang-ki*'s desk, when a devotee offered to donate another small coffin Tua Ya Pek said that it would be better if he could provide a full-sized coffin which could be used for luck-promoting rituals, and a large coffin was thus donated in 2013. However, it was too small to fit either the tall or the obese. A year later, the coffin's donor, Mr Zhang and the owner of a funeral parlour discussed this issue, the latter offering to provide an extra-large coffin at wholesale price for the rituals. In 2015 the police officer again entered the narrative as, in a consultation with Di Ya Pek, he asked for the deity's assistance in securing a promotion. Di Ya Pek agreed to help on the condition that, once promoted, he must organise the purchase of the larger coffin. The promotion soon came and, within two weeks, he had arranged for twenty devotees to contribute, his 50,000-ringgit donation being the largest. Thus, in late 2015, the coffin used for the contemporary rituals was purchased for the temple.

While analysing salvation rituals in Chapter 8, I attributed the all-round greater presence of Buddhist elements in Malaysia's Underworld tradition to the formulation of religious categories in the decennial census, a societal catalyst generating a primarily Buddhist sense of religious self-identity among Malaysia's ethnic Chinese. This, however, relates to Chinese Mahayana Buddhism, common expressions of this being found throughout Malaysia's Underworld tradition, from Dizangwang taking precedence over the City God on Brickfields Chenghuangmiao's main altar to the common inclusion of Buddhist chanting at major temple events throughout Malaysia. While the Mahayana emphasis in Malaysia and the orthodox Taoist in Singapore may be accounted for in the context of emic self-identity resulting in the inclusion of orthodox rituals performed at temple events, at the time of writing the Thai vernacular and Theravada Buddhist influences were unique to Malaysia.

Illustrated at Muar by the inclusion of *luk thep* dolls, and at Brickfields Chenghuangmiao where the coffin rituals themselves were inspired by Theravada Buddhist practices, the transnational flow of Thai religious culture into Malaysia's Underworld tradition has, in comparison to Singapore, increased the options available in the metaphoric knowledge buffet from which Chinese vernacular religion draws. There are several underlying factors which have facilitated these cultural flows and expedited their subsequent appropriation, albeit with reinvented cosmologies, into Malaysia's Underworld tradition – prerequisites which are absent from Singapore's contemporary ethnopolitical environment.

As previously noted, a primary goal of the PAP has been to promote a unified Singaporean identity integrating all ethnicities and religions, a nation-building process exemplified by the ethnicity-based allocation of HDB housing on a pro-rata basis. Exacerbated by land shortage, integration policies have precluded the possibility of Thai immigration, and employment laws regarding Thai migrant workers requires them to return home once their work permits have expired (Kitiarsa, 2014). The Thai population in Singapore is therefore negligible, while, in addition to Thais living in Malaysia without Malaysian citizenship, there are approximately 70,000 Malaysian nationals self-identifying as Thai, with some 20% of Thais laying claim to a Chinese ancestry (Rappa & An, 2006). Ethnicity is therefore a factor contributing to overlaps between Thai and Chinese vernacular religious practices in Malaysia. Malaysia's geographical proximity to Thailand has further facilitated comparatively free transnational cultural flows, while Singapore's limited border crossings and highly regulated religious landscape, which is monitored by the state, has prevented similar cultural flows into Singapore.

The acquisition of Brickfields Chenghuangmiao's coffins and their ritual use suggests a further, thought-provoking opposition rooted in contrasting societal factors between the two locations. While perhaps expectedly, due to their association with death and the afterlife, coffins have made their way into both Singapore and Malaysia's Underworld traditions, they have done so in differing material forms, and with contrasting ritual usage.

In Singapore, due to the ongoing mass exhumation of graves, there has been a plentiful supply of used coffin-wood, and this has been reprocessed for the manufacture of the miniature coffins frequently found on Underworld altars (Plate 13). Due to the *yin* properties of used coffin-wood, their primary uses are as temporary resting places in the human realm for Underworld deities and as prisons to accommodate exorcised spirits and wandering spirits forcibly enlisted by individual Tua Di Ya Pek into their own temples' spirit armies.

Meanwhile, in Malaysia, where Chinese cemeteries remain unthreatened by development and the dead therefore remain interred, these objects remain a rarity. Instead, new, full-sized coffins serve multiple ritual purposes. As in Brickfields City God Temple, an increasing number of Underworld temples in central and northern Malaysia have replaced their thrones decorated with effigies of Ox Head and Horse Face – objects which are still prevalent in Singapore – with coffins. These act not only as substitutes for thrones, but may be used for luck-promoting, luck-changing or exorcistic rituals. In Penang, full-sized coffins are used by several temples offering astral journeys to the Underworld, and in others they play an integral role in healing rituals. Essentially, with Muar's *luk thep* dolls being an exception, Singapore's recycled and scaled-down coffins are generally intended for the use of or to manipulate the souls of the dead, while in Malaysia, new coffins are primarily used by *tang-ki* to increase the good fortune of the living.

The releasing of Yin Fu Tan's exorcised spirits

I returned to Yin Fu Tan for Tua Ya Pek's birthday, which falls annually in the Lunar Seventh Month, to observe the releasing of spirits exorcised by Di Ya Pek over the previous three years. As the party itself contained similar elements to Di Ya Pek's, the ethnography will focus on discussions with Tua Ya Pek and Di Ya Pek and on the releasing of the exorcised spirits. Our discussions began while I was examining the tortures portrayed in their Underworld recreation when Tua Ya Pek entered to order the removal of exorcised spirits from storage. The conversation continued in greater depth over drinks and dinner with Di Ya Pek after their 'sending off'. The topics discussed began with Tua Ya Pek's ethical perceptions of imprisoning spirits and, after Di Ya Pek arrived, turned to Tua Di Ya Pek's Underworld duties; relative time; the construction of deities; and the age and creation of the Chinese Underworld.

> *I was examining the prison cell located diagonally across from the Gates of Hell where soon after the sun had set, Tua Ya Pek beckoned me to join him. The prison cell's entrance consisted of a slatted and rusting iron gate sealed with a heavy padlock and chain and was inhabited by female Caucasian mannequins shrouded in crimson-tinted semi-darkness, and variously chained to walls and chairs, or standing with their hands and feet in shackles. All were dressed in white sheets, this being the colour associated with funerals. One mannequin's hands were reaching out between the bars as if pleading for help, a wig of wavy brown hair partially revealing blank prefabricated eyes facing the corridor 'as if*

expressing the resignation of a soul driven to a catatonic state by the hopelessness of ever attaining reincarnation. Carelessly painted onto the white cloth in black ink over its breast was a single Chinese character, 'ren' (人), literally meaning 'people', but which in situ would more poignantly be interpreted as 'human'.

Tua Ya Pek unlocked the gate, and as it stood ajar, asked me if I would like to spend a night inside. I declined but stepped in briefly followed by two of his assistants who carefully picked up a crate of empty Guinness bottles nestled in the far corner, and then laid it down in the corridor. There were twenty-three bottles in total, each plugged with a crumpled sheet of joss paper filling the bottle's neck and sealed on top with Di Ya Pek's green talisman. I returned to the corridor, and relocking the gate, Tua Ya Pek asked me to guess the contents of the bottles.

"Spirits," I ventured, and putting his arm around me with a grin, Tua Ya Pek announced that Di Ya Pek was going to set them free later that night. I queried the wisdom of this, suggesting that sending them to the Underworld for reincarnation might be a better idea to which he jokingly replied, "Setting them free will give us more business as we can recapture them again in the future." Registering my surprise, he explained that these souls could not reincarnate as they had died too suddenly to enter the Underworld, and that even if they had descendants to perform the correct rituals for them, they must stay in the human realm. I questioned the logic of releasing spirits who could neither enter the Underworld, nor reincarnate, and who, I suggested, would most likely cause further angst. Answering question with question, he asked me if it would be reasonable to keep them trapped inside the bottles for ever. Indicating that I acknowledged the complexity of this problematic, Tua Ya Pek explained that the spirits would be released as an act of altruism, and that having been imprisoned once, it was for the spirits to decide on their own future behaviour. After directing the initial construction of the ritual space, at 11 p.m., Tua Ya Pek retired to the temple as his birthday had ended, and he wished to return to his duties in the Underworld. As one Ah Pek departed, the other, Di Ya Pek took his place to oversee their release.

Approaching midnight, the crate of bottles was carried through the village to the same piece of waste ground where the Jade Emperor's palace had been 'sent off', and where a mound of joss papers approximately four metres in diameter had been laid out with a space in the centre for the bottles. The plan was that as the pyre burned, the seals would be incinerated, thus allowing the spirits to escape. The bottles

9.1 The prison cell

were removed from the crate and stood upright in a closely packed square, and several sacks of pre-folded joss papers in the shape of ancient coinage were emptied over them for their use. As the mound increased in height, various ritual precautions were taken. The flags of the Underworld Generals of the Five Directions were firmly hammered into place marking the boundaries of the ritual space, that of the central camp placed strategically on a mound at some distance to take overall command of the combined Underworld forces. Several metres from the pyre, red candles separated by incense sticks were pressed into the ground in the shape of a 'U' thus surrounding the pyre on three sides. Di Ya Pek ran his flag over these before they were lit, transforming them through the transference of his efficacy into a 'qi' barrier impenetrable to wandering spirits, but which the living could cross at will. Twenty-three bowls of rice, each topped with two eggs and with a lit incense stick in the centre were placed round the edges of the pyre so that the spirits would not leave the area hungry. A chair was set at the open end of the formation for Di Ya Pek who would dutifully patrol the opening to prevent wandering spirits gathered nearby from grabbing the joss money as it burned and to supervise the exorcised spirits as they left.

The fire was lit from all sides, Di Ya Pek walking casually around it as the flames took hold, flinging path money in and around the fire, and advising onlookers to take photos, but not to view them until after midnight as this would give the released spirits time to manifest more clearly in the photos. The fire raged for perhaps ten minutes, after which, the bottles becoming visible, it became apparent that the heat had not ignited the joss paper in all the bottles' stems as some had been too tightly packed. An assistant was then instructed to push the joss money into the bottles with a thick joss stick, thus allowing the spirits to finally escape. This done, two further sacks of joss money were added on top, and once again the flames soared high into the air. When the fire died down, Di Ya Pek inspected the bottles to confirm that the spirits had all been released, and the gathering moved into his Underworld chamber where the party and discussions continued.

A long table had been set up with the customary alcohol, plates of cooked meats, and other delicacies brought from Tua Ya Pek's table of birthday offerings on the second floor. Di Ya Pek sat in the centre, the head of the temple's committee to his left, and Ah Pek invited me to sit to his right. Our glasses were filled with cognac and water, and now relaxed in his own altar room, resting his pipe on his left hand, Di Ya Pek put his arm around me and calling for silence gave me a 'name-in-religion' by which I would be known at his temple "I name

9.2 Di Ya Pek patrolling the area

you 'Lao You'" ('Old Friend') and after proposing a toast said, "Let's chat". It was time to clarify my Understandings of Underworld cosmology, at least from this particular Di Ya Pek's perspective, a Di Ya Pek of the Fourth Court brought from Anxi, and therefore, the soul of the original Fan Wujiu.

"Last week I visited a Tua Di Ya Pek conference in Muar," I began, "and there were ten pairs of Tua Di Ya Pek, one from each Underworld court. As you know, I have spoken with several hundred Ah Pek in Singapore and Malaysia, some with their own family names and some without. I would like to know how many Tua Di Ya Pek there are in the Underworld."

"The real Tua Di Ya Pek, that is the 'hun' of Xie Bian and Fan Wujiu, there can only be one. But in the Underworld, their 'hun' can be divided multiple times, allowing them to exist in numerous places and deal with various duties simultaneously, including those among the living through their 'tang-ki'." Our glasses were recharged, toasts made, and again refilled, and Di Ya Pek continued. "We have many statues in temples across Malaysia and Singapore, and therefore, we help people by possessing our 'tang-ki' in all these temples. When called by other Ah Pek, Xie Bian and Fan Wujiu may also enter their 'tang-ki', and using our authority and efficacy, help solve devotees' problems in their temples."

"I understand that Xie Bian and Fan Wujiu have many names and titles and serve in the Fourth Court of the Underworld under King Wuguan. Who are the other Ah Pek?" I enquired.

"Each Underworld court has a pair of Ah Pek, who, like me, were once human, and each perform different duties. They are all known as Tua Di Ya Pek, but Xie Bian and Fan Wujiu are the original pair."

Curious about the distinction between the material realms and the discarnate retaining physiological attributes and behaviours in a post-mortal state I continued. "So, after death, as with Fan Wujiu, it is an individual's spirit that goes to the Underworld, not their body. So how do spirits communicate in the absence of a body?"

"Spirits can communicate with each other in the Underworld, and with Underworld deities as they are all composed of the same spirit substance."

"Yes, but in the scriptures, and in this recreation of the Underworld, punishments are inflicted on the human body. If it is the 'spirit substance' that survives in the Underworld, how can an Underworld demon gouge out a spirit's eyes or remove its tongue, or, in the 'Hell of Sword Trees', a body become impaled on the blades and have its flesh shredded?"

"The mechanism of change is beyond my understanding," replied Di Ya Pek, "but I can assure you that the pain the spirits feel is as real and equal to that which their bodies would feel when alive."

"That is a terrifying prospect," I replied, and satirically affirming the obvious added with a smile, "and here we are drinking to your good health!" and after pausing to do just that, I queried Di Ya Pek's role in the infliction of punishments.

"The Fourth Court's tortures include being crushed, buried alive, and force-fed quicklime, not to mention the 'Blood Pond Hell'. Do you wake up every morning and visit each sub-hell just to ensure that the Underworld demons are not shirking their responsibilities?" Pausing momentarily to reformulate a more specific question, I continued: "What are your actual duties and your daily routine in the Underworld?"

The party was by now in full swing, with around fifty people gathered in the altar room to eat, drink and pay their respects, and I would have to wait a while for an answer. When our discussion continued some minutes later, Di Ya Pek brought attention to my incorrect a priori assumption that Underworld deities sleep, and, based on material temporality, the inappropriate interposition of 'daily routines' in the Underworld. My unintentional errors, and not the implications of my question, did, however, elicit an unexpected and thought-provoking response.

"My daily routine," joked Di Ya Pek, restating 'daily routine' several times while shaking his head in a jocular fashion. Then returning to seriousness to respond to my first question, he replied: "My main duty is to capture troublesome, lost or escaped spirits and deliver them to the Underworld. There are thousands of jails to lock up these souls ..." and spreading his arms and gazing around to signpost his meaning completed his sentence "under this world!" Then, devoid of humour, he repeated "My daily routine," and pausing momentarily to lend emphasis to the import of his answer, explained, "When it is 5 a.m. in the Underworld, it is 5 p.m. here, but only once a year, as one year on Earth equals one day in the Underworld."

Somewhat perplexed by the exactness and conviction of his analogy, while Di Ya Pek was occupied welcoming new guests, I made some calculations, noting that if a year in the Underworld equalled 365 years on Earth, that an hour on Earth equalled roughly 9.7 seconds in the Underworld.[8] This meant that if Ah Boon channelled Di Ya Pek for six

---

8 One day equals twenty-four hours, so one year equals 8,760 hours. With twenty-four hours in a day, 8,760 divided by twenty-four equals 0.0027 hours. As one hour equals sixty minutes, 0.0027 multiplied by sixty equals 0.162 minutes, which is 9.72 seconds.

hours, less than a minute would have passed in the Underworld, and, as Di Ya Pek possessed Ah Boon at the same time every week, less than half an hour would have passed in the Underworld between each visit.[9]

"Ah Pek, if time moves so much faster on Earth than in the Underworld, how do you perceive time when possessing your 'tang-ki'"?

"When in a human body, I perceive time as a human; when in the Underworld, as a spirit."

"I can understand that, but if time is relative as you have described it, and the Underworld is literally 'under this world', how can prisoners know how long they have been in the Underworld as there are neither clocks nor a sun to measure time's passing?"

"Underworld chickens crow every morning," Di Ya Pek replied.

Having noticed many altars placed just inside a temple's external gates dedicated to Underworld chickens in both Singapore and Malaysia, and, coupling this new piece of data with Di Ya Pek's explanation of Underworld time, I ventured, "So, every time you hear a cockerel, a year has passed on Earth, but only a day in the Underworld." Ah Pek concurred. "And that means," I continued, "in terms of ancestral offerings, if someone's descendants continue to make them annually several times a year, the prisoner will receive a year's offerings over the course of every single day in the Underworld." Ah Pek nodded approvingly at my grasp of Underworld time, even though he knew that I knew that the spirits suffering in the Underworld are 'hungry ghosts' unable to swallow the roasted meats, sweets and other delicacies offered to them. I therefore decided to redirect the conversation and to discuss Di Ya Pek's perceptions of the Underworld and its deities in a historic context.

"Chinese culture is ancient," I suggested, "and many people claim its history dates back 5,000 years. Was the Chinese Underworld there before Chinese history began?"

"Yes, it existed before that," Ah Pek replied, "it is more than 5,000 years old as our Chinese ancestors have lived there since about 10,000 years ago."

"Okay, but modern humans date back to pre-history, maybe 50,000 years ago, so humans were on Earth before the Underworld," I proffered.

"Yes, humans are older than the Underworld," Ah Pek agreed.

Choosing my words with care so as not to offend I replied, "But that suggests that the Underworld may have been created by humans."

---

9 Based on one day in the Underworld equalling a year on Earth, then if one hour equals 9.72 seconds, one day equals 233.28 seconds. Multiplied by seven, one week equals 1,632.96 seconds of time in the Underworld, which equals 27.21 minutes.

"How do deities come about?" Ah Pek answered rhetorically. *"You cultivate yourself, and through that training, you become a deity. Or, you live a meritorious life, accumulate merits, and are worshipped after death. Over the years, through people's beliefs and prayers carried and transformed by offerings of incense, you become a deity."*

I nodded in appreciation and continued, "So, if deities developed from humanity, did people also create the Underworld through prayers and beliefs?"

*"Yes. **Belief** created this Underworld, and **people** created the deities as the deities can **help** them. It is **all real**, and **all** from human culture."*[10] Di Ya Pek was speaking 'anthropology', and the assumed dualities of etic and emic fleetingly dissipated 'sans communitas' as pieces of the metaphoric cosmological jigsaw began to slot into place.

"Ah Pek, you told me that the Underworld is maybe 10,000 years old, but Xie Bian and Fan Wujiu lived much more recently. Can I ask who performed Tua Di Ya Pek's duties in the Underworld before them?"

"Before them, there were other officers like Ah Pek in the Underworld, but the most senior was Gui Wang, the 'Ghost King'. Nowadays most people know him as Da Shi Ye."

I have included the full transcript of the conversation with Di Ya Pek to provide readers with an understanding of the emic perceptions which, consistent within the internal logic of the tradition, account for the mass channelling of Tua Di Ya Pek in one or more locations as described at Di Ya Pek's party in Chapter 7, and at the Tua Di Ya Pek conference at Muar. For practitioners, this cosmology not only legitimises the presence of multiple Tua Di Ya Pek but also allows for *tang-ki* to remain in trance possession for long periods of time without the deities themselves neglecting their duties in the Underworld. However, this Di Ya Pek's perceptions are his own, and while the majority of *tang-ki* that I interviewed between 2010 and 2017 advocated similar understandings of the divisible nature of deities' souls, these views and his understanding of the Underworld's creation do not necessarily reflect the opinions of all *tang-ki* or their followers.

Conclusion

In the Underworld tradition, death is associated with karmic retribution, which, while entering Chinese cosmology through Buddhism, is emphasised most vigorously in the Underworld tradition where Tua Di Ya Pek

10 Di Ya Pek's emphasis.

materialise in the world of the living to furnish their devotees with verbal warnings and material representations of wrongdoers' post-mortal fates. The Buddhist leaning in Malaysia and the Taoist in Singapore are mutually beneficial to all parties, as, among elder devotees, the orthodox presence adds legitimacy to *tang-ki*'s Underworld rituals through their association with religious authority prior to the 'vernacularisation of tradition'. Historically, a primary source of their clerics' income has derived from officiating over funerary rituals, but now their income is largely obtained from participation in *tang-ki* temples' events. If viewed through the lens of commodification, religious consumerism may be partially accredited for the orthodox involvement in, and accommodation of, the Underworld tradition's idiosyncrasies, many of which have ostensibly inverted vernacular religious norms. Legitimacy is therefore not only derived from association with an idealised past or an orthodox presence, but from the resituation of existing traditions within atypical Underworld *tang-ki* temple settings. The commodification of objects, tradition and cosmology will be discussed further in Part IV.

In the following paragraphs I will discuss the influence of Anxi Chenghuangmiao on Malaysia's Underworld temple landscape. First, as illustrated, association with Anxi Chenghuangmiao lends legitimacy to either a temple or temples' ritual events through possessing replicas of Anxi's deity statues or a division of their incense; symbolically through copies of their City God's clothes; or, pragmatically, through Anxi's endorsement of events. In Chapter 1 I emphasised the importance of 'identifiable deities' in the production of the ritual and material cultures constructed around their veneration, and, as Di Ya Pek stressed, Xie Bian and Fan Wujiu are the prototypical archetypes of Tua Di Ya Pek in the modern tradition. Di Ya Pek also noted that each Underworld court has its own Tua Di Ya Pek, a facet of contemporary cosmology amply illustrated by their channelling at temple events in Singapore and Malaysia. However, there is no consensus on who these other Tua Di Ya Pek are, their family names are inconsistently linked to Underworld courts and their mythologies remain unknown. I therefore propose that Xie Bian and Fan Wujiu are perceived to be the original Tua Di Ya Pek in the modern Underworld tradition, as their mythologies and present-day graves in Anxi render them identifiable both as individuals and with a specific location. Therefore, Anxi Chenghuangmiao's primary legitimising factor in the Underworld tradition beyond Penang is not the elevated rank of its City God but that, in its own mythology, the temple's grounds house the graves of Xie Bian and Fan Wujiu.

Anxi has therefore become a pilgrimage site, devotees from Singapore and Malaysia now paying homage at the graves – an act which serves multiple functions in the perpetuation of the Underworld tradition. First, in pilgrimage, as Victor Turner notes, the "Integrality of the individual is indissoluble from the peace and harmony of the community" (Turner, 1973: 218), and pilgrimages to Anxi are mostly communal, organised at a temple level, and therefore serve to strengthen ties between individuals in visiting Underworld temple communities. Moreover, association with Anxi Chenghuangmiao offers Malaysian practitioners access to a larger transnational community which includes Underworld temples, however new or remote, in both Malaysia and Singapore. In all these respects, Anxi Chenghuangmiao contributes to the formation and consolidation of Malaysia's temple communities and, where replicas of its statues or divisions of incense have been provided, to the self-perpetuation of its own City God tradition.

However, the active involvement of Anxi Chenghuangmiao's representatives is a post-1994 phenomenon, and their choice of endorsements is highly selective. This raises a question mark regarding potential underlying economic motives for their attendance at ritual events in small-town and rural Malaysia. The commoditisation of cosmology and the wider political implications of Anxi Chenghuangmiao's presence will be discussed in Chapter 10 in the context of China's changing policies towards international cooperation and religious toleration.

I will therefore conclude this chapter by returning to Dasheng City God Temple and the temple manager's reminiscences. It is of note that even though his temple was relocated to is present site in 1990, only five years after the founding of nearby Muar City God Temple, local residents were unfamiliar and uncomfortable with Underworld deity worship at that time. It was not until 1999, the same year that Muar City God Temple received its City God replica from Anxi, that Dasheng City God Temple's Underworld deities superseded its Heaven deities in terms of ritual veneration and recognition.

These dates are significant, as they help to plot the geographical dissemination of the modern Underworld tradition, a post-1955 phenomenon whose mass popularisation has occurred at individual locations at differing times since the 1990s. The approximate dates of Underworld deities' increasing popularity in Johor State, supplemented by Mr Zhang's claim that in 1996 few *tang-ki* in Kuala Lumpur channelled Tua Di Ya Pek and Yin Fu Tan's founding in 2006 and completion in 2013, all suggest that the Malaysian Underworld tradition may have originated in either Singapore or northern Malaysia, later spreading to multiple locations in central and southern Malaysia from the early to mid-1980s onwards. Lending support to this theory, while there are a high number of Underworld *tang-ki* temples located in Johor State, in terms of their concentration in any given area, Johor State pales in comparison to George Town's outer suburbs, most notably Jelutong, Ayer Itam and neighbouring Bandar Baru Air Itam, an area known locally as Farlim. The diffusion of the tradition will be explored in detail in Chapter 11, and the origins of the contemporary tradition will be sought in George Town, Penang State, the first capital of the British Straits Settlements and home to Malaysia's eldest City God temple. First, though, moving to Anxi in Chapter 10, the popular mythos of the modern Underworld tradition's having originated from Anxi Chenghuangmiao will be analysed and dismissed.

Part IV
Tracing the origins of the modern Underworld tradition

10

Anxi Chenghuangmiao and cultural flows of local mythology

The first part of this chapter addresses general misassumptions held among practitioners in Singapore and Malaysia connecting Anxi Chenghuangmiao and the graves of Xie Bian and Fan Wujiu to the origins of the modern Underworld tradition. My purpose in readdressing this assumption is not to question Tua Di Ya Pek's origin myths in the Underworld tradition, but to highlight the role of Anxi Chenghuangmiao's recent cultural reinvention, which, in elevating its present-day significance, has conferred upon it a unique status among many overseas practitioners. Anxi's post-1990 reinvention has also brought about many positive results. These include providing Tua Di Ya Pek with a generic source of historical continuity, thus endowing the Underworld tradition with a potent symbol in a distinct geographical location in China.

While the temple's fortunes were originally interwoven with the imperial dispensation of licence and authority through state appointed magistrates, since 1990, its growth as a pilgrimage centre has been linked to legitimacy bestowed by local bureaus of the Communist Party of China (CCP) and by the overseas popularisation of Tua Di Ya Pek. These factors are best illustrated by briefly recounting its pre-1989 history and events following its post-1990 relocation. The following data has been pieced together from multiple sources, including the temple's self-published *Anxi County Chenghuang Temple's History*; face-to-face and online interviews with Chen Qixin,[1] Hu Jingzi and Anxi's present temple manager Chen Yiqun;[2]

---

[1] Cultural advisor, historian and co-editor of the temple's history book (Yuan, Jinlai, Qixin & Rongzu, 2007).
[2] Hu Jingzi was temple manager from May 2014 to August 2018, and Chen Yiqun from August 2018 onwards.

interviews at Singapore's first City God temple, Jiucaiba Chenghuangmiao; online data and discussions with Zhongliao Anxi Chenghuangmiao in Taiwan; and interviews with Anxi's local residents.

Historical summary

The area now known as Anxi County was established during the Five Dynasties and Ten Kingdoms era in 955 CE. The administrative and judicial centre was located at Fengcheng and, to reinforce the power of the judiciary, a City God temple was inaugurated there in 956. As local city gods assumed post-mortal authority over the souls of those under their jurisdiction, local magistrates and government officials customarily swore oaths of allegiance to emperor and country before their altars. The inclusion of magistrates and city gods in most Tua Di Ya Pek mythologies most likely stemmed from these associations in the imperial state religion.

According to County records, during the Ming dynasty the temple was rebuilt twice, in 1368 and 1565, and three additional halls were added between 1472 and 1479, all work being undertaken by local magistrates. The 1565 construction by magistrate Cai Changyu followed the temple's destruction in 1560 as a part of a wider trade war waged by Sino-Japanese pirates (*wokou* / 倭寇), and neither the temple nor its latter sixteenth-century statues came under threat again until the Second World War. Throughout its early history, as new administrative districts expanded from Fengcheng to encompass all of present-day Anxi County, the temple's location remained consistent in the heart of Fengcheng's administrative district on what is now Fumin Street. The temple contained ten City God statues, these being primary and vice statues for each district under the temple's jurisdiction: Anxi, Huian, Jinjiang, Nanan and Tongan; statues of Chenghuang's immediate subordinates including Tua Di Ya Pek; and an assortment of Bodhisattvas linking the temple to Chinese Buddhism.

The temple and statues remained safe until 1941, when the Kuomintang's (KMT) republican army entered Anxi and, under the orders of vice regiment commander Qiu Qiuxing, troops were stationed in and around the temple. Utilising the temple as a barracks, Qiu Qiuxing ordered non-combustible deity statues, including those of Tua Di Ya Pek, to be smashed; one elderly gentleman recalled that some wooden statues had been used as firewood for cooking. Only two statues were rescued, the main and the vice statue of the fifth City God, Wu She Chenghuang Gong, and these were temporarily worshipped at a local resident's home. In 1943 a small temple was built by the North Gate Bridge,[3] and Chenghuang's surviving statues were placed there. A decade later, amid renewed fears for their safety under the CCP, they were placed in a then remote hillside temple, Dongyue Si, and worshipped in its east wing. This was the first time in Chenghuangmiao's history that their City God statues had come into close proximity with the graves of Xie Bian and Fan Wujiu, who, according to legend, were buried in a public graveyard high above Dongyue Si, overlooking the town. The devotees' fears were not ungrounded, and, following the destruction of the North Gate Bridge temple during the Cultural Revolution, the two surviving statues were concealed in Dongyue Si's extensive hillside grounds.

Between 1966 and 1969 Dongyue Si was badly damaged, its deity statues destroyed, and both their own and Chenghuangmiao's hand-written historical documents burned. Moreover, the cemetery above was desecrated, the gravestones smashed, coffins exhumed, and their contents scattered. As a result, no written or material evidence recording the interment of Xie Bian and Fan Wujiu, the exact locations of their graves or details of their headstones' inscriptions have survived. Chen Qixin confirmed this, adding that applications to build new tombs in the cemetery began in 1998, that the location of the new graves was guessed and their inscriptions newly composed, and that the current graves contain unidentified bones and should therefore be considered only as monuments.[4] All details of Fan Wujiu and Xie Bian's lives and their final resting places therefore lie in the annals of mythology rather than in recorded local history.

Meanwhile, the two hidden City God statues remained unscathed and in 1985, seven years into Deng Xiaoping's 'reform era', they were again placed on public view on Dongyue Si's Sandalwood Altar. This 'marriage of convenience' would soon lead to Dongyue Si being incorporated into Anxi Chenghuangmiao's administrative structure. In the same year, after a fortyfour-year absence, new statues of Tua Di Ya Pek were carved, although, as the temple's records had been burned, these were generically styled and their tongues remain opium free. Plate 14 illustrates the differences between their statues and those commonly found in Singapore and Malaysia's temples.

However, as records of Anxi's overseas deity statues confirm, only their Chenghuang tradition had been promoted. Their distribution of replica statues illustrates two further poignant facts: first, and reflecting early emigration patterns, that initially the temple was focused on spreading its Chenghuang tradition to Taiwan rather than to Southeast Asia; and second, that, prior to the modern Underworld tradition, no replicas of their Tua Di Ya Pek were ever exported, the only recorded cases being in the twenty-first century:

---

3 Demolished in the 1970s, previously located near the intersection of present-day Hebin North Road and Fengshan Road.
4 Online conversations with Chen Qixin, 9 March 2018.

to Singapore's Zhenren Gong and Shanlong Miao in 2001 and 2005, and to Linghai Dian in Jelutong, George Town in 2007.

The first replica statues were exported by individuals emigrating from Fujian to Taiwan in the late seventeenth century, Anxi's second Chenghuang being brought by the 'Shi' family and their third by Zhang Dan, both of whom settled in Zhongliao in the southwest of Chaiyi County. Initially worshipped on home altars, both statues were placed in Zhongliao Anxi Chenghuangmiao after its construction in 1775. Two further replicas were brought to Chiayi in the early Qing dynasty and worshipped at home altars, being later placed in Dongshiliao Dongan Gong in 1821. There are a further fifteen temples in Taiwan containing Anxi's Chenhuang, but, of these, fourteen received their original replica statues from Zhongliao Anxi Chenghuangmiao, the fifteenth being brought from Anxi around 1901 and placed in Chaiyi County's Shenglin Gong in 1981.

Anxi's only City God replica statue in Singapore is Wu Shi Chenghuang Ye which was brought to Singapore in 1917 by a Taoist priest named Xiao Tianping and a scholar, Xie Liwen. The statue found a permanent home at Jiucaiba Chenghuangmiao when it was relocated to its present position in 1989.[5] Anxi's interest was only turned to Malaysia late in Deng Xiaoping's 'opening up' era, with Muar City God Temple and Zhenlinshan Jieyuan Tang Chenghuangmiao in Johor State being the first temples to be given Chenghuang replicas in the mid-1980s, and Linghai Dian in Penang receiving its replica in 2007. Nonetheless, their comparatively late cultural investment in Malaysia's temple landscape has recently resulted in unexpected material returns, details of which will follow.

First, though, returning to the temple's recent history, a new era began in 1989 when a Singaporean devotee from Jiucaiba Chenghuangmiao, Mrs Chen Meiying, visited Anxi with an offer of 400,000 ringgits to rebuild the temple. As the original building on Fumin Street was being used as a library for an adjacent primary school, she initially approached the 'Anxi Dongyue Si Cultural Relics Repairing and Construction Committee', which had been established in 1987 for the restoration of Dongyue Si, where Chenghuang's statues were located. Using the traditional method of casting divination blocks in front of the deity's statue, when the City God was asked if he would like his new temple to be located east of Dongyue Si, nine consecutive 'yes' answers were received. However, divination blocks can be manipulated by the wording and choice of questions asked, and it is likely that foreknowledge of Tua Di Ya Pek's overseas mythologies influenced their choice of relocation, making it the temple located closest to the desecrated cemetery. This

---

5 The temple's history is detailed in chapter twelve.

notion is supported by the hypothesis that Anxi's mid-1980s involvement in Malaysia's temple landscape and visits from Jiucaiba Chenghuangmiao provided their foresight, and that Tua Di Ya Pek's rapid overseas popularisation in the 1990s following its relocation provided the societal catalysts required for Anxi's later pragmatic promotion of Xie Bian and Fan Wujiu's graves.

Architectural plans were therefore presented to Anxi County government for approval, and construction began in February 1990. Three halls were completed in eleven months, and an inauguration ceremony was held on 16 January 1991. According to Chen Qixin, only after the new temple was opened did overseas temples begin to take divisions of incense from their Underworld deity censers back to Singapore and Malaysia. With the City God temple's new-found popularity, 'Anxi Dongyue Si Cultural Relics Repairing and Construction Committee' was replaced by the 'Anxi Dongyue Si Chenghuangmiao Committee' in 1994. The new committee submitted an application to Anxi County government requesting them to manage the temples, and Fengcheng Town government took over the administration of the two temples as a single unit 'Dongyue Si Chenghuangmiao'. Thereafter, appointed managers have been CCP cadres paid directly by Fengcheng Town government, with the management offices located in Chenghuangmiao.

Registering the temple as either Buddhist or Taoist would grant it official legitimacy by virtue of association with one of the five religions recognised in China, in which freedom of worship is constitutionally protected. However, up to now, religious leaders, including the administrative staff of registered temples, are vetted for political allegiance to the CCP and the state and are therefore necessarily atheists. It has been suggested that this enables the government to harness "The benefits of religion to advance broader CCP economic, political, cultural, and foreign policy goals" (Cook, 2017: 4). In the context of the commodification of culture, registered temples are at liberty to promote both national and international tourism, with pilgrimage centres in particular increasing local economic growth. Therefore in 1998, Anxi Dongyue Si Chenghuangmiao registered with 'Anxi County Bureau of Ethnic and Religious Affairs' as a Taoist complex. In the same year Anxi Chenghuangmiao obtained the ground above its existing temple complex and was given planning permission for the reconstruction of Fan Wujiu and Xie Bian's graves, and these were completed in 2000. The temple's expansion and the construction of the new graves illustrates Anxi City government's assessment of local temple developments, essentially "By their functional utility understood in secular [economic][6] terms" (Chau, 2009: 214).

---

6 Author's addition.

10.1 Ba Ye Gong (Xie Bian) and Jiu Ye Gong's (Fan Wujiu's) new graves

Incompatible mythologies and titles

Anxi Chenghuangmiao's mythology is quite different from the Tua Di Ya Pek narrative prevalent among practitioners in Singapore and Malaysia. Most notably, in Anxi's version not only did Xie Bian and Fan Wujiu never meet, but they also lived in earlier and different periods. As will be seen, there is nothing in Anxi's mythology linking Xie Bian and Fan Wujiu to opium, catching or being criminals, nor regarding their sworn oath of brotherhood, essentially, the most common elements of their mythos in the contemporary Underworld tradition.

In Anxi's narrative, Xie Bian was born into a poor family and often begged in order to support his mother. His family lived near the government office (*yamen* / 衙门), and one day the county magistrate saw him catching lice that were presumably afflicting his mother and, impressed by his devotion, offered him work in the government office. Xie Bian was a filial son and his mother was elderly, so it was his habit to help her put on her shoes. One day as he was doing so, he heard a commotion coming from the ofice and someone yelling that he was late for work, so he rushed there with his mother's shoe still in his hand. Seeing Xie Bian running while holding an item of a woman's personal clothing, the county magistrate assumed that he had behaved indecently and therefore beat him to death without trial. Many people felt aggrieved as Xie Bian was seen as a model of filial piety, and so they petitioned the Jade Emperor on his behalf, which resulted in King Yama investigating his death. Following the discovery of the truth, the county magistrate was postmortally punished and Xie Bian was posthumously promoted as one of Anxi Chenghuang's lictors. In the temple's mythology he was granted the honorific title of 'imperial envoy' (*qinchai dachen* / 钦差大臣).

By contrast, Fan Wujiu was a brave man famed for putting himself in danger to save others. There was a tyrant living in Fan Wujiu's neighbourhood who had seized land on which to build his own house, who claimed the village well as his own and who charged neighbouring villagers to fetch water from it. The villagers soon became rebellious over the 'water tax', so the landowner decided to drop poison into the well. Fan Wujiu discovered this plan and, guarding the well, told villagers not to draw water from it. However, the villagers were unconvinced, so to save the innocent from poisoning, Fan Wujiu drank some himself and promptly died. Struck by his heroic action and furious with the tyrant, the villagers forced the tyrant to drink the water too. When Fan Wujiu's soul reported to the Underworld, King Yama, impressed by his selflessness and upright character, as with Xie Bian, granted him the position of 'imperial envoy' in Anxi Chenghunag's local retinue.

When I asked Chen Qixin to account for the incompatibility of their two mythologies, he replied, "When people took incense aboard, they relied on their memory to remember the legend but knew very little about the real story. Over time, the legend got distorted, but as long as it sounds plausible, it will do. There is *even* a version of the story that says Xie Bian and Fan Wujiu were opium sellers! The Xie Bian and Fan Wujiu in this temple were from the Song dynasty, that was a *thousand* years ago, and there *wasn't* any opium in China then!"[7] Further compounding the incompatibility of the mythologies, Anxi does not identify Xie Bian and Fan Wujiu as First and Second Grand Elder (Tua Di Ya Pek), but as Eighth and Ninth Lords (Ba Ye Gong and Jiu Ye Gong). Nonetheless, while their own Fan Wujiu and Xie Bian mythology has remained constant, it has in no way rewritten or replaced common perceptions of Fan Wujiu and Xie Bian in the Underworld tradition in Singapore and Malaysia.

Anxi's new Underworld altar temple annex

An unexpected result of Anxi's ritual investments in Malaysia came to fruition on 12 December 2018. On the 11th, an official banquet was held to celebrate the opening of Anxi's new temple annex immediately below Fan Wujiu and Xie Bian's graves. Joining me at the banquet table were Hu Jingzi, Chen Qixin and Anxi Chenghuangmiao's new manager, Chen Yiqun; local politicians; Dato Yong Mun Tong, the director of the Malaysian charity the 'Sin Hock Min Foundation'; and Ah Boon and his wife. Of the fifteen remaining tables, two catered exclusively for members of Yinfu Tan who had come to attend the opening of the new Underworld altar room, where visiting *tang-ki* would be allowed to channel their Underworld masters. The annex is called Anxi Chenghuangmiao fushu Yinfu Tan, and both its initial conception and the funds donated for its construction had originated at Yinfu Tan in Klang.

In May 2017, two of Di Ya Pek's godsons, Dato Yong Mun Tong and the owner of the Asian Gaming Foundation, Dato Goh Yong Hau, had visited Di Ya Pek in Klang. During their consultations, Di Ya Pek informed them that he longed to return to Anxi. As the channelling of deities was prohibited in Anxi Chenghuangmiao, they soon established that what Di Ya Pek actually wanted was to open a branch of Yinfu Tan in Anxi, and both promised to assist. Dato Goh Yong Hau's uncle was an official in the Anxi City council, so they met him in Anxi, where he introduced them to Anxi Dongyue Si Chenghuangmiao's management committee to present the

---

7 Interviewed at Anxi on 12 December 2018.

idea. It was received favourably and, with Chen Yiqun accompanying them around the temple's surrounds, they decided that the empty plot of land beneath the graves was the most suitable location.[8] As this land belonged to the local government, Anxi's management committee, themselves government employees, negotiated its free acquisition for the temple's expansion. The final stamp of approval was granted by the Major of Fengcheng Town and the Secretary of Fengcheng Town government in June, and a ground-breaking ceremony attended by Ah Boon and Dato Goh Yong Hau was held on 11 July 2017.

An agreement had been reached whereby funds from Malaysia would be used to build the 283 stairs leading to the new annex and the annex itself, while the temple in Anxi would pay for the purchase of land belonging to local farmers that would be encroached upon by the staircase. In total, two million ringgits came from Malaysian donations, and Anxi Chenghuangmiao spent an equivalent of one million ringgits on the expropriation of land, the walls around the construction, and the annex's design fees, all of which had to be approved by Anxi County's Bureau of Construction.

From the outset, Malaysia and Anxi had differing interpretations of rights of use and control over the temple which was about to be constructed. In an interview in Klang in July 2018 Ah Boon explained, "When Dato Yong Mun Tong and Dato Goh Yong Hau contacted Anxi Chenghuangmiao they were speaking for Yinfu Tan. So, both Anxi Chenghuangmiao and the Chinese government knew it was Malaysia's Yinfu Tan building the new temple. After it is built, we will therefore put a 'Klang Yinfu Tan' plaque on the temple." I asked how Anxi's management felt about having a branch of Yinfu Tan in their grounds, and Ah Boon replied, "They think it is good. They said it is okay to build Yinfu Tan there, but they also asked us to build a stairway for them." Ah Boon then acknowledged that he perceived the annex as a 'Yinfu Tan – two', so I asked about Anxi's perceptions. "Of course, they would think it is a part of Anxi Chenghuangmiao, but we have different opinions."

However, by the time of the opening, it was clear that Klang Yinfu Tan had no choice but to relinquish all control over the annex to Anxi Chenghuangmiao. While the consensus among the contingent of devotees that had travelled from Klang for the opening was that the new annex was 'Klang Yinfu Tan – two', the political realities were clear to both Ah Boon and Dato Yong Mun Tong. On the morning of 12 December 2018 Anxi's new manager had informed me that, to the best of his knowledge, there had never been talk of a 'Klang' Yinfu Tan in Anxi, and that as the annex's

8 Interview in Anxi with Chen Yiqun, 12 December 2018.

10.2 The lowest section of the new staircase

name indicated, it is was the sole property of Anxi Chenghuangmiao. Later that evening I mentioned this to the Dato, who replied with resignation, "I am fully aware that after I worked so hard to raise two million ringgits, the temple still belongs to Anxi. We have no right to claim any authority. Today they needed to acknowledge us because we have raised so much money, but after today, we have no role here."

To grasp Chen Yiqun's claim, the name itself, 'Anxi Chenghuangmiao fushu Yinfu Tan' requires some clarification. While Yinfu Tan *is* the name of the temple in Klang, its literal translation is 'Underworld altar', so those unfamiliar with Klang Yinfu Tan would not connect the annex with Ah Boon's temple. More confounding still is that there are several Malaysian temples called 'Yinfu Tan', and several more that include the words 'Yinfu Tan' in their name. Furthermore, a full translation of the annex's name may be rendered as 'The Underworld altar affiliated to Anxi City God Temple' or 'Anxi City God Temple's affiliated Underworld altar', neither of which identifies Klang Yinfu Tan with its conception and construction. To compensate for this, Dato Yong Mun Tong had requested that a sign reading 'Klang Teluk Pulai[9] Yinfu Tan' be placed over the new deity altar inside the annex, but this idea was rejected.

Moving on to the inauguration ceremony itself, it was brief and performed by Chen Qixin in his function as head of Anxi's Buddhist Service Group (*Xiude Foshi Tuan*). Therefore, even though the temple complex is registered as Taoist, he performed the rituals with five assistants all wearing Buddhist robes. However, as he lacked formal training, the rituals were of his own design and contained borrowed elements from both the Taoist and vernacular traditions. The first was performed in the main temple facing Chenghuang's altar.

> *Together with his assistants, an invocation was chanted to a musical accompaniment inviting all the temple's deities from the City God and his Underworld retinue to heavenly Bodhisattvas to bestow blessings on all gathered. Behind them stood the temple's management and invited guests each holding three incense sticks, and in front lay a table of offerings central to which was a raw pig's head, and cooked duck, goose, chicken and fish (Plate 15). Chanting completed, and incense placed in Chenghuang's censer, the gathering moved up to the new annex. After a short address by Anxi's ex-manager, Ah Boon and Dato Goh Yong Hau, clearly irked by the ironic position in which they had been placed, unveiled the building's new name plaque with looks of mild distaste.*

---

9 The area of Klang in which Yinfu Tan is located.

Once inside, the second ritual was to 'open the eyes' of the cast plastic Tua Di Ya Pek statues. In front of a table littered with similar meaty offerings, Chen Qixin invoked deities hailing from the Taoist, Buddhist, imperial and vernacular pantheons to bear witness, and then chanted four Buddhist sutras.[10] In the Taoist fashion he then drew a talisman on a small round mirror to attract wealth to the temple through the mirror's light, and then employed the mirror to reflect light onto the deity statues to increase their efficacy as each vital point was dotted with red ink. With the offerings, music, mirror and talisman, sutras aside, both rituals resembled those typically found in the Taoist and vernacular traditions.

Once the rituals had been completed, with only Klang's contingent remaining inside, Ah boon removed his shirt and put on Di Ya Pek's black silk trousers. Sitting behind a desk placed to the right of the altar room and surrounded by followers, Ah Boon made history as the first 'tang-ki' to channel a deity in the new annex. When Di Ya Pek arrived, he was not however his usual confident self, but nervous and reserved, and he explained in a trembling voice that this was because his original master, Anxi's Chenghuang was there observing him.

Conclusion

There is a dichotomy of opinions between Tua Di Ya Pek's devotees from Malaysia and Anxi Chenghuangmiao's management regarding the relative significance of Anxi's set of deities, with Anxi maintaining that their City God is of paramount importance. Chen Yiqun suggested: "People from Taiwan mainly come here for the City God. As for Singaporeans, I think they come here first to worship Chenghuang and then Ba Ye and Jiu Ye. For Malaysians, I think they mostly come just for Ba Ye and Jiu Ye. In the 1980s and 90s, there were even fewer people worshipping Ba Ye and Jiu Ye. The number of worshippers has only increased in the last ten years or so."[11] In contrast, interviews in Singapore and Malaysia showed that, bar the small minority of temples actually containing Anxi's City God, other temples and devotees travelled to Anxi primarily to pay homage to Xie Bian and Fan Wujiu, individuals they perceived as the original Tua Di Ya Pek.

Anxi's capitalisation of their new location and graves is an intentional commodification resulting from the Underworld tradition's inversion of cosmological emphasis, so the same inversion which thrust Tua Di Ya Pek into the spotlight of the ritual stage has subsequently facilitated Anxi

10 Da Bei Zhou, Lu Xian Zan, Xin Jing and Yangzhou Jing Shui.
11 Interview in Anxi, 12 December 2018.

Chenghuangmiao's new supporting role in the tradition's narrative. In relocating the temple and building the new graves, Anxi Chenghuangmiao has physically identified itself with an existing mythological symbol, a powerful means in itself of gaining and maintaining influence. Having reconstructed the temple and its accompanying mythology in tangible forms, their ongoing cultural significance within the Underworld tradition relies somewhat on whether overseas practitioners' self-identities remain primarily linked to their ancestral roots. If they do, the graves linking Xie Bian and Fan Wijiu's (and therefore Tua Di Ya Pek's) legend to Anxi Chenghuangmiao may maintain its cultural integrity. However, if overseas nationalism eventually succeeds in promoting citizenship over ethnic origins as a primary factor in identity formation – a distinct possibility in Singapore, though unlikely in Malaysia's foreseeable future – Anxi's status in the Underworld tradition may diminish. I mention this as, in an era described as the "'Cultural turn' of secular governance in China" (Wang, 2019: 155), where county and provincial-level bureaucrats market religious sites as cultural commodities, this would explain to some degree Anxi's timely involvement and ongoing cultural investment in Malaysia's temple landscape.

I will conclude by reiterating the facts most pertinent to the modern Underworld tradition's origins. Anxi's City God Temple Tua Di Ya Pek mythologies conflict with those conveyed by Malaysian and Singaporean Chinese practitioners: pre-1990, there was no geographical connection between Anxi Chenghuangmiao and the graves of Xie Bian and Fan Wujiu; the contemporary graves are neither in their original locations, nor do they contain the actual corpses of Xie Bian and Fan Wujiu; and, with neither censers nor statues of Tua Di Ya Pek in Anxi between 1943 and 1985, during the first three decades of the Underworld tradition's development no replicas of its deity statues or divisions of incense of Anxi's Tua Di Ya Pek could have been taken to either Singapore or Malaysia. Therefore, while Anxi Chenghuangmiao may lay claim to being the singularly most famous temple among Singapore and Malaysia's practitioners, it is clear that the modern Underworld tradition could not have originated from Anxi.

11

Penang: the earliest recollections of Tua Di Ya Pek embodied

Introduction

Throughout the last two years of my fieldwork, as I had visited in excess of two-hundred Underworld temples, from Singapore in the south to Alor Setar in Malaysia's most northern state, Kedah, one specific question was posed to me by many interested *tang-ki*, temple owners and management committees and during lengthy interviews over tea with the eldest members of various temple communities. It was a question to which, until towards the end of my research, I was unable to suggest a satisfactory answer. The question was simply this. Did I know where, or at which temple, Tua Di Ya Pek had first been channelled through a *tang-ki*? There was a general consensus among Malaysia's elders that the tradition may have dated back to the mid-1950s, and among those in Singapore to the early 1960s. The number of individuals actively involved in the early channelling of Tua Di Ya Pek would have been small. Also, as they would have been born pre-1950, when life expectancy was short (rising to only 48 years in 1950, and 59.5 years among the Chinese male population by 1957[1]), any distant memories would have to be recalled by those who had lived to enjoy an unexpectedly long life. Therefore, if any recollections were to be found and recorded, they would be of historical significance because, within a decade or so, this aspect of the modern Underworld tradition's history would no longer be able to be researched.

Initially the trail was cold, but, prompted by these practitioners' own curiosity and asking the same question at each temple I visited, in the eighth year of my research – specifically, on return visits to Kuala Lumpur

---

1 Source: 1957 Population Census of the Federation of Malaya, Report No. 14.

and George Town in 2017 – I found the trail to get warmer. As outlined in Chapter 6, the burning of Da Shi Ye integral to Underworld temple's Seventh Month rituals originated from Penang in the 1920s. Moreover, as Penang houses the highest percentage of ethnic Chinese in Malaysia, and George Town the greatest concentration of Chinese temples, perhaps influenced by Da Shi Ye's history, George Town is now associated by many practitioners with the invention of traditions associated with Underworld deity worship. The narrative therefore moves to George Town and its suburb of Ayer Itam, and to events which occurred there in the 1950s. In the absence of locally written records providing concrete evidence of the modern tradition's origins, the accounts reproduced represent the earliest recollections that I have collected regarding not only where but also how the tradition may have begun. However, as narratives may be influenced over time by individual temples' own elaborations of events, and in the absence of testimonies by those involved who have already passed away, the conclusions drawn are based on the available evidence and are not intended as definitive historical facts.

Penang Chenghuangmiao

Established in 1862, Penang Chenghuangmiao is the eldest City God temple in Malaysia, predating Singapore's Jiucaiba Chenghuangmiao by fifty-six years. Tua Di Ya Pek have been worshipped there since its inauguration and, as this was rarely found outside of City God temples prior to the advent of the modern Underworld tradition, it is likely that their Tua Di Ya Pek statues are among the eldest in Malaysia. The Penang Chenghuangmiao statues can moreover lay claim to be the longest continually worshipped Tua Di Ya Pek statues in a public temple in either Singapore or Malaysia, and the first to be 'fed' daily with an unerring supply of opium. According to the present temple keeper, Mrs Lin, the procedure dates back at least one hundred years whereby, along with incense offerings, it has been the practice to feed these statues with opium when petitioning them for assistance.[2] The practice may have started due to the impression held in Malaysia at the time of lower-ranked Chinese court officials, including magistrates' lieutenants and messengers, being opium addicts, and therefore easily corrupted with bribes of opium.[3]

Although opium has been illegal since the Dangerous Drugs Ordinance of

[2] Her father-in-law witnessed this as a teenager from the 1920s, and the tradition was already well established at that time.
[3] From conversations with Professor Wang Chengfa, a Taoist priest and folklore specialist born and based in Penang.

1952, devotees continue to purchase it along with incense to satisfy Tua Di Ya Pek's insatiable appetites when they ask for prosperity or luck, or, once favours have been received, to offer as a gesture of gratitude. Most devotees buy two one-gram wraps, one for each of Tua Ya Pek and Di Ya Pek. The small plastic wraps are handled only by a temple assistant, who, using a sharpened butter knife, scrapes off the opium and feeds the deity statues by smearing it on their tongues while devotees, sometimes with their families, kneel down with three incense sticks and worship each deity. So much opium has accumulated that, during the hottest part of the day, the top layer liquefies and drips down onto a plastic bib covering Tua Ya Pek's white robes, and from Di Ya Pek's shorter tongue onto his chin, from where it slides down to solidify on his protruding belly. The faces of both deities have therefore become darker over time from the countless layers of opium which have over time been absorbed into the wood, rendering the lower sections of their faces particularly dark and shiny. Although Dizangwang sits on the central altar, the City God Weiling Gong flanked by Ox Head and Horse Face on the right altar, and the 'Goddess of Midwives' Zhu Sheng Niang-niang on the left, the primary focus for most visitors, both past and present, has been the veneration of Tua Di Ya Pek. Tua Ya Pek's human-sized statue is thus the largest in the temple and stands in front of the City God's altar (Plate 16), and Di Ya Pek's hefty statue is placed parallel, in front of Zhu Sheng Niang-niang.

The oral evidence therefore indicates that the application of opium to Tua Di Ya Pek's tongues originated at this temple and only later spread throughout the *tang-ki*-centric Singapore–Malaysian Chinese Underworld tradition. Moreover, the following narratives suggest that Penang Chenghuangmiao's Tua Ya Pek mythology not only initiated the later opium-smoking tradition among *tang-ki* but also helped to furnish the deity's prototypical behavioural characteristics, Tua Ya Pek's joviality and Di Ya Pek's comparative seriousness, both now easily observable when channelled through their respective *tang-ki*.

Ordinarily, temple mythologies, rather than being common knowledge, are known by temple insiders and by those who use the temple for daily worship. Only when an individual deity becomes widely worshipped due to imperial or Taoist promotion within the celestial pantheon, as for example Mazu,[4] or is depicted in novels and on stage through operatic or puppet performances such as Sun Wukong and Guan Gong,[5] does their mythology enter the wider public realm. Penang City God's Tua Ya Pek mythology is

---

[4] Promoted multiple times, from 'Aunty Lin' in the eleventh century to 'Empress of Heaven' in 1737 (Adler, 2002).
[5] Made household names through the novels *Journey to the West* and *Romance of the Three Kingdoms*, both of which have been dramatised through stage and puppet performances, and later through films and television series.

an exception to this rule. Within days of the following events first occurring, the story had been spread by Penang's rickshaw riders, and became widely known throughout George Town as later events unfolded.

The account of the temple's mythology is as related to me by Mrs Lin and supplemented with details from two further sources, the first being a newspaper article 'Respectful thanks to Black and White Impermanence' (*Daxie shen en xun Hei Bai Wuchang*) (Junren, 1989) published in the *Guangming Ribao* and itself based on an earlier article in the same publication by Professor Wang Chenfa; the second being conversations with Professor Wang, who is a long-time friend of Mrs Lin, her husband and her deceased father-in-law.

I first visited the temple with Professor Wang who introduced me to Mrs Lin, and when I asked Mrs Lin on a later occasion to recount the temple's mythology, she immediately retorted "It's real history! It happened a long time ago, just before I got married, but it really did happen!" Settling down she continued, "We called Tua Ya Pek 'Lang Cia Ah Pek', that is, 'Rickshaw Ah Pek',[6] and he was famous at the time."

The year was 1955, and their Tua Ya Pek was already associated with selecting winning combinations of numbers between 1 and 999 for the 3D lottery. These lotteries had been illegal since the Betting Act of 1953, in which 'common betting houses'[7] had been deemed a "nuisance and contrary to law",[8] with owners and employees, on conviction, being liable to a fine of between 20,000 and 200,000 ringgit and up to five years' imprisonment.[9] Their clients, if convicted, were fined up to 5,000 ringgit or sentenced "to imprisonment for a term not exceeding six months or … both".[10] However, neither the law nor the fact that 3D lotteries were run by multiple bookmakers with individual clan and gangland connections impacted on their popularity. Ironically, both gamblers and bookmakers elicited Tua Ya Pek's assistance, the former to request winning numbers and the latter to prevent the winning numbers requested from being chosen. Hanging from Tua Ya Pek's right shoulder is a cream-coloured cloth bag, and gamblers would either take numbers from his bag or write the numbers that they had chosen on a piece of paper and drop them into the bag with promises of opium if

6 Rickshaw in Hokkien is '*lang cia*'.
7 "Any place kept or used for betting or wagering […] which the public or any class of the public has, or may have, access […] whether such bets or wagers reach the bookmaker by the hand of the person placing the bet or his agent or the bookmaker's agent" (Act 495: Betting Act 1953: Interpretation (i) and (iii)).
8 Act 495: Betting Act 1953, section 3.
9 Act 495: Betting Act 1953, section 4. (1).
10 Act 495: Betting Act 1953, section 6. (1).

their numbers were selected. Concurrently, bookmakers would also place multiple numbers in Tua Ya Pek's bag and feed him opium while requesting that these numbers would not be selected, and then return after the weekend draw to offer him more opium as thanks. Not only would gamblers take these numbers thinking that they were lucky, but the bookmakers put in the numbers that were popular among gamblers and therefore most commonly chosen, those being numbers containing the digit 8, as its pronunciation *'ba'* sounds similar to *'fa'* (发), meaning 'prosperity'. Bookmakers would then write a list of these numbers and place it beneath the statue's feet, which they believed, along with sufficient offerings of opium, would prevent these numbers from being selected in the weekly draw. However, these proceedings were a Penang custom, and at the time, before Tua Di Ya Pek started to be channelled by *tang-ki*, were distinct to this temple. In the absence of similar data from other locations, it can be surmised that the association between Tua Di Ya Pek and gambling originated from this City God temple in the early days of lotteries in Penang.

Then, in 1955, when their Tua Ya Pek manifested in human form to enjoy carnal delights, local history morphs into a local mythology.

> *Mrs Lin resumed her narrative.* "One evening, soon after dark, a pleasant-looking middle-aged man with downward-sloping eyebrows and dressed in fresh white clothes hailed a cycle rickshaw outside the temple. After making himself comfortable, he asked the rickshaw driver to take him to the closest place to find happiness, wealth and bliss. The astute driver therefore headed towards the Chulia Street area of Chinatown and took him first to a brothel, then to a bookmaker, and finally to an opium den. The passenger was delighted by the evening's excursion and persuaded the driver to accept three lucky numbers in lieu of cash, and then disappeared from sight as he walked back towards the temple." *With a knowing smile she continued:* "The driver had made a good choice as at noon the following day, the prostitute, bookmaker and opium seller found that the money they had received had transformed into Hell banknotes, and that weekend, the driver won a 3D lottery. As news of the Hell banknotes and winning numbers spread, it became common knowledge that if you met our Rickshaw Ah Pek around the City God temple, prosperity would come. Therefore, increasing numbers of rickshaws would park outside the City God temple every evening waiting for him. This went on for several months, the passenger always visiting different establishments, the proprietors and vendors finding their ringgit replaced by Hell banknotes the next day, and the rickshaw drivers winning 3D prizes."

As these tales of Tua Ya Pek's efficacy spread across Penang, for the first time, the broader ethnic Chinese populace became interested in Underworld deity veneration.

"Every night the temple square was crowded with rickshaw drivers and members of the public hoping to meet the Hell deity, and this soon prompted complaints from the temple's neighbours. The 'man in white' therefore began to leave the temple in the daytime to visit Cecil Street market to buy snacks before his night-time excursions as the rickshaw drivers waiting for him in the daytime would not be able to loiter until night.

"One day when he went to buy rice dumplings (rou zong / 肉粽), he asked the vendor to collect the money from him later at our temple. The dumpling seller thought that the man looked familiar, so agreed, but when he came to the temple, instead of finding his customer, he found dumpling wrappers by Tua Ya Pek's feet. Looking up and seeing the statue's face and long sloping eyebrows, he realised why the man had seemed familiar, and having heard of the rickshaw drivers' winnings, interpreted the incident as auspicious. Applying a local tradition, he consulted the 'Tua Pek Kong cian li to', a picture book matching words to numbers, and found 'rou zong' equated with the number 645, and 'eat rice' ('chifan' / 吃饭) with 389. The following weekend his numbers were selected, winning him the second prize in a 3D lottery."

Professor Wang Chengfa later completed the narrative as told to him by Mrs Lin's father-in-law before he died.

"Within a few months of the 'man in white' venturing out of the temple, along with neighbour's complaints came those from the proprietors of opium dens and brothels aggrieved by the transformation of their earnings into Hell banknotes. Mrs Lin's father-in-law, the temple abbot, Lin Maosheng, therefore called in the assistance of his father, a Taoist priest from Zhangzhou in Fujian, Lin Zhangshan. Employing his orthodox talismanic training, he drew and pasted talismans on the side of Tua Di Ya Pek's statues and placed a chain sealed with a talisman around each, in effect preventing either from leaving the temple except in spirit form on the City God's instructions. So," he continued, *"the mythology ends there, but from 1955 until now, Penang's gamblers, bookmakers, prostitutes and gangsters have continued to feed opium to the temple's Tua Di Ya Pek in return for their protection, and by doing so have adopted them as their own patron deities. Moreover, many of Penang's underground*

gambling dens, brothels and seedier bars still contain statues of Tua Di Ya Pek. This was initially a Penang tradition, but has since spread across Kedah State in northwest Malaysia, and as far as Ipoh 150 kilometres south in Perak State."

Significantly, neither the temple's City God nor its Tua Di Ya Pek originated from Anxi, their City God 'Weiling Gong' being the post-mortally promoted soul of a local physician, Xu Xiaoshan, and Tua Di Ya Pek his locally appointed assistants. Combined with the following narrative and Anxi's historical distribution of replica deity statues, the data shows that there is no connection between Anxi Chenghuangmiao and the origin of the modern Underworld tradition in Malaysia. In contrast to Anxi Chenghuangmiao, who have actively promoted their own City God, Penang Chenghuangmiao, uninterested in building an expanded temple network, have never provided replicas of their deity statues. According to Mrs Lin, other temples only approached them for Tua Di Ya Pek's incense ash after the night-time excursions had become common knowledge, first coming from Penang State, and soon after from Singapore.

Ayer Itam: Penang's eldest Underworld temple

Built in its present location in the Farlim area of Ayer Itam around 1920, Tiandeyuan Xunyin Fu is Penang's eldest temple where Underworld deities have been channelled. Prior to 1955, their first *tang-ki* was a rickshaw driver who channelled an Underworld deity similarly called Lang Pek, 'Rickshaw Uncle', as the deity first entered him while he was riding his rickshaw from a Datuk Gong shrine in the mountains to his home. The rickshaw rider and his wife then purchased some land and established Tiandeyuan Xunyin Fu with a single altar. According to the temple's mythology, the *tang-ki* decided to return to China with his family, selling the temple and surrounding land to finance the trip. The temple was immediately expanded by its new owners; a local Tua Ya Pek possessed the *tang-ki* just before the latter's emigration, and soon afterwards the events reported at the City God temple began.

The elders of the temple's committee[11] recall that their first new *tang-ki* was visiting the City God temple around the time of Tua Ya Pek's outings and, entering a spontaneous trance state, claimed to be channelling the City God's Tua Ya Pek. A picture of the City God's Tua Di Ya Pek was therefore placed on their temple altar, where new devotees started worshipping them as Underworld gods of gambling and wealth and consulting Tua Ya

11 Interviewed December 2016.

Pek through his new *tang-ki*. Tiandeyuan Xunyin Fu therefore holds the claim of having the first *tang-ki* to regularly channel Tua Ya Pek in Penang, and while this is likely, due to the fame of the City God temple's mythology, other *tang-ki* in Penang began channelling Tua Di Ya Pek in the same period. Nonetheless, according to oral accounts, during the 1950s and 1960s, it became the most popular temple in Penang for Underworld deity worship, second only to Chenghuangmiao. Since 1955, Tua Ya Pek has been channelled there continuously by a line of *tang-ki*, each one mentored by the last, and, at the time of writing, by the temple's sixth *tang-ki*.

Professor Wang Chengfa considers the channelling of Tua Ya Pek at Tiandeyuan Xunyin Fu as the start of a new cult, noting: "If they have the first *tang-ki* to trance Tua Ya Pek as a god of gambling, they challenge the status of both the priest Lin Zhangshan and of orthodox Taoism."[12]

Soon after Tua Ya Pek was first channelled at Tiandeyuan Xunyin Fu, two further Underworld deities entered their *tang-ki*, the 'Laughing God' Lo Qio Sian Pek, referred to as Qio Pek, and the 'Bone God' Pai Gu Pek.[13] Always portrayed in statue form as a pair, the Bone God and Laughing God had popular appeal and, since the 1990s, their statues have become increasingly common on Penang's Underworld temple altars. The Laughing God, channelled through his *tang-ki* in Farlim, recalled that when the Laughing God was alive he was an extremely joyous and philanthropic businessman from China, Mr Wang Wenjiu, who had financial interests in Penang. Although he looks stern in iconic form, he arrives laughing when channelled through his *tang-ki*.

The Bone God has two mythologies, one promoted by each of his best-known *tang-ki*. They credit the difference to the Bone God first channelled at Tiandeyuan Xunyin Fu hailing from the Fourth Court of the Underworld, and the other, channelled by the second *tang-ki*, hailing from the Tenth Court. Holding the same rank as Tua Di Ya Pek in the Underworld, when channelled through their *tang-ki* the two Pai Gu Pek appear to be close friends. Their histories were related to me by the two *tang-ki* when not in trance possession states, the second verified by the *tang-ki*'s father, who commissioned Tiandeyuan Xunyin Fu's first Pai Gu Pek statue.

The gentleman deified as the Fourth Court Pai Gu Pek was channelled for over thirty years by Lee Huck Chye at Tiandeyuan Xunyin Fu and has been channelled by him in Farlim's Xunyin Miao since 2010. Prior to his death and deification in the Underworld, the gentleman lived in Penang but, as he looked and spoke Japanese, he was detained by police on suspicion of

---

12 Conversation on 20 February 2018.
13 Literally 'Rib Uncle', as his ribs are visible in his iconography.

spying. Mistreated and underfed, he lost weight rapidly, his rib cage becoming clearly visible under his skin. Not long before Tua Ya Pek's first exploits at the City God temple he was reported as missing from his prison cell but had actually died there.

In contrast, the Tenth Court Pai Gu Pek was originally a high-ranking Japanese officer who served in Penang during the Second World War. Both a vegetarian and a humanitarian, he was executed for trying to prevent Chinese civilians from being shot. When channelled at Qingyun Dian in Jelutong, instead of consuming Guinness or cognac, he drinks Japanese rice wine (*sake*), receives offerings of *sushi* and proudly displays a *samurai* sword in a cabinet next to his altar table. Qingyun Dian opened in 1998; although its *tang-ki* is known as far afield as Kuala Lumpur and Singapore through reciprocal ritual networks, at the time of writing, outside of Penang there are no other dedicated Pai Gu Pek temples.

Elsewhere in Penang, the channelling of Tua Di Ya Pek became popularised at house altars, and later in established temples where Underworld altars had been added to meet the increasing supply of Underworld *tang-ki* and the demand for their services. In the majority of temples dedicated to Heaven deities and built before 1970, Underworld altars were added after their popularisation from the mid-1970s onwards, while temples built in Penang after the mid-1970s commonly included a dedicated Underworld altar room adjoining the temple. There was a general surge in the popularity of Underworld temples in Penang in the 1970s and 1990s. According to temple owners, this corresponds to the second generation of *tang-ki* mentored in the 1960s, and third generation mentored by them in the 1980s who either established their own temples or channelled Underworld deities in older temples. These temples commonly contain a large collection of Underworld deity statues, many of whom are not worshipped outside of Penang. In addition to the locally renowned Laughing God and Bone God, these include 'Uncle North' (Bak Ya Pek), 'Uncle Red' (Ang Ya Pek) and 'Uncle Wealth' (Zai Ya Pek). Also, the earliest statues of Underworld deities who are now worshipped more widely, including the 'Ghost Emperors of the Five Directions' (Wu Fang Gui Di), Sa Ya Pek and Hell's treasurer 'Uncle Gold' (Kim Ya Pek) are said to be housed in Penang.

There are three further features prolific in Penang's Underworld temple landscape which are less common elsewhere in Malaysia and seldom found in Singapore. First, while in all locations flags representing the external camps of the Generals of the Five Directions are placed beyond a temple's threshold, in Singapore, and regulated by the HDB, a parcel of land reserved for one religious group may not be used by another. By law, "Legal provisions demarcate appropriate physical public spaces as places of worship for various religious groups" (Gee, 2011: 10), and therefore the flags are generally placed in corners of the temple's grounds. In the numerous HDB home temples, the flags are commonly bunched together with a censer outside the apartment's entrance. Under the 2001 revised edition of the Maintenance of Religious Harmony Act, placing them in a public space would risk causing friction between different religious groups and is therefore forbidden. However, most Malaysian temples place one set of flags within their grounds, and a second set up to a kilometre from the temple, with the central camp's flag used to determine the location of the others, thereby vastly extending the perimeter of a temple's spiritual protection. Each flag is accompanied by a censer at which incense is lit daily, once again the ritual act being shaped by the material culture and the material culture by official regulations.

The second and related element is the inclusion of a hollow bamboo post representing either the external camps of the Underworld Generals of the Five Directions or the outside camp of Tua Di Ya Pek's combined ghost armies (*wai ying* / 外营). Placed at the furthest position from the temple proper, either on the perimeter of the temple's grounds or at the closest road intersection,[14] both varieties of external altars to Underworld Camps are a ubiquitous feature of Penang's Underworld temple landscape, and commonly found in Underworld temples elsewhere in Malaysia. Both contain a second army of Underworld bamboo spirits (*yin zhu jun* / 阴竹军) who are sinister, unpredictable and vicious in nature. The post itself is a section of one to three internodes cut from the culm of a mature plant, commonly measuring one to two metres in height and ten to fifteen centimetres in diameter. Containing various ritual objects, its 'eyes are opened' at a temple's inauguration. Inside, the bottom layer consists of incense ash either from the censer of the deities whose spirit soldiers it contains, or occasionally from a censer dedicated to the warrior deity the Emperor of the Dark Heavens who has the power to control the bamboo spirits. Five stylised Chinese coins (*gu tongqian* / 古铜钱) are embedded in the ash, representing the four cardinal directions of the compass, with the central coin rooting a vertical axis connecting the Heaven, Earth and Underworld realms. The upper section is filled with sand, with the head of a white cockerel placed in the centre. The head represents the bamboo spirit's commanding officer and is severed as a reminder of the fate awaiting in the Underworld for disloyalty or disobedience. The entire contents are then drenched with the blood of a black dog until no more can be absorbed. The blood serves two purposes, as an ingredient thought to bridge the void between the physical and spirit worlds,

---

14 Most commonly in Farlim, where, due to the high concentration of temples, they also serve as a ritual marker designating the jurisdiction of the temple's outside camps.

thereby allowing the bamboo spirits to summon more brethren to protect the ritual space when required, and as a means to control the bamboo spirit's souls inside by preventing them from reincarnating. The top of the bamboo is sealed with red cloth, and flags of the deities in command of the camps are attached, along with a talisman drawn by their *tang-ki* when channelling the most senior deity. Yellow talismans are rare, as they represent Heaven deities; red and white talismans represent the elements of fire and metal, which the bamboo spirits fear and which therefore keep them subservient; and the more common green talismans represent the power and authority of a Hell deity. The configuration is completed with a censer, an open area to place offerings of food and drink for the soldiers, and an umbrella, as the bamboo spirits belong to the subterranean *yin* world and shun the sunlight. Due to the restrictions of the Religious Harmony Act, external altars to the Underworld Camps play a minimal and secretive role in Singapore's temple landscape.[15]

The third difference lies in the adornment of the thrones that *tang-ki* use to channel Underworld deities. While in both locations the arm-rests are commonly decorated with images of Ox Head and Horse Face, in Malaysia, and particularly ubiquitous in Penang, their backs are overlaid with decorative spirals of carefully folded joss money up to four metres in length. Some thrones are so heavily laden with them that from behind they obscure the deity channelled.

It is also a common practice for devotees to hang bags of gold and silver ingots constructed from joss money over the backs of these thrones, and, after they have been blessed with Ah Pek's name chop and a talisman has been drawn on the bag, they are taken home by devotees to attract wealth to their dwellings. These two features distinguish Tua Di Ya Pek specifically as gods of wealth in the Malaysian tradition, but not in Singapore's, where the features were only later adopted by Bao Bei Ya temples and their *tang-ki*.

The analytical significance of these three features, in common with feeding Tua Di Ya Pek opium through their statues' tongues, is that they indicate Penang as the most likely source of much of the tradition's material culture. Penang's role in the origins of the modern Underworld tradition will discussed further in the following chapter.

---

15 If included, they are placed just inside a temple's grounds, or, as at Yu Feng Nan Fu Xuanshan Miao, placed outside the temple gates only when the temple is open during Seventh Month and at the temple's anniversary.

11.1 Underworld throne in Penang

12

Analysis and conclusions

The historical dissemination of the Underworld tradition

The evidence from Penang, pointing to the modern Underworld tradition in Malaysia originating from its City God temple and Tiandeyuan Xunyin Fu, is compelling. This conclusion is supported by the fact that Penang hosts both the greatest assortment of Underworld deities to be worshipped and channelled in any location, and George Town the highest density of Underworld temples in Malaysia. This suggests that Penang's Underworld tradition has had the longest time in which to diversify. In addition, the 'sending off' of Da Shi Ye, the channelling of Underworld deities and Tua Di Ya Pek's actual rather than mythological opium consumption all originated in Penang. However, while much of the ritual and material roots of the contemporary Underworld tradition clearly originated in Penang, this is not to say that the tradition's post-1955 developments did not evolve in multiple locations.

With divisions of incense from Penang Chenghuangmiao's Tua Di Ya Pek's censers taken to Singapore soon after 1955, of analytical interest is the degree and duration of the influence of Penang's Underworld tradition on Singapore's, and the timeline of its cultural transmission both in and between Singapore and other locations in Malaysia. Even though Singapore had achieved *de facto* self-rule by 1958[1] and became a part of Malaysia only from 1963 to 1965, neither ritual links nor family ties between ethnic Chinese in Singapore and Malaysia were uncommon, and these likely contributed to a largely shared material culture based on the same inversion of cosmological emphasis. While Anxi Chenghuangmiao can be dismissed

1 Britain maintained control of foreign affairs and defence until 1963.

as the origin of the modern tradition, given its early links with Singapore's Jiucaiba Chenghuangmiao, and Jiucaiba Chenghuangmiao's influence on both Singapore's Underworld tradition and the transformation of Anxi Chenghuangmiao into a pilgrimage site, I will take Singapore and Malaysia's eldest City God temples as a starting point.

In contrast to Penang, where the local City God and Tua Di Ya Pek have been venerated since 1862, when the first Chenghuang statue was brought from Anxi to Singapore in 1917, due to its association with the Underworld, no one wanted to keep it in their house.[2] It was therefore first housed in the business premises of a puppet theatre[3] on Craig Road, Tanjung Pagar. Only after one of the two owners, Mr Zhang Wuwen, opened his own theatre company in the early 1920s was the statue placed in a public temple, first in a small Jade Emperor temple[4] before moving to the original Jiucaiba Chenghuangmiao in 1938. This temple was built in Lorong Khoo Chye, between present-day Pereira Road and Little Road, but was relocated several times, the statue finding a permanent home only when the present-day Jiucaiba Chenghuangmiao was completed in 1989. As Anxi Chenghuangmiao's connection with Singapore predates that in Malaysia, it may be surmised that Singapore's Underworld tradition was initially more closely associated with Anxi than Malaysia's. However, as was shown in Chapter 10, while Anxi Chenghuangmiao promoted its City God tradition internationally, only after the popularisation of the Underworld tradition did it promote its own Tua Di Ya Pek or become physically associated with the site of their graves.

Given the initial reaction to an Underworld deity arriving in Singapore, it is perhaps not surprising that when Tua Di Ya Pek were first channelled in the late 1950s[5] the practice was both uncommon and frowned upon.[6] There were also major differences between the early Underworld traditions, with Singapore's Tua Di Ya Pek being addressed as Ba Ye Gong and Jiu Ye Gong, the same titles as in Anxi Chenghuangmiao. Neither did their *tang-ki* smoke opium or drink alcohol, instead drinking three cups of hot tea before speaking, and eating five pieces of red bean cake, *dousha bing* (豆沙饼), with Guinness and cognac introduced into the material culture only in the early 1980s. Moreover, when new temples wanted replica statues of Anxi's Ba Ye Gong and Jiu Ye Gong, they had to be obtained through Singapore's

---

2 Interviews with Jiucaiba Chenghuangmiao's management committee, 2016.
3 Laoquanan Zhangzhong Ban.
4 Fenglishan Tiangong Tan, now Maris Stella High School.
5 The elders at Jiucaiba Chenghuangmiao interviewed in 2016 first recalled them being channelled in 1957 and 1958.
6 Interviews with Jiucaiba Chenghuangmiao's management committee, 2016.

City God temple, who were reluctant to provide them to unknown *tang-ki*, so most of Singapore's early statues were imported from Malaysia.[7] The process of material acquisition was accompanied by cultural transmission, and by the 1970s Ba Ye Gong and Jiu Ye Gong had become largely obsolete titles, the two deities commonly being referred to by devotees as Tua Di Ya Pek as in Malaysia.

While Tua Di Ya Pek in both locations have been associated with gambling and financial gain, in Singapore the Underworld God of Wealth Bao Bei Ya has become increasingly prominent both in statue form and channelled by *tang-ki*. As a result, Tua Di Ya Pek are now more frequently turned to for healing, luck changing and foetus assistance rituals; Seventh Month graveyard salvation rituals; conflict resolution between parents and children; blessings; and providing protective talismans. Devotees in Malaysia also consult Tua Di Ya Pek for a plethora of reasons, but gambling, the accumulation of wealth and business success, along with exorcisms, feature more prominently.

The question therefore arises of whether the modern Underworld tradition's ritual and material cultures in Singapore were initially transferred directly from Penang, moved gradually south through Malaysia first, or developed independently in one or the other location. There is no absolute answer to this, as, while Jiuciba Chenghuangmiao's recollections suggest that in the late 1950s there were significant differences in the material culture, commonalities with the Penang tradition include Underworld deities' shared association with opium and gambling, and similarities in Tua Di Ya Pek's iconography incorporating their black faces, ferocious looks and Tua Ya Pek's exaggerated lolling tongue that all differ from Anxi's more conservative representations.

The diversities between the two traditions, including different interpretations of post-mortal cosmology, the centrality of cemetery rituals and Sinification of Datuk Gong in Singapore, and Malaysia's large-scale Ah Pek parties and inversions of the Heaven–Underworld hierarchy, are all later developments, self-perpetuating mechanisms that have emerged in response to adversity caused by differing combinations of societal catalysts. The implication of this is that, after the *tang-ki*-centric Underworld tradition was first brought to Singapore from Penang, the channelling of Underworld deities in Singapore developed independently along a similar timeline to Penang, and therefore prior to the development of the Underworld tradition in central and southern Malaysia. This is confirmed by evidence from the City God temples in Kuala Lumpur and Muar of the Underworld tradition not being fully accepted and incorporated into the local religious landscapes until the

7 Ibid.

late 1980s. Given the earlier popularisation of Tua Di Ya Pek in Penang and Singapore; Penang's 'Laughing God', 'Bone God' and other Underworld deities remaining locally worshipped; and the Johor–Singapore Causeway providing convenient road and rail links between Singapore and Johor State, it is probable that Singapore's Tua Di Ya Pek tradition bore a significant influence on the development of the Underworld tradition in the southern half of peninsular Malaysia prior to Anxi's later involvement.

Self-perpetuating technologies of religious synthesis: Singapore, Malaysia and Taiwan

Returning then to technologies of religious synthesis, the autonomous development of the two Underworld traditions following Singapore's independence in 1965 accounts for the deviations between them brought about by two distinct sets of societal catalysts. These can be categorised by appropriation, absorption, transfiguration, hybridisation and transfiguring hybridisation, and the invention, reinvention, reinterpretation, inversion and Sinification of tradition in three principal areas. These include ritual and material cultures; new, reconstructed and re-emphasised cosmologies; and forms of temple networking in the religious and secular arenas. Many of the diversifications fall into overlapping categories, for instance where an absorbed or appropriated tradition has been reinvented, or where reinterpretations of cosmology have led to the addition of material objects necessitating the invention of new ritual forms. Examples of the former include Datuk Gong in Singapore (Chapter 4) and *luk thep* dolls at Muar (Chapter 8), while examples of the latter include the 'sending off' of Da Shi Ye in Singapore's cemetery rituals (Chapter 6) and luck-promoting coffin rituals in Kuala Lumpur (Chapter 9). With the catalysts to individual differences between Singapore and Malaysia's Underworld traditions having been accounted for either in the ethnography or concluding discussions in each chapter, to avoid uncalled-for repetition, and taking into account that Anxi's first replica statues arrived in Taiwan long before their presence in Southeast Asia, the analysis will address the question of why a similar Underworld tradition has not developed in Taiwan.

The answer is best illustrated by comparing the societal catalysts that have shaped Taiwan's religious landscape over a corresponding timeframe with those that have shaped Singapore and Malaysia's. This will show how different traditions and institutions fulfilling comparable functions to the *tang-ki*-centric Underworld tradition have flourished in Taiwan, and how societal catalysts in Taiwan have precluded the likelihood of a comparable Underworld tradition materialising there. The following analysis is therefore intended to illustrate the value of combining historical sociology with a framework of self-perpetuating technologies of religious synthesis to provide causal explanations for differential patterns of religious evolution in multiple locations.

As a starting point, in Chapter 2 I noted that the Japanese 'purge through purification' (1941–1945), where "Japanese massacres left the whole island[8] [and peninsular Malaysia][9] littered, in the imagination of many Chinese, with countless unsatisfied ghosts" (Elliott, 1990: 18), had the causative effect of creating a deep-rooted fear of ghosts, albeit subliminal, and a perceived need to control them. With Tua Di Ya Pek's responsibilities including the capture and return of ghosts to the Underworld, I suggested that a collective historic memory of the massacres facilitated the initial and gradual rise to dominance of Underworld deities over the Heaven deities in the post-war period. In contrast, during the Second World War there were very few deaths in Taiwan, and those conscripted into the Japanese army died overseas, meaning that the ghosts of the war dead were thus detached from Taiwan's religious landscape.

Of greater significance, though, is that, long before Tua Di Ya Pek's popularisation, the power of potentially malicious ghosts and wandering spirits had already been harnessed in Taiwan by their reinvention as individual deities comprised of multiple anonymous souls, venerated ghosts known as 'Ten Thousand Good Gentlemen'. Commonly created from the bones of unclaimed and forgotten bodies buried together with a small shrine, after receiving sufficient worship a hybridisation occurs and the ghosts take on the attributes of a deity. An early example dating from 1822 can be found in Tainan County's Nankunshen Temple, personified as 'The Young Duke' Jianzi Gong. Venerated ghosts may be worshipped for varied reasons, but are most often associated with good luck, especially so in gambling.[10]

As described in Chapter 4, by the 1980s ghost temples were playing an important role in Taiwan's vernacular temple landscape, and before the 1990 stock market crash these temples were visited as frequently as the eldest and often palatial Heaven temples dedicated to deities including Mazu, Guanyin and Taiwan's 'Royal Lords', Wangye. Two coinciding societal catalysts have previously been identified with ghost temples' 1980s popularity, the first being a change in moral values that was influenced by the disintegration of the traditional extended family and lineage structures in the shift from a rural to industrial economy (Clart, 2003), and the second being government

---

8 Singapore.
9 Author's addition.
10 Interviews with Nankunshen's management committee, February 2007.

policy promoting an export-orientated economic policy combined with "minimal state support beyond education and infrastructure" (Weller, 2000: 494). Rapid industrialisation and increasing exports generated a huge excess of expendable private wealth, a phenomenon often referred to as Taiwan's 'economic miracle' (Gold, 1986). In Taiwan's 'gambler's economy', with a stock market boom and vast amounts of capital literally being gambled on shares, ghost temples gained a reputation for choosing profitable stock market investments and for selecting winning lottery numbers. Therefore, Taiwan's ghost temples and Tua Di Ya Pek *tang-ki* served similar functions, and both reasserted perceived control over potentially malicious spirits, the former by providing them with offerings and veneration and the latter through their ability to subdue them.

Returning to the Japanese influence on Taiwan, during the colonial era (1895–1945) as a modern infrastructure of roads, railways, schools, sewerage and hospitals were built, it is unlikely that either Taiwan's post-war economic miracle and the new belief circles that emerged from it, could have proceeded at such a rapid pace without these Japanese contributions. The 'Japanisation Movement' that emerged in the late 1930s sought to transform the residents of Taiwan into Japanese citizens, and many local residents adopted Japanese names, while in return Taiwan produced food supplies to support Japan's war machine. Due to the thirty-eight years of martial law under the KMT which followed (1949–1987), the Japanese colonial era is still perceived by elders as a 'golden age', and transnational flows of Japanese popular culture have remained fashionable into the present. One such flow has resulted in another unique feature of Taiwan's temple landscape, namely, foetus ghost appeasement temples. These have precluded the need for Underworld deities to speed foetus spirits' reincarnation (Chapter 5) and rendered the possibility of their enlistment into a temple's private spirit army through appropriation and reinvention as malicious foetus ghosts (Chapter 7) insupportable in Taiwan's vernacular tradition.

The first foetus-appeasement rituals occurred after 1945 among new religious movements in Japan. By the 1970s the tradition had evolved, greater emphasis being placed on the influence of spirits over human affairs, foetus ghosts being attributed with the power, "unless ritualised appropriately" (Hardacre, 1997: 58), to punish and menace their own would-have-been parents. Soon after, popularised by emotive visual imagery in Japanese tabloids, malevolent foetus ghosts were first appropriated into Chinese vernacular religion along with other cultural imports including soap operas, comic books and fashion items from Japan in the 1970s (Moskowitz, 1998, 2001; Hardacre, 1997). Initially foetus ghosts played a minor role in Taiwan's religious landscape; the societal catalyst which propelled foetus-appeasement rituals into a 'national phenomenon' was the eugenics legislation of 1985, which essentially decriminalised abortion – a fact reflected by the coincidence of the increasing popularisation of new foetus-appeasement rituals marketed to provide spiritual support for parents and the step-by-step process of fully legalising abortion.

By the 1990s appeasement rituals were in high demand, but, with no customary format or set duration, new rituals were variously invented by temples' proprietors. Illustrating this and the Sinification of tradition, Moskowitz (2001) compares several temples, reporting that at one Taoist temple one to three days of burning incense to Guan Gong and Qingshui Zushi was sufficient, while at a Buddhist temple[11] burning oil lamps before a Bodhisattva statue for one to two months was prescribed. At Taiwan's oldest and largest foetus ghost temple, Longhu Gong in Miaoli County, where since opening in 1978 in excess of 16,000 foetus ghost statues have been housed, the process of appeasement takes three years. It includes a printed appeal to Heaven deities, including an admission of guilt and an apology, burning ghost money, prayers at two ceremonies per year and the naming of a small metal foetus ghost statue, with the potential for the foetus ghost to gain deity status for an additional charge of 10,600 Taiwan dollars.[12]

Differing combinations of societal catalysts have prevented Taiwan's foetus ghost tradition from developing in Singapore and Malaysia. First, the Underworld tradition was becoming established when the Japanese tradition first entered Taiwan's religious landscape, and by the mid-1980s Tua Di Ya Pek had already been accredited with the ability and moral responsibility of assisting the souls of foetus spirits in their post-mortal journeys. Second, ghost temples had become among the most popular in Taiwan and, as it was already normative to make offerings at ghost temples, making similar offerings to foetus ghosts was an extension, albeit with a hybridisation of meaning, of an existing precedent. This was not the case in either Singapore or Malaysia. In Singapore, a fear of wandering spirits, later exacerbated by the ongoing removal of graves in the urban renewal process, left little appetite or space for the addition of a new 'imported' vindictive ghost into its local cosmology. Political factors also bore a significant influence. Turning to international relations, in contrast to Taiwan's 'Three-Noes Policy' ('*San bu zhengce*' / 三不政策) of 'no contact, no compromise and no negotiation' with China

---

11 In these examples, Taoist and Buddhist refer to their primary deities, not to membership of orthodox associations.
12 Conversations with Longhu Gong's manager, 26 December 2018.

instigated by President Chiang Ching-kuo between 1979 and 1986, affable Sino-Singapore relations were firmly established in the same era. Prime Minister Lee Kuan Yew visited China in 1976, 1980 and 1986, and Deng Xiaoping and the Chinese Premier Zhao Ziyang paid reciprocal visits to Singapore in 1978 and 1981. Thus, while cultural flows from China to Taiwan were minimal, so were cultural flows into Singapore from Taiwan. Therefore, although Singaporean abortion laws developed along similar lines to Taiwan's, with the 1968 Abortion Bill first legalising abortions and the 1980 amendments simplifying the process,[13] neither Taiwan's foetus ghost-appeasement rituals nor the Japanese concept of malicious foetus ghosts entered Singapore's religious landscape.

In Malaysia, in contrast, beyond the bias against Japanese cultural flows into Malaysia, after 1957 the only legal basis for abortion was to save the life of a pregnant woman. Then, in April 1989, section 312 of Act 727 of the Penal Code was amended permitting abortion, but only if a registered doctor deemed that the pregnancy might risk the life of the mother or cause mental or physical injury to the patient. The penalty for violating this law was up to seven years' imprisonment for both the abortionist and abortee. Essentially, the lack of sufficient foetus spirits to placate prevented their commoditisation and, as noted, Malaysia's sizeable Thai population and proximity to Thailand were the primary societal catalysts to the reinvention of foetus spirits and Thai *kuman thong* as malicious foetus ghosts in its Underworld tradition.

Before I move on to ritual network formation in Taiwan's broader temple landscape, the influence of early KMT legislation in the Republic of China on Taiwan's post-war *tang-ki* tradition should be noted, and compared to the absence of equivalent laws in Singapore and Malaysia's historical influences, as the KMT restrictions on *tang-ki* later contributed to the popularisation of Taiwan's belief circles.

During British colonial rule in Singapore, unless rituals caused social disorder through either blocking traffic or causing too much noise, the British colonial government "left the Chinese completely free to organize their religious groupings and express their religious beliefs in any way they chose, manifesting an indifference to religion which amounted to a tolerance not provided in the Chinese homeland" (Freedman & Topley, 1961: 12). This also allowed spirit-mediums "more space to innovate in Southeast Asia" (Dean, 2019: 76) and enabled their practices to flourish relatively unhindered as compared to either Taiwan or Anxi under the CCP. In Taiwan's Japanese era, *tang-ki* "were forbidden to exist" (Jordan, 1972: 69), after which, based

---

13 Abortion Bill No. 40/1968, and Abortion (Amendment) Bill No. 20/1980.

on earlier legislation, *tang-ki* traditions were discouraged by the Nationalist government after 1948. The 1928 Standards for Preserving and Abandoning Gods and Shrines, promulgated by the KMT in Mainland China, was maintained under KMT rule in Taiwan, and superstition was set apart as an obstacle to social progress. Two further laws reinforced this, the Procedure for the Abolition of Occupations of Divination, Astrology, Physiognomy and Palmistry, Sorcery and Geomancy (1928) and the Procedures for Banning and Managing Superstitious Objects and Professions (1930), both of which discriminated against *tang-ki* vis-à-vis historical non-*tang-ki* temples. While they were initially a political move to take control of anti-government groups and extend the power of the state into the villages in China, the prohibitions affected the vernacular tradition in Taiwan, until the advent of democracy, through promoting older temples of historical significance while restricting spirit-medium practices. This had the effect of making temples themselves central to Taiwan's religious landscape and, while *tang-ki* continued to channel Heaven deities in Taiwan, it effectively prevented *tang-ki*-centric deity cults from dominating Taiwan's temple landscape in the same period that the *tang-ki* tradition came to prominence Singapore's and Malaysia's.

Contemporary ritual networks among southern Malaysia's Underworld *tang-ki* temples evolved from the previously guarded British settlements which transformed into ethnic Chinese communities in 1958, along with earlier Chinese temples in larger towns. From the mid-1980s in Singapore, new reciprocal ritual networks between temples were most commonly formed through *tang-ki*, large numbers of whom channelled Underworld deities at new HDB home altars. Similar *tang-ki* networks have been forming in post-1990 Malaysia, and these have fortified links in and between emerging temple-based ethno-religious communities. In addition, following urban relocation, Singapore's earlier ceremonial circles have all but been replaced by a secondary form of temple networking based on past proximity in demolished villages. Lacking the societal catalysts triggering these developments, namely, forced urban relocation in Singapore and the implementation of the NEP in Malaysia, Taiwan's temple landscape developed quite differently over a corresponding period.

The underlying catalysts to change included a steep rise in living standards in Taiwan since the 1950s, "shared not just by private families and individuals, but also by virtually all Taiwan institutions, including religious institutions" (Jordan, 1994: 139), and the custom in Taiwan for devotees to make temple donations in the form of gold objects to adorn temple altars. However, the actual catalyst to change came from overseas when, in 1971, the United States abandoned its fixed exchange rate of gold at US$35 per ounce, causing gold prices to rise significantly. This multiplied the value of gold assets held by temples which could be put to use in constructing new, grander buildings and an infrastructure of roads and guesthouses for those who wished to visit them. Thus, coinciding with the economic boom of the 1970s, "Temple building has increased in tempo and scale beyond belief" (Pas, 1996: 133). Land prices in major cities skyrocketed during the 'Taiwan miracle', so new temples were mostly built on non-agricultural land and in developing urban districts. Increasing temple construction reshaped the religious landscape by facilitating the growth of Taiwan's temple networks in the form of expanding belief circles, with the same economic forces that had inflated land prices also providing the means to visit them. The number of registered motor vehicles in Taiwan increased from 819,104 in 1970 to 4,665,433 a decade later, and by 2015 the total number had reached 21,400,897.[14] Of these, the number of buses increased from 7,954 to 34,890,[15] many owned directly by temples servicing new, media-sponsored religious tourism. Nankunshen has among the largest ritual networks,[16] its growth facilitated by Taiwan's infrastructure projects. Before 1986 it had no road linking it to any major towns, received few pilgrims and served only six local rural communities. However, since the construction of a major road and both parking and tourist facilities built by the temple in 1996, at least half a million pilgrims have visited each year.[17] In relation to the expansion of its belief circle, in 2007 approximately 1,300 replicas, each representing a connected temple, returned to 'recharge' their statues' spiritual efficacy,[18] with each temple having bought their replica statues and making donations on return visits. By 2018 the number had reportedly increased to over 27,000.[19]

Belief circles based on the worship of replicas of Taiwan's eldest deity statues from historic temples have come to dominate the temple landscape over a corresponding timeframe to the Underworld tradition's popularisation in Singapore and Malaysia. This has left little room for other new deity cults or traditions to emerge. When they have done so, new vernacular traditions have been primarily profit driven and temple based rather than *tang-ki* centric, the new foetus-appeasement temples typifying this trend.

---

14 From *Taiwan statistical data book 2016*, National Development Council ROC.
15 Ibid.
16 Two Mazu temples, Beigang Chaotian Gong and Dajia Zhenlan Gong, have similarly extensive networks based on replica statues.
17 Interviews with Wu Yiming, Head of Public Relations, December 2006 and February 2007
18 Ibid.
19 https://n.yam.com/Article/20180629283342, cited on 20 December 2018. The difference between earlier temple networks based on replica statues and divisions of incense and Taiwan's new belief circles is that the latter resulted from modern communications and transportation, and the breakdown of older traditional temple networks.

A second example exemplifying the commodification of religious culture are Taiwan's new money god temples, which have reinterpreted, ritualised and successfully marketed money gods' prevailing cosmology.[20]

Fulfilling a similar function to Bao Bei Ya in Singapore, 'Uncle Wealth' (Zai Ya Pek) and 'Uncle Gold' (Kim Ya Pek) in Malaysia and Tua Di Ya Pek in both locations in their role as Underworld gods of wealth, Taiwan's new money god temples have thrived since the end of Taiwan's economic boom. In these temples, devotees use divination blocks to ask the deities to lend them small amounts of actual Taiwan dollars, designated as fortune money (*facai jin* / 发财金), which symbolise a deity's intention to positively influence the recipient's financial well-being. The borrowed money is commonly returned with interest at a later date.[21] Money god temples thus act as banking intermediaries between deities and devotees and reap the financial rewards. The first temple to do so was Sheliao Zinan Gong in the 1930s, the bargaining process becoming ritualised in the 1950s, with the temple lending between 100 and 600 Taiwan dollars, depending on the fall of practitioners' divination blocks. According to the temple's vice-manager, Mr Chen,[22] between 1940 and 1950 the number of visitors lent money rose from approximately twenty to two hundred. Coinciding with better transportation links and private vehicle ownership, the number increased to an estimated one million visits by 1990 and approximately six million by 2000. Mr Chen estimated that in 2013 there were ten million visits, and added that in 2013 the temple earned approximately NT$200 million (£4.23 million) profit, that is, interest paid on the initial amounts lent. The societal catalyst triggering the more recent conversion of existing temples or construction of new money god temples was the 1990 stock market crash. With quick and almost certain profits from share trading no longer available to everyday investors, a primary function of ghost temples was transferred to money god temples, whose deities offered to provide good fortune for a minimal fee. Two newer money god temples are worthy of mention. These are Shiding Wu Lu Caishen Miao, as it has formed its own belief circle based on replicas of its 'Money Gods of the Five Directions', central to which is the deity Zhao Gongming, and Taichung Guangtian Gong, where the financial exchange is immediate, visitors paying the temple a minimum of 360 Taiwan dollars for 168 Taiwan dollars of 'fortune money'. With ghost temples still providing possible combinations of

---

20 The same money gods are commonly found on other temples' altars, most notably Tudi Gong and Zhao Gongming, but money is not borrowed from them.
21 The recipient decides how much money to return, several hundred interviews in 2013 revealing that the interest rates paid varied between 100% and 2,500%, depending on the amount borrowed and the perceived good fortune experienced.
22 Interviewed in 2013.

winning lottery numbers, and money god temples offering deific assistance in the accumulation of wealth, other deity cults would be redundant in this pragmatic ritual sphere.

As was noted in Chapter 4, Underworld deities are not entirely absent from Taiwan's religious landscape, but, rather than channelled or worshipped, are portrayed through their participation in the Eight Infernal Generals performance troupes and as giant puppets, and as peripheral statues in Taiwan's City God temples. However, as the Underworld in general and its lower-ranking enforcers in particular remain a taboo subject in Taiwan, Tua Di Ya Pek's mythologies remain largely unknown, and the primary task attributed to them in the Underworld tradition, of collecting the souls of the dead, remains associated with Ox Head and Horse Face in Taiwan.[23]

On a similar note, a famous morality tract called *Journeys to the Underworld* (*Diyu Youji*) was composed by planchette divination at Shengxian Tang in Taichung, Taiwan between 1976 and 1978 by the medium Yang Zanru.[24] The book describes multiple visits which the author made in spirit form to the Underworld with Jigong as his guide. In the tradition of morality tracts, *Diyu Youji* was widely distributed in Taiwan, Singapore and Malaysia. While this tract may have had some influence on the Underworld tradition in the late 1970s, its impact in Taiwan has been minimal, as the Underworld has remained a taboo topic.[25] When I first asked Singaporean practitioners about the book in 2010, I was advised to 'take it with a pinch of salt', as it was widely perceived as written for the self-promotion of Yang Zanru and his temple. Most often, I was told that if I wanted to know the truth about the Underworld, Underworld deities were always at hand to ask. This advice resonated with the research methodology I was already employing, local perceptions of *Diyu Youji* reconfirming my own commitment to a dialogic approach in researching *tang-ki* in the Underworld tradition.

Final reflections

Modernity has become an inevitable backdrop to religious change, changes which are manifesting in multiple guises in most, if not in all, of the world's major spiritual and religious traditions. In Chapter 2 I set out the hypothesis

---

23 As it did in Singapore and Malaysia before Tua Di Ya Pek's popularisation.
24 Not a *tang-ki*, as, rather than channelling deities, he went on spirit journeys.
25 Any influence that *Diyu Youji* may have had in all three religious landscapes was nullified in 2013. Yang Zanru was ordained as a Buddhist monk in 1997 and founded a monastery in Taichung, where he abused his power to obtain sexual favours. In 2013 he was sentenced to ten years in prison for multiple counts of sexual indecency and for sexual assaults against five women. This effectively discredited the author and the contents of *Diyu Youji*, both in the Underworld tradition and in Taiwan.

that religious developments occur in response to societal catalysts triggering technologies of religious synthesis, resulting in subsequent developments serving to perpetuate the broader religious tradition. In this instance, the framework of analysis has illustrated where, why, when and how the modern Underworld tradition originated, and has accounted for subsequent divergences in Singapore and Malaysia's cosmological interpretations and in their ritual and material cultures. To illustrate the analytical framework's versatility, it was then employed to explain why a similar tradition has never evolved in Taiwan. However, the three religious landscapes share one significant commonality, namely, that each new tradition which has emerged has evolved in a form that serves to perpetuate the vernacular tradition in the prevailing socio-political environment in which it has developed.[26] My aspiration is that further studies linking societal catalysts to religious developments both in Chinese vernacular religion and in other religious and spiritual traditions will provide insights which enable the analytical framework to be transformed into a predictive model to assess the most likely consequences of future societal catalysts on religious development.

Moving on, I would like to comment further on the combination of approaches that my research methodology has entailed.

Both the dialogic and participatory approaches were particularly rewarding, as they allowed me to form a bond of trust based on mutual respect and information exchanges between myself and *tang-ki* both in and out of trance possession states and, by extension, with their temples' communities. In the process, the boundaries between being an observer and a participant in the participant observation paradigm became malleable, providing close proximity access to, and often experiential knowledge of, the rituals performed. Central to this was the incorporation of an underlying ontological approach to religious phenomena, an approach supported by the universality of spiritual traditions both historically and geographically. Cognitive anthropologists have argued that this universality is inherent to human evolution, as, "Regardless of local histories or cultural innovation and transmission, our fixed, generic cognitive capacities churn out more or less the same kinds of religious outputs in all places at all times (the 'universal religious repertoire')" (Whitehouse, 2007: 229). Due to the vagaries of the words 'more or less

---

26 Taiwan's money god temples are self-perpetuating because if a devotee prospers after receiving 'fortune money' they will return to borrow more to increase their future wealth, and if they do not prosper, devotees usually return to pay interest to prevent further misfortune. Similarly, Underworld deity culture in Singapore reinforces the belief in and the fear of ghosts while providing a ritual means and physical presence through *tang-ki* to control them. The same logic applies to Malaysia's Underworld temples and events where growing ethno-religious communities and attached *guanxi* networks rely on the maintenance of a temple's prosperity and integrity and for their own continuity.

the same kinds of religious outputs', I would further qualify Whitehouse's observation by adding the caveat that no commodity can be successfully marketed without a pre-existing demand, and, in relation to many spiritual and religious traditions, this demand stems from concerned inquisitiveness concerning one's own mortality, ameliorated by the generic cognitive desire for the continuation of the human soul after physiological death. The nature of traditions and cosmologies predominant in any given time and location is therefore also dependent on historical antecedents and ongoing societal catalysts to change, both necessitating the inclusion of historical sociology in analysing contemporary spiritual and religious traditions.

Moving on to the reproduction of visual images in ethnographic texts, as the study has shown, a ritual is not a single act but a process of sequential events, where each enacted element, in the process of becoming, itself becomes a past event which cannot be duplicated with exactitude. Margaret Mead (1973) has argued that it is an ethical responsibility of anthropology as a discipline to preserve records of disappearing 'irreproducible behaviours', and therefore the photographs selected for this book illustrate the ritual and material culture at static moments in time, allowing the reader to more vividly appreciate the nuances of the tradition as captured in their moments of becoming. As with Mead's 'irreproducible behaviours', it is tautological within the framework of analysis that, as new societal catalysts emerge, the ritual practices and material culture of traditions studied will inevitably develop, and previously enacted rituals will either evolve into new forms or be supplanted.

At the time of writing, I would suggest that the mass worship of Underworld deities both at dedicated altars and animated through the embodiment of *tang-ki* is reaching a zenith, the commodification of Chinese purgatorial cosmology elevating the Underworld tradition to among the most dominant forms of lived ritual traditions in Singapore and Malaysia. Taking the framework of analysis as a future predictive model, it can be said with certainty that when the necessary societal catalysts evolve that render the Underworld tradition in one or both locations no longer the optimal self-perpetuating mechanism for the wider vernacular tradition, new deity cults with their own cosmological emphasis and ritual and material cultures will rise to ascendancy as the Underworld tradition's importance diminishes. As the analysis of Taiwan's temple landscape suggests, new traditions or deity cults will evolve, their shape, form and cosmological emphasis largely determined by the societal catalysts triggering their development. Moreover, I would expect that, as the era of 'digitalised modernity' advances, with 5G mobile networks in the making and affordable virtual reality devices already entering the consumer market, increased proficiency in the use of creative media to disseminate 'digitalised history in the making' will effectively increase the speed of cultural dissemination and actual development of future traditions. In what I have described as 'the vernacularisation of tradition', where the transmission of new ritual forms and traditions has been transferred into the public domain, it is likely that the previously slow-moving influences of transnational cultural flows will be largely replaced by smartphone culture, with future cultural flows disseminated through live online feeds and other forms of instant digital media.

Returning to the Underworld tradition, I would like to conclude by sharing two insights, both of which are open to readers' interpretation and intended to stimulate further reflection. The second was formed reflexively, regarding my own perceptions of the study's deeper-rooted significance which I shall come to shortly, and the first is transcribed from a voice recording I made in Klang during Di Ya Pek's birthday.

> *I have returned to my position on the upper-floor balcony after revisiting the party area below, and was amazed by the array of emotions shown towards Di Ya Pek by hundreds of people here: some kneeling down for blessings, others presenting him with gifts and drinking toasts, and many treating him 'as if' a film idol or pop star and collecting his autograph on their personal possessions which he signed with his thumb print. The overriding emotions I saw were adoration, devotion, respect, admiration and happiness, and these were reciprocal, not just within this community, but on reflection, between devotees and deities throughout the Underworld 'tang-ki' temples that I have visited.*
>
> *Di Ya Pek is walking up to the balcony now, so I will give him my own birthday present, a 160-million-year-old ammonite that I found on Charmouth beach,[27] and a bottle of my favourite liqueur unavailable in Malaysia. It feels appropriate to give something back, something of myself, something personal, as fieldwork should be based on a mutual relationship of give and take.*
>
> *Di Ya Pek was delighted with the fossil, and happily passed it around his inner circle of devotees to admire. I had expected him to open the bottle and share its contents, but instead he passed it to the temple's manager instructing him to place it in his Underworld altar room for safekeeping. Noting my surprise, he explained, "Today this bottle only contains alcohol, so I will wait ten years to share it with you, because then it will also contain meaning, a decade of our own friendship, and will reveal a new story to be written."*

27 In Dorset on England's Jurassic coast.

In the introduction I stated my intention of providing readers "with unique insights into the lived tradition and into the cosmology upon which contemporary ritual practices are based" and "insights into both the mindsets and the vibrant and often intense life-worlds of the religious practitioners described". I hope that I have achieved both goals. However, over the lengthy processes of writing and editing this book I have come to understand that it has traversed into unexpected territory, addressing issues which are perhaps more fundamental to the human condition. First, the quest for well-being, wealth, good fortune, belonging and codes of ethical behaviour, and second, the challenges of dealing with environmental destruction, corruption, discrimination, social self-determination, self-identity and ethnic and national identity. Beyond this, it demonstrates the invention of a tradition based on an inversion of cosmological emphasis which has evolved to deal with many of life's most emotionally wrought uncertainties: the fear of death, disposing of corpses, death itself, the possibility of life after death, the existence of spiritual beings and potential manifestations of their efficacy and, most poignantly, the possible nature of the human soul itself. Therefore, in the broadest sense, I am optimistic that this study has provided readers with an alternative methodological approach and lexicon of terminology to describe spiritual and religious phenomena, and I hope that it will inspire some to conduct further research into ritual practices and traditions, and others to question their own spiritual and doctrinal beliefs or doubts, open-mindedly, from comparative and alternative perspectives.

Appendix of Chinese names

Ah Boon	亚文
Ah Pek	阿伯
Ang Ya Pek	红爷伯
Anxi	安溪
Anxi Chenghuangmiao	安溪城隍庙
Anxi Chenghuangmiao fushu Yinfu Tan	安溪城隍庙附属阴府坛
Anxi Dongyue Si Chenghuangmiao	安溪东岳寺城隍庙
Ba Jiajiang	八家将
Ba she chuan sai xiao diyu	拔舌穿腮小地狱
Ba Ye	八爷
Ba Ye Gong	八爷公
Bai Wuchang	白无常
Bak Ya Pek	北爷伯
Bao Bei Ya	包贝爷
Bao feng bojue wu yi wushuang	褒封伯爵五邑无双
Bao Gong	包公
Beidi	北帝
Beigang Chaotian Gong	北港朝天宫
Biancheng Wang	卞城王
Cai Changyu	蔡常毓
Chen	陈
Chen Meiying	陈美英
Chen Qixin	陈其新
Chen Yiqun	陈益群
Chenghuang	城隍
Chengzong	成宗
Choa Bao Bei Ya	蔡包贝爷
Chong xi pao guan Bamin di yi	宠锡袍冠八闽第一
Chujiang Wang	楚江王
Chun	春
Cixi	慈禧
Da Bei Zhou	大悲咒

APPENDIX OF CHINESE NAMES 231

Da qi ge	大旗歌
Da Shi Ye	大士爺
Dajia Zhenlan Gong	大甲镇澜宫
Daxie shen en xun Hei Bai Wuchang	答谢神恩熏黑白无常
Di Guan Dadi	地官大帝
Di Ya Pek	二爷伯
Difang Fu	地方府
Diji Gong	地基公
Diji Zhu	地基主
Ding shi li feng xiao diyu	钉石立峰小地狱
Diyu Youji	地狱游记
Dizang pusa benyuan jing	地藏菩薩本願經
Dizangwang (Bodhisattva)	地藏王
Dong	冬
Dongshiliao Dongan Gong	东势寮东安宫
Dongyue Dadi	东岳大帝
Dongyue Si	东岳寺
Dongyue Si Chenghuangmiao	东岳寺城隍庙
Doumu Gong	斗母宫
Doumu Niang-niang	斗母娘娘
Dushi Wang	都市王
Fan Di Ya	范二爷
Fan Jiangjun	范将军
Fan Wujiu	范无救
Fazhu Gong	法主公
Fei dao huo shi diyu	飞刀火石地狱
Fengcheng	凤城
Fengdu	酆都
Fenglishan Tiangong Tan	凤梨山天公坛
Fo Shuo shiba ni li jing	佛说十八泥犁经
Foshuo Dazang zhengjao xuepen jing	佛说大藏正教血盆经
Fujian Province	福建
Gan	干
Goh Yong Hau (Dato)	吴勇豪
Guan Gong	关公
Guan Sheng Dijun	关圣帝君
Guangming Ribao	光明日报
Guanyin	观音
Gui Wang	鬼王
Guo Dacheng	郭大诚
Hao Zhu Ya	孝子爷

APPENDIX OF CHINESE NAMES

Hei Bai Wuchang	黑白无常
Hei Ling Jiangjun	黑令将军
Hei Wuchang	黑无常
Heishi Xiansheng	黑石先生
Hokkien	闽南语
Hu Jingze	胡金泽
Huaguang	华光
Huaguang Dadi	华光大帝
Huangquan	黄泉
Jian shu diyu	剑树地狱
Jianzi Gong	囝仔公
Jigong	济公
Jin Shui Gang	洴水港
Jiu Bao Bei Ya	周包贝爷
Jiu Ye Gong	九爷公
Jiucaiba Chenghuangmiao	韭菜芭城隍庙
Kang Di Ya	江二爺
Kim Ya Pek	金爷伯
Kou yan xiao diyu	抠眼小地狱
Kuomintang	国民党
Kuzhu qiao	苦竹桥
Lai Dong Sen	内东成
Laisheng Gong	来圣宫
Lang Cia Ah Pek	人车阿伯
Lang Pek	人伯
Lao You	老友
Laojun	老君
Laoquanan Zhangzhong Ban	老泉安掌中班
Lee Huck Chye	李学财
Leigong	雷公
Li Shimin	李世民
Liangfu	梁父
Lim Bao Bei Ya	林包贝爷
Lin	林
Lin Maosheng	林茂盛
Lin Yayuan	林亚源
Lin Zhangshan	林长杉
Lina	丽娜
Lingbao	灵宝
Lingguan Ma Yuanshuai	灵官马元帅
Linghai Dian	灵海殿

APPENDIX OF CHINESE NAMES 233

Liu	刘
Liutian	六天
Lo Qio Sian Pek	老笑仙伯
Longde Tang	龙德堂
Longhu Gong	龙湖宫
Lu Xian Zan	炉香赞
Mamian	马面
Mazu	妈祖
Meng Po	孟婆
Mile Pusa	弥勒菩萨
Minnan	闽南语
Minxiong Zhuang zongjiao tuanti taizhang	民雄庄宗教团体台帐
Muar Dasheng Gong Chenghuang Dian	麻坡大圣宫城隍殿
Naihe (Bridge)	奈何桥
Nan Bei Dou Xingjun	南北斗星君
Nankunshen	南鲲鯓
Nanlai Dian	南莱殿
Neicang Baibao jing	内藏百宝经
Nezha	哪吒
Nie jingtai	孽镜台
Niutou	牛头
Nong xie diyu	脓血地狱
Pai Gu Pek	排骨伯
Pangu Xianshi	盘古仙师
Pangzu	旁足
Pingdeng Wang	平等王
Qi e'ah So	青蚵仔嫂
Qi Ye	七爷
Qian Bao Bei Ya	千包贝爷
Qielan Pusa	伽蓝菩萨
Qingshui Zushi	清水祖师
Qingti	目連, 青提
Qinguang Wang	秦廣王
Qingxi Chenghuang Xianyou Bozhu wenhua zhi ye	清溪城隍显佑伯主文化之夜
Qingyun Dian	清云殿
Qio Pek	笑伯
Qiu	秋
Qiu Qiuxing	邱秋星
Sa Ya Pek	三爷伯
San Taizi	三太子

Sanbao Gong	三宝宫
Sanguan	三官
Sanqing Zushi	三清祖师
Santian	三天
Sanzhong Gong	三中宫
Shancai Tongzi	善才童子
Shangdi	上帝
Shangqing	上清
Shanlong Miao	善龙庙
She meiren	蛇美人
Sheliao Zinan Gong	社寮紫南宫
Shengan Dian (Temple)	圣安殿
Shenglian Gong	圣莲宫
Shenglin Gong	圣林宫
Shengxian Tang	圣贤堂
Shensi bu	生死簿
Shi	施
Shi Dian Da Er Ye Bo wenhua jiaoliu hui	十殿大二爷伯文化交流会
Shi Dian Yenwang	十殿阎王
Shiba nili jing	十八泥犁經
Shiba Wang Gong	十八王公
Shiding Wu Lu Caishen Miao	石碇五路财神庙
Shiwang jing	十王經
Siming Panguan	司命判官
Sin Hock Min (Foundation)	申学明
So	苏
Songdi Wang	宋帝王
Songji Zhi Zha Dian	松记纸扎店
State of Lu	鲁
Sun Wukong	孙悟空
Tai Shan	泰山
Tai shang ling bao ba du wang shan shishi keyi	太上灵宝拔度望山施食科仪
Tai shang qing shen ke	太上請神科
Tai yi jiu ku miao jing	太乙救苦妙经
Taichung Guangtian Gong	台中广天宫
Taipingjing	太平经
Taishan Fu Jun	泰山府君
Taishan Wang	泰山王
Taisui	太岁
Taiyi Jiuku Tianzun	太乙救苦天尊

APPENDIX OF CHINESE NAMES

Tan	陈
Tan Tua Lao	陳大炮
Tan Tua Ya	陈 大爷
Tao Hongjing	陶弘景
Tiandeyuan Xunyin Fu	天德园巡阴府
Tua Di Ya Pek	大二爷伯
Tua Pek Kong Beo	大伯公庙
Tua Pek Kong cian li to	大伯公千字图
Tua Pek Kung	大伯公
Tua Ya Pek	大爷伯
Tudi Gong	土地公
Wang Chengfa	王琛发
Wang Wenjiu	王文九
Wang Yijie	王益杰
Wangsi Cheng	枉死城
Wangye	王爷
Wanshan Ye	万善爷
Weiling Gong	威灵公
Wu Dan Zhou	五丹咒
Wu Fang Gui Di	五方鬼帝
Wu Jing	五经
Wu She Chenghuang Gong	五舍城隍公
Wu Yiming	吴易铭
Wuguan Wang	五官王
Wulu Caishen	五路财神
Xia	夏
Xiao Fo	笑佛
Xiao Tianping	萧天平
Xie	谢
Xie Bian	谢必安
Xie Jiangjun	谢将军
Xie Liwen	谢礼文
Xin Jing	心经
Xinjiawang Chenghuangmiao	麻坡新加望城隍庙
Xiude Foshi Tuan	修德佛事团
Xiwangmu	西王母
Xu Xiaoshan	许晓山
Xuanhuang Dian	玄皇殿
Xuantian Shangdi	玄天上帝
Xunyin Miao	巡阴庙
Yang	楊

Yang Zanru　　　　　　　　　　　　　杨赞儒
Yangzhou Jing Shui　　　　　　　　　杨枝净水赞
Yanluo Wang　　　　　　　　　　　　阎罗王
Yaozhan xiao diyu　　　　　　　　　腰斩小地狱
Yilan Jinxing Gong　　　　　　　　　宜兰进兴宫
Yinfu Tan　　　　　　　　　　　　　阴府坛
Yinyuan jing　　　　　　　　　　　　因缘经
Yong Mun Tong (Dato)　　　　　　　　杨瞒冬
You guo diyu　　　　　　　　　　　　油锅地狱
Yu Feng Nan Fu Xuanshan Miao　　　　玉封南府玄善庙
Yuanshi tianzun jidu xiehu zhengjing　　元始天尊济度血湖真经
Yulanpen (Sutra)　　　　　　　　　　盂兰盆
Yuli chao chuan　　　　　　　　　　玉历钞传
Yunshan Dian　　　　　　　　　　　云善殿
Yushan Temple　　　　　　　　　　　玉善殿
Zai Ya Pek　　　　　　　　　　　　　财爷伯
Zeng　　　　　　　　　　　　　　　曾
Zeng Zhongying　　　　　　　　　　　曾仲影
Zhang Dan　　　　　　　　　　　　　张旦
Zhang Daoling　　　　　　　　　　　张道陵
Zhang Songba　　　　　　　　　　　张松峇
Zhang Wuwen　　　　　　　　　　　张乌文
Zhao Gongming　　　　　　　　　　　赵公明
Zheng He　　　　　　　　　　　　　郑和
Zhengao　　　　　　　　　　　　　　真誥
Zhenling weiye tu　　　　　　　　　真灵位业图
Zhenlinshan Jieyuan Tang Chenghuangmiao　振林山结缘堂城隍庙
Zhenren Gong　　　　　　　　　　　真人宫
Zhong Kui　　　　　　　　　　　　　钟馗
Zhongliao Anxi Chenghuangmiao　　　中寮安溪城隍庙
Zhongyuan　　　　　　　　　　　　　中元
Zhongyuan Dadi　　　　　　　　　　中元大帝
Zhu Sheng Niang-niang　　　　　　　註生娘娘
Zhuangzi　　　　　　　　　　　　　庄子
Zhuanlun Wang　　　　　　　　　　转轮王

References

Adler, J. 2002. *Chinese religions*. London and New York: Routledge.
Ahern, E. 1973. *The cult of the dead in a Chinese village*. Stanford: Stanford University Press.
Ancuta, K. 2014. 'Asian gothic'. In J. E. Hogle (ed.), 208–223, *The Cambridge Companion to the Modern Gothic*. Cambridge: Cambridge University Press.
Aspen, H. 2001. *Amhara traditions of knowledge Spirit mediums and their clients*. Wiesbaden: Harrassowitz Verlag.
Baker, C. J. & Pusuk, P. 2010. *The Tale of Khun Chang Khun Phaen: Siam's great folk epic of love and war, Volume 1*. Chiang Mai: Silkworm Books.
Bell, C. 1992. *Ritual theory, ritual practice*. New York: Oxford University Press.
Blackburn, K. 2009. 'Nation-building, identity and war commemoration spaces in Malaysia and Singapore'. In R. Ismal, B. Shaw and G. K. Ooi (eds), 93–114, *Southeast Asian culture and heritage in a globalising world: Diverging identities in a dynamic region*. London, New York: Routledge.
Bokenkamp, S. R. 2008. 'Lingbao'. In F. Pregadio (ed.), 663–669, *The encyclopedia of Taoism*. Abingdon, New York: Routledge.
Boltz, J. M. 2008. '*Pudu*: Universal salvation. 2. The ritual'. In F. Pregadio (ed.), 793–794, *The encyclopedia of Taoism*. Abingdon, New York: Routledge.
Bowie, F. 2013. 'Building bridges, dissolving boundaries: toward a methodology for the ethnographic study of the afterlife, mediumship, and spiritual beings'. *Journal of the American Academy of Religion*, 81:3, 698–733.
Bradshaw, B. 2002. *Change across cultures: A narrative approach to transformation*. Grand Rapids, MI: Baker Academic.
Cao, D. 2006. 'Key words in Chinese law'. In A. Wagner & W. Pencak (eds), 35–50, *Images in law*. London, New York: Routledge.
Carstens, S. A. 2005. *Histories, cultures, identities. Studies in Malaysian Chinese worlds*. Singapore: Singapore University Press.
Chan, M. 2006. *Ritual is theatre, theatre is ritual. Tang-ki: Chinese spirit medium worship*. Singapore: Singapore Management University.
Chan, M. 2008. 'Bodies for the Gods: image worship in Chinese popular religion'. Singapore: Singapore Management University. https://ink.library.smu.edu.sg/cgi/viewcontent.cgi?article=2487&context=soss_research.
Chau, A. Y. 2006. *Miraculous response. Doing popular religion in contemporary China*. Stanford, CA: Stanford University Press.
—— 2009. 'Expanding the space of popular religion: Local temple activism and the politics of legitimation in contemporary rural China'. In Y. Ashiwa & D. L. Wank (eds), 211–240, *Making religion, making the state: The politics of modern religion in China,*. Stanford, CA: Stanford University Press.

Cheng, U. W. 1961. 'Opium in the Straits Settlements, 1867–1910'. *Journal of Southeast Asian History*, 2:1, 52–75.
Choi, M. 2017. *Death rituals and politics in Northern Song China*. Oxford, New York: Oxford University Press
Clark, A. & Chalmers, D. J. 1998. 'The extended mind'. *Analysis*, 58:1, 7–19.
Clart, P. 2003. 'Chinese tradition and Taiwanese modernity: Morality books as social commentary and critique'. In P. Clart & C. B. Jones (eds) , 84–97, *Religion in modern Taiwan*, . Honolulu: University of Hawai'i Press.
Cohen, A. P. 1977. 'A Chinese temple keeper talks about Chinese folk religion'. *Asian Ethnology*, 36:1, 1–17.
Cook, S. 2017. *The battle for China's spirit. Religious revival, repression and resistance under Xi Jinping*. New York, Washington DC: Freedom House.
Dean, K. 2000. 'Daoist ritual today'. In L. Kohn (ed.), 650–682, *Daoism handbook*. Leiden, Boston, Koln: Brill.
—— 2018. 'Spirit mediums and secular-religious divides in Singapore'. In K. Dean & P. van der Veer (eds), 51–82. *The secular in South, East, and Southeast Asia*. Cham, Switzerland: Palgrave Macmillan.
DeBernardi, J. 1987. 'The God of War and the Vagabond Buddha'. *Modern China*, 13:3, 310–332.
—— 1995. 'Tasting the water'. In D. Tedlock & B. Mannheim (eds), 179–197, *The dialogic emergence of culture*. Urbana, Chicago: University of Illinois Press.
—— 2002. 'Malaysian Chinese religious culture: past and present'. In L. Suryadinata (ed.), 301–324, *Ethnic Chinese in Singapore and Malaysia*. Singapore: Times Media Private Limited.
—— 2004. *Rites of belonging. Memory, modernity and identity in a Malaysian Chinese community*. Stanford, CA: Stanford University Press.
—— 2006. *The way that lives in the heart. Chinese popular religion and spirit mediums in Penang, Malaysia*. Stanford, CA: Stanford University Press.
—— 2013. *Beyond nature and culture*. Janet Lloyd (trans.). Chicago: University of Chicago Press.
—— 2014. 'Modes of being and forms of predication'. *Hau: Journal of Ethnographic Theory*, 4:1, 271–280.
Elliott, A. J. A. 1990 (1955). *Chinese spirit-medium cults in Singapore* (LSE monographs on social anthropology). London & Atlantic Highlands, NJ: The Athlone Press.
Eng, K. P. 2003. *State, society and religious engineering: Towards a reformist Buddhism in Singapore*. Singapore: Eastern Universities Press.
—— 2007. 'Diversities and unities: Towards a reformist Buddhism in Singapore'. In L. A. Eng (ed.) , 505–523, *Religious diversity in Singapore*. Singapore: Institute of Southeast Asian studies, National University of Singapore.
Escolar, D. 2012. 'Boundaries of anthropology: Empires and ontological relativism in a field experience with anomalous entities in Argentina'. *Anthropology and Humanism*, 37:1, 27–44.
Feuchtwang, S. 1991. *The imperial metaphor: popular religion in China*. London and New York: Routledge.
Foucault, M. & Miskowiec, J. 1986. 'Of other spaces', *Diacritics*, 16:1, 22–27.
Freedman, A. L. 2001. 'The effect of government policy and institutions on Chinese overseas acculturation: The case of Malaysia'. *Modern Asian Studies*, 35:2, 411–440.
Freedman, M. & Topley, M. 1961. 'Religion and social realignment among the Chinese in Singapore. *The Journal of Asian Studies*, 21:1, 3–23.

Gee, F. L. K. 2011. 'The Eternal Mother and the State: circumventing religious management in Singapore'. Asia Research Institute working paper series no. 161. Singapore: Asia Research Institute.

Giddens, O. & Giddens, S. 2005. *Chinese mythology*. New York: The Rosen Publishing Group.

Giles, H. 1926. 'The yü li ch'ao c'huan'. In S. L. Pu (ed.), 2013, H. A. Giles (trans.), 388–41, *Strange tales from a Chinese studio* (Kindle edition). North Clarenden, Singapore, Tokyo: Tuttle Publishing.

Goh, D. P. S. 2009. 'Chinese religion and the challenge of modernity in Malaysia and Singapore: syncretism, hybridisation and transfiguration'. *Asian Journal of Social Science*, 37, 101–137.

Gold, T. 1986. *State and society in the Taiwan miracle*. London and New York: Routledge.

Gold, T., Guthrie, D. & Wank, T. 2002. 'Introduction'. In T. Gold, D. Guthrie & T. Wank (eds), *Social connections in China: Institutions, culture, and the changing nature of Guanxi*. Cambridge, New York, Melbourne, Madrid, Cape Town: Cambridge University Press.

Gomes, C. 2009. 'Keeping memories alive: maintaining Singaporean nationalism abroad'. *Asia Journal of Global Studies*, 3:1, 37–50.

Goodrich, A. S. 1981. *Chinese hells. The Peking Temple of Eighteen Hells and Chinese conceptions of Hell*. Sankt Augustin, Germany: Institut Monumenta Serica.

Grant, B. & Idema, W. 2011. 'Introduction'. In B. Grant & W. Idema (trans.), 3–34, *Escape from Blood Pond Hell. The tales of Mulian and woman Huang*, Seattle: University of Washington Press.

Hannerz, U. 1996. *Transnational connections: Culture, people, places*. London, New York: Routledge.

Hardacre, H. 1997. *Marketing the menacing foetus in Japan*. Berkeley, Los Angeles, London: University of California Press.

Harrell, S. 1979. 'The concept of the soul in Chinese folk religion'. *The Journal of Asian Studies*, 38:3, 519–528.

Harrell, S. & Perry, E. 1982. 'Syncretic sects in Chinese society: an introduction'. *Modern China*, 8:3, 283–303.

Henare, A., Holbraad, M. & Wastell, S. 2007. 'Introduction: Thinking through things'. In A. Henare, M. Holbraad & S. Wastell (eds), 1–31, *Thinking through things*. London & New York: Routledge.

Hill, M. & Lian, K. F. 1995. *The politics of nation building and citizenship in Singapore*. London, New York: Routledge.

Hobsbawm, E. & Ranger, T. 1983. *The invention of tradition*. Cambridge: Cambridge University Press.

Holbraad, M. & Pedersen, M. A. 2017. *The ontological turn. An anthropological exposition*. Cambridge, UK, New York: Cambridge University Press.

Hook, D. et al. (2004). *Critical psychology*. Lansdowne: UTC Press.

Howell, S. 1996. 'Cosmology'. In A. Barnard & J. Spencer (eds), 157–159, *The Routledge encyclopedia of social and cultural anthropology (second edition)*. London, New York: Routledge.

Hue, G. T. 2012. 'The evolution of the Singapore united temple: The transformation of Chinese temples in the southern Chinese diaspora'. *Chinese Southern Diaspora Studies*, 5, 157–174.

Jenx, P. 2016. *The Thai occult*. France: Timeless.

Johnson, A. A. 2016. 'Dreaming about the neighbours: magic, orientalism, and entrepreneurship in the consumption of Thai religious goods in Singapore'. *South East Asian research*, 24:4, 445–461.

Jones, J. J. 1949. 'The Mahāvastu', J. Jones (trans.), *Sacred books of the Buddhists, Vol 14*. London: Luzac.

Jordan, D. K. 1972. *Gods, ghosts and ancestors: The folk religion of a Taiwanese village*. Berkeley, Los Angeles, London: University of California Press.

—— 1994. 'Changes in postwar Taiwan and their impact on the popular practice of religion'. In S. Harrell & C. C. Huang (eds), 137–160, *Cultural change in postwar Taiwan*. London, New York: Routledge.

Junren (俊仁). 1989. *Daxie shen en xun Hei Bai Wuchang* (答谢神恩熏黑白无常). Kuala Lumpur: Guangming Ribao (光明日报).

Kamau, L. J. 2001. 'Liminality, communitas, charisma, and community'. In S. L. Brown (ed.), pages, *Intentional community: An anthropological perspective*. New York: State University of New York Press.

Kitiarsa, P. 2008. 'Introduction'. In P. Kitiarsa (ed.), 1–13, *Religious commodifications in Asia: Marketing gods*. Abingdon: Routledge.

Kitiarsa, P. 2014. *The "bare life" of Thai migrant workmen in Singapore*. Chiang Mai, Thailand: Silkworm Books.

Kohn, L. 2001. *Daoism and Chinese culture*. Cambridge, MA: Three Pines Press.

—— 2009. *Introducing Daoism*. London, New York: Routledge.

Kohn, L. & Kirkland, R. 2008. 'Daoism in the Tang (618–907)'. In L Kohn (ed.), 339–383, *Daoism handbook*. Leiden, Boston, Koln: Brill.

Kong, L. 1992. 'The sacred and the secular: EXPLORING contemporary meanings and values for religious buildings in Singapore'. *Southeast Asian Journal of Social Sciences*, 20:1, 18–42.

Kong, L. & Yeoh, B. S. 2003. *The politics of landscapes in Singapore: Constructions of nation*. Syracuse, NY: Syracuse University Press.

Lagerway, J. 2009. 'Introduction'. In J. Lagerwey & M. Kalinowski (eds), 1–52, *Early Chinese religion. Part one: Shang through Han (1250 BC–220 AD), Volume two*. Leiden, Boston: Brill.

Landa, J. T. 2016. *Economic success of Chinese merchants in Southeast Asia: Identity, ethnic cooperation and conflict*. Heidelberg, New York, Dordrecht, London: Springer.

Lee, H. G. 2002. 'Malay dominance and opposition politics in Malaysia'. *Southeast Asian Affairs*, 177–195.

Lee, J.-D. 2003. 'Gender and medicine in Tang China'. *Asia Major*, 16:2, 1–32.

Lin, M. R. 1986. 'You jisiquan laikan Caotun Zhende defang Zuzhi' (Ceremonial circles as forms of local organization in Caotun Township). *Bulletin of the Institute of Ethnology, Academia Sinica*, 62, 53–114.

—— 1989. 'Zhanghua Mazude xinyangyuan' (Belief circle of Zhanghua Mazu). *Bulletin of the Institute of Ethnology, Academia Sinica*, 68, 41–104.

Maspero, H. 1932. 'The mythology of modern China'. In J. Hackin (ed.), 252–384, *Asiatic mythology*. London, Bombay, Sydney: George G. Harrap & Co. Limited.

McDaniel, J. 2014. *The lovelorn ghost and the magical monk: Practicing Buddhism in modern Thailand*. New York, Chichester, West Sussex: Columbia University Press.

Mead, M. 1973. 'Visual anthropology in a discipline of words'. In Hockings, P (ed.) 2003, 3–12, *Principles of visual anthropology*. Berlin, New York: Mouton de Gruyter.

Miller, A. L. 2008. 'Hell'. In F. Pregadio (ed.), 69–71, *The encyclopedia of Taoism*. Abingdon, New York: Routledge.

Mohamad, M. 1970. *The Malay dilemma*. Singapore: D. Moore for Asia Pacific Press.

Moskowitz, M. 1998. 'The haunting foetus: greed, healing, and religious adaptation in modern Taiwan'. *Bulletin of the Institute of Ethnology, Academia Sinica*, 86, 157–196.

—— 2001. *The haunting foetus: Abortion, sexuality, and the spirit world in Taiwan*. Honolulu: University of Hawai'i Press.

Mueller, D. M. 2014. *Islam, politics and youth in Malaysia: The Pop-Islamist reinvention of PAS*. Abingdon, UK, New York: Routledge.

Nickerson, P. 2008. 'Taoism and popular religion'. In F. Pregadio (ed.), 145–150, *The encyclopedia of Taoism*. Abingdon, New York: Routledge.

Nikaido, Y. 2015. *Asian folk religion and cultural interaction*. Gottingen, Taipei: V&R Unipress & National Taiwan University Press.

Noremy, M. A., et al. 2012. 'Physical child abuse: what are the external factors?' *The Social Sciences*, 8:9, 83–91.

Paleček, M. & Risjord, M. 2013. 'Relativism and the ontological turn within anthropology'. *Philosophy of the Social Sciences*, 43:1, 3–23.

Paper, J. 2009. 'The role of possession trance in Chinese Culture and religion: a comparative overview from the Neolithic to the present'. In P. Clart & P. Crow (eds), 327–48, *The people and the Dao: New studies in Chinese religions in honour of Daniel L. Overmeyer*. Sankt Augustin, Germany: Institut Monumenta Serica.

Pas, J. 1979. 'Religious life in present-day Taiwan: a preliminary report'. *Journal of the Royal Asiatic Society Hong Kong Branch*, 19, 176–191.

—— 1996. 'Religious life in present day Taiwan: a field observations report, 1994–1995' *Journal of Chinese Religions*, 24, 131–158.

Pedersen, M. A. 2012. 'Common nonsense: a review of certain recent reviews of the "ontological turn"'. *Anthropology of THIS CENTURY*, 5. (Available online at: http://aotcpress.com/articles/common_nonsense/)

Primiano, L. N. 1995. 'Vernacular religion and the search for method in religious folklife'. *Western Folklore*, 54:1, 37–56.

Prinz, J. J. 2004. *Gut reactions: A perceptual theory of emotion*. Oxford: Oxford University Press.

Rappa, A. L. & An, L. W. H. 2006. *Language policy and modernity in Southeast Asia: Malaysia, the Philippines, Singapore and Thailand*. New York: Springer.

Robinson, J. B. P. 1956. *Transformation in Malaya*. London: Secker & Warburg.

Schachter, S. & Singer, J. 1962. 'Cognitive, social, and physiological determinants of emotional state'. *Psychological Review*, 69, 379–399.

Scott, I. & Gong, T. 2016. *Routledge handbook of corruption in Asia*. London, New York: Routledge.

Scott, J. C. 1985. *Weapons of the weak: Everyday forms of peasant resistance*. New Haven and London: Yale University Press.

—— 1990. *Domination and the arts of resistance: Hidden transcripts*. Yale: Yale University Press.

Scott, J. L. 2007. *For gods, ghosts and ancestors: The Chinese tradition of paper offerings*. Hong Kong: Hong Kong University Press.

Scott, M. W. 2007. *The severed snake: Matrilineages, making place, and a Melanesian Christianity in Southeast Solomon Islands*. Durham, NC: Carolina Academic Press.

—— 2013. 'What I'm reading. The anthropology of ontology (religious science?)'. *Journal of the Royal Anthropological Institute*, 19, 859–872.

—— 2013a. 'Steps to a methodological non-dualism'. *Critique of Anthropology*, 33:3, 303–309.

—— 2016. 'To be Makiran is to see like Mr Parrot: the anthropology of wonder in Solomon Islands'. *The Journal of the Royal Anthropological Institute*, 22:3, 474–495.

Skoggard, A. 1996. *The indigenous dynamic in Taiwan's post-war development: The religious and historical roots of entrepreneurship*. Armonk, NY, London: East Gate Book.

Sowell, T. 2016. *Wealth, poverty and politics (revised and enlarged edition)*. New York: Basic Books.

Stafford, C. 2000. *Separation and reunion in modern China*. Cambridge: Cambridge University Press.

Stewart, C. 2004. 'Relocating syncretism in social science discourse'. In M. Leopold, & J. Jensen (eds), 264–285, *Syncretism in religion*. London: Equinox.

Stewart, C. & Shaw, R. 1994. *Syncretism / Anti syncretism. The politics of religious synthesis*. London, New York: Routledge.

Strauch, J. 1981. *Chinese village politics in the Malaysian state*. Cambridge, MA, London, England: Harvard University Press.

Sutton, D. S. 2003. *Steps to perfection. Exorcistic performers and Chinese religion in twentieth-century Taiwan*. Boston: Harvard University Press.

Tajuddin, A. 2012. *Malaysia in the world economy (1824–2011): Capitalism, ethnic divisions, and 'managed' democracy*. Lanham, Boulder, New York, Toronto, Plymouth UK: Lexington Books.

Tan, E. K. B. 2002. 'Reconceptualizing Chinese identity: the politics of Chineseness in Singapore'. In L. Suryadinata (ed.), 109–136, *Ethnic Chinese in Singapore and Malaysia*. Singapore: Times Media Private Limited.

—— 2008. 'Keeping God in place. The management of religion in Singapore'. In L. A. Eng (ed.), 55–82, *Religious diversity in Singapore*. Singapore: Institute of Southeast Asian Studies, National University of Singapore.

Tedlock, D. & Mannheim, B. 1995. 'Introduction'. In D. Tedlock & B. Mannheim (eds), 1–32, *The dialogic emergence of culture*. Urbana, Chicago. University of Illinois Press.

Teiser, S. 1988. *The Ghost Festival in medieval China*. Princeton, Chichester: Princeton University Press.

—— 1995. 'Popular religion'. *Journal of Asian Studies*, 54:2, 378–395.

—— 2003. *The scripture of the ten kings and the making of purgatory in medieval Chinese Buddhism*. Honolulu: University of Hawai'i Press.

Teo, P. et al. 2004. *Changing landscapes of Singapore*. Singapore: McGraw Hill.

Thompson, L. G. 1979. *Chinese religion*. Belmont, CA: Wadsworth Publishing Company.

—— 1989. 'On the prehistory of hell in China'. *Journal of Chinese Religions*, 17:1, 27–41.

Tong, C. K. 1989. 'Child diviners: religious knowledge and power among the Chinese in Singapore'. *Southeast Asian Ethnography*, 8, 71–86.

—— 2004. *Chinese death rituals in Singapore*. London, New York: Routledge Curzon.

Tong, C. K. & Kong, L. 2000. 'Religion and modernity: ritual transformations and the reconstruction of space and time'. *Social and Cultural Geography*, 1:1, 29–44.

Turner, E. 1993. 'The reality of spirits: a tabooed or permitted field of study?' *Anthropology of Consciousness*, 4:1, 9–12.

Turner, V. 1973. 'The center out there: pilgrim's goal'. *History of Religions*, 12:3, 191–230.
van der Veer, P. 2016. *The value of comparison (The Lewis Henry Morgan lectures)*. Durham, NC, London: Duke University Press.
von Glahn, R. 2004. *The sinister way: The divine and the demonic in Chinese religious culture*. Berkeley: University of California Press.
Wang, X. 2019. '"Folk belief," cultural turn of secular governance and shifting religious landscape in contemporary China'. In K. Dean & P. van der Veer (eds), 137–164, *The secular in South, East, and Southeast Asia*. Cham, Switzerland: Palgrave Macmillan.
Wang, Z. 2012. 'The Taoist concept of the Six Heavens'. In Z. Mou (ed.), 119–148, *Taoism*. Leiden, Boston: Brill.
Weller, R. 1987. *Unities and diversities in Chinese religion*. Basingstoke, London: The Macmillan Press.
—— 1999. 'Identity and social change in Taiwanese religion'. In M. Rubenstein (ed.), 339–365, *Taiwan: A new history*. Armonk, New York, London: Eastgate.
—— 2000. 'Living at the edge: religion, capitalism, and the end of the nation-state in Taiwan'. *Public Culture*, 12, 477–498.
Werner, E. T. C. 1922. *Myths and legends of China*. London, Bombay, Sydney: George G. Harrap & Co. Ltd.
Whitehouse, H. 2007. 'The evolution and history of religion'. In D. Perkin & S. Ulijaszek (eds), 212–233, *Holistic anthropology: Emergence and convergence*. New York, Oxford: Berghahn Books.
Wikan, U. (1989). 'Managing the heart to brighten face and soul: emotions in Balinese morality and health care'. *American Ethnologist*, 16:2, 294–312.
Winzeler, R. L. 2010. *The peoples of Southeast Asia today: Ethnography, ethnology, and change in a complex region*. Lanham, New York, Toronto, Plymouth UK: Altamira Press.
Wolf, A. 1974. 'Introduction'. In A. Wolf (ed.), 1–18, *Religion and ritual in Chinese society*. Stanford, CA: Stanford University Press.
Xing, G. 2010. *The concept of the Buddha: Its evolution from early Buddhism to the trikaya theory*. London, New York: Routledge Curzon.
Yamada, T. 2000. 'The Lingbao school'. In L, Kohn (ed.), 225–255, *Daoism handbook*. Leiden, Boston, Koln: Brill.
Young, C. C 1981. 'The *Shih-pa Ni-li* Ching'. In A. S. Goodrich (ed.), 128–134, *Chinese hells. The Peking Temple of Eighteen Hells and Chinese conceptions of Hell*. Sankt Augustin, Germany: Institut Monumenta Serica.
Young, J. & Brunk, G. 2009. 'Introduction'. In J. Young & G. Bunk (eds), 1–10, *The ethics of cultural appropriation*. Chichester, Oxford: Wiley-Blackwell.
Yu, Y. S. 1987. '"O soul, come back!" A study in the changing conceptions of the soul and afterlife in pre-Buddhist China'. *Harvard Journal of Asiatic Studies*, 47:2, 363-395
Yuan, L., Jinlai, S., Qixin, C. & Rongzu, L. 2007. *Anxi Xian Chenghuangmiao Zhi* (安溪县城隍庙志). Anxi: Anxi County Chenghuang Temple Compilation Committee.

Index

Ah Pek parties in Malaysia 114, 127–135 *passim*, 139, 141, 152–160 *passim*, 216
Ah Pek parties in Singapore 104, 131–132, 138, 139
alcohol 8, 9, 25, 41, 47, 49, 59, 60, 61, 65, 79, 131, 139, 158–159
  and *communitas* 140
  in opposition to Islamic sobriety 138, 162
  social discontent in Singapore 138
  toasting with Underworld deities in Malaysia 129, 130, 135, 139, 140, 179, 228
  transference between realms 57–58, 59, 60, 159
altars 19, 51, 52, 75–76, 90, 93, 118
  Buddhist 147–148
  cemetery 89, 90, 93, 98, 102, Figure 6.1, Plates 4 and 5
  City God 143–144, 157, 190, 204
  external camps of the Generals of the Five Directions 51, 210–211
  external Datuk Gong 114, 153, 164
  Jade Emperor 118–119, 129, 134
  rank and positioning on 52, 128, 129
  Underworld 47, 52, 128–129, 153, 155, 164, 173, 210, Plates 10 and 13
  wandering spirits 90, 165
ancestor / ancestral
  burial / graves 87, 108, 109
  cosmology 19, 87–88
  cult and filial piety 107, 125, 135
  palaces for 147, 151
  offerings 19, 76, 83, 84, 87, 90, 96, 99, 101, 102–103, 138, 141, 151, 181
  salvation rituals 9, 98, 101, 107 142, 147
  spirits 19, 155
  tablets 96, 101, 102, 147, 149, 151
  worship 16, 36, 96, 99

anthropology of consciousness and paranthropology 6
anthropomorphic 19, 45, 66
anthropomorphising 64, 64–66 *passim*
Anxi Chenghuangmiao 8, 10–11, 17, 43, Figures 10.1 and 10.2, Plate 15
  Ba Ye Gong and Jiu Ye Gong 194, 196, 200
  channelling deities 196, 200
  City God 143, 152, 156, 157, 183, 192, 200
  City God statues 190–191
  City God tradition overseas 161, 191
  commoditisation of cosmology 184
  destruction of Fan Wujiu and Xie Bian's original graves 191
  destruction of Tua Di Ya Pek's statues in 1941 190
  division of City God's incense 183
  division of Tua Di Ya Pek's incense 193, 201
  Dongyue Si 191, 192
  Dongyue Si Chenghuangmiao 193, 196
  exhumation of Fan Wujiu and Xie Bian's graves 191
  Fan Wujiu and Xie Bian's mythologies and titles 183, 190, 191, 195–196
  Fan Wujiu and Xie Bian's new graves 191, 193, 196, 201, 215, Figure 10.1
  graves of Fan Wujiu and Xie Bian 43, 183, 189, 191, 201, 215
  history prior to relocation 190–193
  Malaysia 142, 152, 156, 161, 183–184, 192, 193, 196–200 *passim*, 201
  mythos and origins of the Underworld tradition 184, 201, 214–215
  new Tua Di Ya Pek statues 191, Plate 14
  opium 191, 195, 196

INDEX

origins of the modern Underworld tradition 189, 201, 208
pilgrimage site and tourism 183–184, 189, 193, 200, 215
post-1990 reinvention 189, 192–194
reinvention and historical continuity 189
relocation 193
replica City God statues in Malaysia 152, 192, 208
replica City God statues in Singapore 192
replica City God statues in Taiwan 191, 192
replica Tua Di Ya Pek statues 191–192
rituals in 199–200
self-perpetuation / promotion of its own City God tradition 184, 191, 215
Singapore 184, 190, 192, 193, 196, 215
symbolic importance of 141
Tua Di Ya Pek's overseas popularisation 189, 193
Yinfu Tan annex 'Anxi Chenghuangmiao fushu Yinfu Tan' 196–200, Figure 10.2

blessing 48
objects 55, 56, 82, 131, 149, 166
people 53, 103, 144, 151, 156, 168, 169, 199
blood
black dog's 211–212
bloodline cosmology / patrilineal descent 125, 160–162 *passim*
tang-ki's blood 56, 99, 116, Plate 3
Bodhisattvas
Dizangwang 52, 68, 104, 147–148, 204
channelled by *tang-ki* 145, 147
and physical embodiment in a natural form 144–5, Figure 8.1
on Underworld altars 129, 145, 164, 172
Mile / Xiao Fo (Future Buddha / Laughing Buddha) 62, 71, 72
Guanyin 52, 144, 164, 218
channelled by *tang-ki* 144, 145
and Da Shi Ye 85, 97
Qielan 71 (note 6), 164
Bowie, F. x, xiv, 6
British
and Malaysia 27–28, 185, 222
and opium 45, 46
and Singapore 23, 148, 221

Buddhism
and Confucianism / Confucian ethics 18, 62, 82, 84, 135, 137
and filial piety 84
and judgemental Underworld 32–33, 35
and karmic retribution 1, 34–35, 182
and lay religious practitioners 17
and Lunar Seventh Month 9, 83–84
and merits 32, 72, 82
and morality tracts 35–36, 84
and religious identity in Malaysia 148
and six paths of reincarnation 35
Theravada 10, 171–172, 173
and Underworld cosmology 1, 16, 32–34, 35, 123, 125
and universal salvation / salvation rituals 35, 106, 147
Buddhist chanting 147, 148, 172, 200
Buddhist clerics / monks 84, 104, 147–148
Buddhist evangelism and New Reformist Buddhism 104, 106
Buddhist influence on Taoism 16, 34–36
Buddhist sutras
Blood Bowl / Pool Sutra of the Correct Teaching of the Great Canon as Preached by the Buddha 116–117
Da Bei Zhou, Lu Xian Zan, Xin Jing and Yangzhou Jing Shui 200 (note 10)
Mahavastu-Avanda Sutra 33
Lokanuvartanasutra 35
Sutra of the Fundamental Vows of the Bodhisattva Kṣitigarbha 147
Sutra on the Eighteen Hells 33, 122
The countless Buddhas of the ten directions 35
Yulanpen Sutra 84, 117 (note 4)

cemeteries 9, 25, 26, 82, 174
altars 89, 90
burial plots 9, 83, 88, 89, 90, 102, 107–109 *passim*
cremation 26, 88
crypt burial system 108
exhumation of graves 26, 87–88, 108–109, 173, 220
gravestones / tombstones 89, 93, 102
sites of resistance 109
cemetery rituals *see* Lunar Seventh Month night-time cemetery rituals in Singapore

Chinese vernacular religion definition 17–18
City God temples. For individual temple names *see* temples in Malaysia / Singapore / Taiwan
  and Underworld deity statues 16, 16 (note 4), 41, 73, 225
  in Malaysia 10, 141 152, 161, 203, 215, 216
  in Singapore 215–216
  in Taiwan 190, 192
City Gods (Chenghuang)
  and post-mortal authority 190
  and Tua Di Ya Pek's mythologies 44, 195
  Anxi *see* Anxi Chenghuangmiao, City God
  on Underworld altars 52, 68, 129, 153, 164
  robes 143, 152, 157
coffin rituals *see* rituals, coffin rituals in, *and*, Lunar Seventh Month night-time coffin rituals in Malaysia
coffins
  child's 151, 164, 172
  for the good fortune of the living 174
  for the souls of the dead 174
  full sized 165, 172, 174
  miniature 118, 173
  substitutes for thrones 164, 169, 172, 174
  used coffin wood 118, 173
commodification / commoditisation
  and Anxi Chenghuangmiao 184, 193, 200–201
  and foetus ghosts in Taiwan 81, 219–220
  and money god temples in Taiwan 224–225
  and orthodox traditions 183
communitas 101, 140
communities ethno-religious / temple communities in Malaysia
  Ah Pek parties and community creation 127–135 *passim*
  creation / formation and maintenance 10, 30–31, 107, 109, 113–114, 127, 140, 141, 152–153, 161, 162
  guanxi, *guanxi* networks and community cohesion 132, 139, 140, 226 (note 27)
  intentional communities 139–140, 153
  and self-identity 138, 162
  and self-perpetuating mechanisms 30, 140, 161, 226 (note 27)
Confucian ethics *see* ethics / morality, Confucian

Da Shi Ye
  and Bukit Mertajam, Penang, Malaysia 86, 203, 214
  cosmology 85, 97–98
  as Ghost King before Tua Di Ya Pek 182
  and paper statues for burning 86, 97, 147, 203
  Taiwan 86
  on temple altars 85–86, 164
  sending off 86, 97–98, 102–103, 203
Datuk Gong
  altars / shrines / tombs 49, 51, 145, 153, 164, 165
  channelled by *tang-ki* 9, 54, 130
  and ethnicity 52–53
  and Islam 114, 130 (note 21)
  natural / animistic form 145, 161
  status in Malaysia and Singapore 114, 139, Plate 6
Dean, K. xii, xiv, 33, 105
death
  associations with 25, 64, 81, 173, 182
  birthdays / age after 81, (81 note 10), continuation of the human soul after xi, 227, 229
  in Chinese cosmology 19, 32–34, 42, 59, 84, 86, 87, 94, 128, 179–180
  permanent 126
  physicality / desires at the time of death 90, 96
  Register of Births and Deaths 128
  symbolic 168–171 *passim*
deific efficacy 97–99 *passim*
  assimilated through ritual piercing 99, 101
  carried in blood 99
  carried in incense (*fenxiang*) 142, 142 (note 2), 143
  see also deity statues, replica
  carried in incense / opium smoke 156, 182
  and the cosmology of *ling* and *hun* 18–19
  directed through / embodying objects 4, 5, 48, 53, 54
  directed through / embodying talisman 80, 97, 155
  directed through *tang-ki* 15, 48, 82, 179

INDEX

embodying statues 96, 98, 223
  see also deity statues, replica (*fenling*)
  invested in or manifested through flags 68–69, 95, 103, 166, 169, 177
  and new terminology 5–6
  and prophecy / predictions 60, 116, 117
  and proxy deities 97–98
deification 19, 52, 64, 70, 148, 209–210
  see also Tua Di Ya Pek, mythologies
deities
  contractual agreements with 42, 117, 132
  creation of new 8, 20, 64, 66, 69–71 *passim*, 220
  creation of new from novels 130 (note 20), 204, 204 (note 5)
  human deity / deity–devotee relations 80, 139, 140
  Heaven deities *see* Heaven deities
  human creation of 19, 182
  identification 5, 15, 46, 47, 70, 98, 183
  proxy deities 97–98
  Underworld deities *see* Underworld deities
deity statues Plate 14
  opium *see* opium, feeding deity statues with
  rank on altars 52, 129
  replica (*fenling*) 30, 142, 144, 152, 184, 191–192, 208, 215–216, 217, 223, 223 (note 17 / 20)
  replica (*fenxiang*) 142, 143–144, 183, 201, 208
descendants 26
Descola, P. 3, 4
Di Ya Pek
  birthday celebrations 9, 127–135 *passim*, 228–229
  conversations with Di Ya Pek *see* dialogic approach, conversations with Di Ya Pek
  identifying features and names 46
dialogic approach to religious phenomena xii, xiv, 2, 5, 6, 7, 8, 11, 225, 226
  conversations with Di Ya Pek 158–160, 179–182
  conversations with Tua Ya Pek 49–50, 57–58, 69–71, 78–79, 158–160, 170, 175
digitalised modernity 107, 227
  digitalised history in the making 37, 228
  and economy of spectacular moments 106
  internet and online social media 37, 106, 107, 197, 228
  internet and online social media and Underworld punishments 122, 126
  photos of spirits 177
  speed of cultural dissemination and development of future traditions 228
  and the vernacularisation of tradition 37, 228
discarnate
  barriers 77, 96
    see also, *qi*, barrier
  efficacy 5, 68
  entities 15, 48
  forces 6, 97
  human control over discarnate forces 20
  human spirit and bodily tortures 179–180
  realms 46, 85, 102, 169
  material objects for use in discarnate form 4, 95, 98
  transition from discarnate to incarnate 4, 78
divination and coins in rituals 76–77, 92, 93, Figure 6.2
divination blocks 19, 42 134, 153, 192, 224
dragon imagery 143, 144–145, 147
efficacy
  of ancestors and deities 18–19
  assimilating heavenly efficacy 101
  temples and spiritual efficacy 127, 129, 223
embodiment
  deific 5, 97, 144–145
  iconography and human embodiment 65
  objects and efficacy 4, 48, 68
  physical 144–145
emic
  ontologies 4
  perspective / understanding 4, 5, 6, 15, 48, 53, 60, 72, 80, 182
  voice 4, 5
ethics and morality
  Confucian 18, 82, 84, 90, 93, 98, 125–126, 135, 137
  degrees of morality 59, 61

ethics and morality (*cont.*)
  disregarding Confucian ethics / decorum 134–135
  dual / multiple moralities 59, 159
  filial piety 84, 98, 107, 123, 125–126
  Jade Record and modernisation of 113–115, 119–127 *passim*
  modernisation of moral causality in Malaysia's post-mortal cosmology 121–127 *passim*
  officially sanctioned morality 138
  opium consumption by Underworld deities 158–159
  universal (laws of) morality / sins 57, 59, 61
ethnography 6
  participant observation paradigm 6, 226
  participatory approach / active participation xii, xiii, 6, 56, 88, 93, 94–103 *passim*, 128–132, 135, 165–169, 174–179 *passim*, 226
  visual images / photographs 7, 227
exorcism
  and imprisonment of exorcised spirits 118, 119, 172, 173
  and release of exorcised spirits 10, 118, 174–178 *passim*
extended mind hypothesis 48

Fan Wujiu and Xie Bian
  as Ba Ye Gong and Jiu Ye Gong 194, 196, 200, 215–216
  burial / graves *see* Anxi Chenghuangmiao, graves of Fan Wujiu and Xie Bian
  mythologies *see* Tua Di Ya Pek, mythologies; Anxi Chenghuangmiao, Fan Wujiu and Xie Bian mythologies and titles
  rank / status 143
  as Tua Di Ya Pek or other Hell deities 17, 43, 47, 179, 183
five elements 90–91, 95
foetus
  and abortion laws / eugenics legislation 220, 221
foetus ghosts (malicious) (*ying ling*) 9 (note 7)
  and appeasement rituals / temples in Taiwan 10, 74, 81, 219–221 *passim*, 223
  and cemetery rituals 9, 83, 87–93, Figure 6.1, Plates 4 and 5
  and Confucian ethics / conventions of filial piety 90, 93
  deifying foetus ghosts in Taiwan 220
  enlisted into a temple's spirit army in Malaysia 8, 10, 74, 150–151, 161, 221, Plate 9
  see also Thai, *luk thep* dolls and *kuman thong*
foetus spirits (harmless) (*taishen*) 9 (note 7)
  alters and offerings and Confucian conventions of filial piety 98
  and foetus spirit assistance rituals 8, 74–78, 81, 82, 150
  and Tua Di Ya Pek in Singapore 74, 81, 82, 216, 220
Foucault, M. and heterotopias 9, 105, 108–109
framework of analysis 2, 11, 21–23
  as a future predictive model 226, 227

gambling 8, 57–58, 60, 61, 82, 216, 218
  3D lotto 81, 205–207 *passim*
  4D lotto 60, 65
  history and origins in the modern Underworld tradition 204–208, 209
Ghost Month *see* Lunar Seventh Month
ghost temples *see* Taiwan, ghost temples
ghosts
  capturing wandering spirits 88
  entertainment for wandering spirits 128, 135
  foetus *see* foetus ghosts
  houses for 94, 95–96, 97, 102
  hungry ghosts 35, 84, 121, 181
  inviting ghosts / spirits 102, 151, 155
  malevolent spirits 25, 26, 41, 48, 53, 54, 86, 96, 98
  and morality 60–1
  venerated ghosts (Wanshan Ye) 60–1, 218
  wandering spirits 9, 25, 85, 86, 93, 94–96 *passim*, 98, 102–103, 109, 118, 134, 142, 155, 155, 165–166, 169, 173, 177, 218, 220
  water ghosts 86
guanxi 132, 139, 140, 226 (note 27)
Guinness 50, 57, 58, 59, 60, 64, 68, 69, 79, 88, 89, 90, 94, 104, 130, 149, 151, 157, 158, 169, 215
  bottles for exorcised spirits 11, 118, 119, 175, 177
  offerings to Underworld deities /

INDEX

spirit armies 89, 97, 143, 149, 155, 164
the drink of the gods 158

Han dynasty 34, 35, 36, 62, 83
Heaven deities
  Bao Gong 52, 68, 129, 153
  Buddha 33, 84, 144, 171
  city gods *see* city gods
  Di Guan Dadi / Zhongyuan Dadi 84
  Doumu niang-niang 52, 72
  Eight Bagua Marshals 101
  Eight Taoist Immortals 54, 101
  Fazhu Gong 130
  Jade Emperor *see* Jade Emperor
  Generals of the Five Directions 72, 80, 134, 210–211
  Guan Gong / Guan Sheng Dijun / Qielan Pusa 52, 71 (note 6), 164, 204, 220
  Hei Ling Jiangjun 69
  Huaguang Dadi (Lingguan Ma Yuanshuai) 71 (note 7)
  Jigong 52, 130, 164
  Leigong 23
  Lords of the Northern and Southern Dipper 51, 54, 121
  Lord Lao (Laojun) 33, 52
  Mazu 204, 204 (note 4), 218
  Money Gods of the Five Directions 73, 224
  Nezha 130
  Nine Emperor Gods 52, 72
  Pangu 52
  Qingshui Zushi 220
  San Taizi 130
  Sanguan 33
  Shancai Tongzi 52
  Sun Wukong 52, 130, 204
  Royal Lords / Wangye 218
  Shangdi 32
  Taisui 51, 51 (note 14), 165
  Taiyi Jiuku Tianzun 35
  Taoist Marshals 71 (note 6), 164
  Thirty-Six Celestial Armies 69
  Three Pure Ones 52
  Three Taoist Luminaries 123
  Tua Pek Kong 89, 114
  Tudi Gong 114, 128, 164
  Weiling Gong 204, 208
  Xiwangmu 118
  Xuantian Shangdi / Emperor of the Dark Heavens 52, 68, 69, 72, 80, 211
  Zhao Gongming 72, 224
  Zheng He 115
  Zhong Kui 153
  Zhu Sheng Niang-niang 204
    see also Bodhisattvas
Heaven deity worship vis-a-vis Underworld deity worship xii, 1, 17, 21, 23, 25, 61, 107, 113, 184, 210, 218, 222
Heaven deity's relinquishment of both moral and actual authority 139
hierarchy
  Heaven–human–Underworld 10, 14, 114, 139, 140
  Heaven–Underworld 130, 134, 138, 139, 216
Hinduism 42, 50, 51
  Madurai Veeran 53, 54
historic memory 25, 218
historical dissemination of the modern Underworld tradition 214–217
  and Anxi Chenghuangmiao 214, 215, 217
  and cultural transmission from Malaysia to Singapore 86, 184, 214, 216
  and cultural transmission from Singapore to Malaysia 184, 217
  and cultural transmission within Malaysia 184
  and cultural transmission in central and southern Malaysia 184, 216–217
  and cultural transmission in Singapore 215–217 *passim*
  and the influence of Jiucaiba Chenghuangmiao 215–216
  and the influence of Penang's Underworld tradition on Singapore's 214
  and self-perpetuating technologies of religious synthesis 217–225 *passim*
historical sociology 2, 22, 23, 142, 218, 227
homonyms 168 (note 4), 170, 206
human
  effigies and exorcism 118
  human control over deities 20, 117
  human creation of deities and Underworld 182
  human–deity contractual agreements 42, 117, 132
  human-deity relations and changing human status 139
  human–deity social interactions and bonding 19, 139, 140

human (*cont.*)
  mortality and continuation of the human soul after physiological death 227
  promotion of human souls 19, 34, 64, 182
  proxy self (*tishen*) 133–134

imperial state religion 18, 34, 36, 83, 204
  and city gods 43 (note 3), 189
  and Han imperial blood sacrifices 34, 36
  and Tua Di Ya Pek mythologies 190
incense
  benzoin 49, 51, 52
  cigarettes as 60, 143
  division of incense *see* deity statues, replica (*fenxiang*)
  external Underworld camps 211
  offered to deities by deities 94, 134, 151, 156
interpretative analysis / approach 2, 3, 11
invention of tradition 22, 151–152, 203, 217, 229
  and coffin rituals 165–169, 171–172
  and deities and the Underworld 181–182
  and Hell deities as ritual masters 105
  and malicious foetus ghosts in Malaysia 149–151, 161
  and new ritual forms 21, 22–23, 145, 147, 171–172, 217, 220, 227
  and 'sending off' Da Shi Ye 86
inversion of tradition 1, 22, 107, 151–152, 217
  and authority in the Heaven–human–Underworld hierarchy 10, 114, 134, 139
  and authority in the Heaven–Underworld hierarchy 130, 134–135, 138, 139, 216
  and Confucian ethics and filial piety 62, 93, 125–6, 134
  and cosmological emphasis from Heaven to Hell deity worship 1, 17, 20, 21, 23, 25, 65, 113, 114, 200, 214, 229

Jade Emperor 36, 51, 56, 99, 103, 118–119, 127, 129, 133–134, 143, 153, 164, 169, 175, 195
Jade Emperor temples 119, 134, 215

Jade Record (*Yuli chao chuan*) 9, 16, 35, 36–37, 113, 114–115, 119–127 *passim*, 135, 136
  Bridge of Pain 36
  Broth of Oblivion 36
  ledgers of reincarnation 36
  Underworld Courts 121–127
  Underworld enforcers 98
  Yama-Kings of Ten Tribunals (*Shi Dian Yenwang*) 36
joss money
  gold and silver 96, 101, 102, 133, 166–168 *passim*, 170
  Hell banknotes 76 (note 9), 77, 90, 93, 94, 101, 102, 155, 166 (note 2), 206, 207
  path money 166, 166 (note 1), 169, 177
  pre-folded and ancient coinage 101, 102, 134, 177, 212 Figure 11.1
  Underworld spirit army and *luk thep* dolls 149

land spirits
  Diji Gong 148, 149, 153, 161
  Diji Zhu 148
  diling 145
lexicon of terminology xiv, 5, 6, 229
ling 19, 30
Lunar Seventh Month
  Buddhism 84
  cosmology 83–86
  Da Shi Ye *see* Da Shi Ye
  taboos 86
  Taoist *Zhongyuan* festival 84
Lunar Seventh Month night-time cemetery rituals in Singapore 9, 83–112 *passim*, Figures 6.1 and 6.2, Plates 4 and 5
  and aborted foetuses, still-born babies and dead children 83, 87–93
  and ancestors and wandering spirits 93–104
  and everyday forms of resistance 83, 107, 108
  and exhumation 87, 88
  and National Environment Agency 87, 88, 94
Lunar Seventh Month night-time coffin rituals in Malaysia 164–174 *passim*
  and experiencing 167–169, Plate 12
  and observing 166–167
  and preparing the ritual space 165–166
  and *qi* talisman and flags 165–169
  and Theravada Buddhism 171

INDEX 251

Lunar Seventh Month releasing of exorcised spirits 174–182 *passim*
  and discussing Underworld cosmology with Di Ya Pek 179–182
  and preparation and sending off 175, 177
Lunar Seventh Month salvation rituals in Malaysia 145–151 *passim*
  and Anxi Chenghuangmiao 142
  and Buddhist identity 147–148
  and coffins 151
  and Dizangwang 144–147
  and land spirits 148–149
  and *luk thep* dolls, malicious foetus ghosts and spirit armies 150–151
Lunar Seventh Month Tua Di Ya Pek conference in Malaysia 142, 152–160 *passim*, Plate 11
  and Anxi Chenghuangmiao 152, 156, 157, 161
  and community formation / temple communities 152–153
  and Gates of the Underworld 155
  and opium 156–158 *passim*, 160

Malaysia
  bumiputra and ethnic exclusion 26, 26 (note 5), 28–29, 137, 162–163
  Chinese cultural, ethnic and religious identity 10, 29, 30, 138, 148, 161, 162
  Chinese temples 27
  community formation *see* communities ethno-religious
  corruption 137–138
  crime 121–127 *passim*
  decennial census and religious identity 148, 161, 172
  environmental damage / destruction 115, 123–125 *passim*, 137
  Independence Constitution and Malay special rights 28, 137, 162
  internet scams 126
  Islamic sobriety and ethno-religious self-identity 138
  Japanese massacres during occupation 27, 218
  language policies 29, 30, 162
  New Economic Policy (NEP) and National Development Policy (NDP) 28, 29, 124, 161, 162, 222
  race riots 28, 30
  socio-political developments 21
  Thai population and proximity to 150, 173, 221
Mead, M. 7, 227
modernity 2 (note 4), 79, 106, 107, 225
  digitalised *see* digitalised modernity
  postmodernity 107
morality *see* ethics and morality
morality tracts 16, 36
  Jade Record (*Yuli chao chuan*) *see* Jade Record
  Journeys to the Underworld (*Diyu Youji*) 225, 225 (note 26)
  Scripture of the Ten Kings (*Shiwang jing*) 33, 35–36
  The transformation text on Mulian saving his mother from the dark regions 84

nature gods and spirits 64, 65

offerings
  ancestral *see* ancestor / ancestral, offerings
  of cigarettes 60, 96, 143, 155
  of food 84, 90, 96, 102, 149, 177, 199
  of joss money *see* joss money
  of opium *see* opium, feeding deity statues
  and transformation *see* realms of existence, transference between realms through burning / immolation
  to wandering spirits 90, 93, 102, 166
  of wine and tea 95, 157
  to Underworld spirit army / soldiers 149, 151, 212
ontological
  alterity 4, 7
  approach to efficacy and religious phenomena 2, 3, 5, 226
  discourse 3
  denial / integrity of emic ontologies 4
  method xvi, 3
  non-human worlds 3
  ontological other 6, 7
  ontology 2, 3, 4
  predication 3
  turn 2, 3, 5
opium
  3D lottery 205–206, 216
  Anxi Chenghuangmiao 195
  coffin ritual 167, 168, 169, 170

opium (*cont.*)
  feeding deity statues with 45, 60, 143, 203–204, 206, 207, 212, Plate 16
  floating between dimensions 158
  history and origins in the modern Underworld tradition 203–208 *passim*, 212, 214
  and karmic retribution 159
  laced cigarettes 46, 130, 153, 156–158 *passim*, 160, 166–169 *passim*
  and trance possession 9, 138, 156–159 *passim*, 161
  and Tua Di Ya Pek's mythology 43, 45
origins of the modern Underworld tradition xiii, 11, 184–185, 189, 202–212 *passim*, 214
  and Anxi Chenghuangmiao 185, 189, 201, 215–216
  dissemination *see* historical dissemination of the modern Underworld tradition
  and Penang Chenghuangmiao 185, 203–208 *passim*, 214
  and Penang Tiandeyuan Xunyin Fu 208–210 *passim*, 214
orthodox traditions and legitimacy 148, 183, 193

Paleček, M & Risjord, M. 3–4, 5, 48
Pedersen, A. M. 3, 5
piercings 48, 72, 99–101
pingan (peace) bridge 133
po 19
post-mortal
  cosmology 10, 16, 32–37 *passim*, 53, 87–88, 160, 161–162
  deities as post-mortal incarnation 47, 64, 208
  ethnically inclusive / exclusive Underworlds 53, 59, 125, 160–163
  execution 126
  inevitability / fate 53, 137, 163, 183
  journey of the soul 6, 35, 43, 46, 79, 83, 128, 220
  karmic retribution 1, 34–36, 114–115, 121–127 *passim*
  merits 72, 73
  modernisation of post-mortal cosmology in Malaysia 114–115, 121–127 *passim*
  physicality / physiological attributes and behaviours 90, 179–180
  promotion 34–35, 195
  punishments 1, 20, 32, 35, 59, 81, 121–127 *passim*, 160
  punishments and filial piety 123, 125–126
  spirit body and physical punishments 179
  tastes and desires 81 (note 10), 96
  worshiping one's own post-mortal torturers 2, 43, 46

qi
  barrier 177
  cleansing 166
  and the power of a temple 144
  proxy self in *qi* form 133
  talismans 166–169 *passim*

realms of existence
  connecting the Heaven, Earth and Underworld realms 211
  cosmic / discarnate 46, 102, 105
  intercommunication between human and heavenly realms 69, 80, 115 (note 2)
  links / transference between the Underworld and human realms 46, 47, 71, 155
  physical links between the human and Underworld realms 46, 47, 83, 85, 155, 211–212
  spirits in the human realms 86, 103, 118, 119, 133, 155, 173, 175–177, 206–207
  symbolic transference to the Underworld 165–170 *passim*
  tang-ki transferring alcohol / opium from human to Underworld realms 57–58, 59, 60, 159
  transference between realms through burning / immolation 73, 76, 76 (note 9), 77, 90, 93, 102–103, 133, 169, 177
  transference through contiguity 45, 60, 143, 204, 206, 207, 212, Plate 16
reflexivity xii, 80, 228
reincarnation 1, 33, 35, 36, 43 57, 59, 87, 121, 126, 175, 219
  as an animal 35, 57, 59
  and foetus spirits 74, 77
  and inability to reincarnate 121, 126, 175, 212
reinterpretation
  of cosmology 53, 73, 224
  of ethics / morality 16, 121–127 *passim*

of the Jade Record 113–115, 119–127 *passim*
of tradition 22, 50, 217
reinvention 22, 217
   and Anxi Chenghuangmiao post-1990 11, 189, 192–194
   of celestial money gods 73, 81, 224
   of foetus ghosts and Thai *kuman thong* 150–151, 161, 221
   of the Jade Record 114–115, 121–127
   of Thai coffin rituals 163, 171
   of Underworld enforcers / Tua Di Ya Pek 9, 73, 79–80
   of vulnerable foetus spirits in Taiwan 81, 150, 220–221
   Xie Bian and Fan Wujiu's graves 191
relative time
   and ageing in the Underworld 78, 81
   and ancestral offerings in the Underworld 181
   and birthdays in the Underworld 78, 81, 129
   and Buddhist hells 33
   on Earth and in the Underworld 174, 180–181
religious phenomena 2, 5, 226, 229
resistance 104, 138
   Bukit Brown Cemetery 108
   everyday forms of resistance 9, 83, 107–109 *passim*, 138
ritual and new ritual forms 21, 22–23, 145, 147, 171–172, 217, 220, 227
ritual and sequential events in the process of becoming 227
ritual objects
   bagua 51, 54, 56, 94
   black flag (*ohr leng*) 68–69, 72, 80
   coffins 118, 164, 169, 172, 173, 174, Plate 13
   flags 48, 51, 72, 94–95, 103, 134, 155, 166, 169, 177, 210–211, 212
   markers 54, 177
   protective 98–99
   skewers 48, 72, 99, 101, Figure 6.3
   talismans *see* talismans
   thrones 42, 51, 56, 66, 68, 74, 119, 134, 147, 172, Figure 11.1
   weapons 5, 46, 48, 130, 134
   whips 22–23, 48, 51, 54, 130
ritual paper objects
   feeding paper horses / steeds 94–95, 102
   horses / steeds 95, 134

   houses / palaces for ancestors or wandering spirits 94, 95–96, 97, 102, 112, 147
   lotuses 96, 101, 102
   joss money *see* joss money
   shops 149
   the Jade Emperor's palace 127, 133–134, 175
ritual / sacred space
   barriers 77, 96, 155, 177
   creating 54–55, 77, 90, 147, 155, 165–166, 177
   inviting deities / spirits into 54, 96, 102, 151
   protecting 51, 53, 151, 212
   Underworld recreation as 9, 114, 118, 128–130
rituals 61
   cemetery rituals in Singapore 9, 87–104 *passim*, 107, 216 Figures 6.1 and 6.2, Plates 4 and 5
   coffin rituals in Malaysia 164–174 *passim*
   coffin rituals in Thailand 171–172
   eye opening 52, 95, 129, 155, 200, 211
   foetus appeasement in Taiwan 219
   foetus assistance in Malaysia 74–78 *passim*
   oil wok in Singapore 54–56, Plate 1
   releasing of exorcised spirits in Malaysia 163, 174–178 *passim*, Figure 9.2
   salvation (*pudu* and *chaodu*) 9, 10, 86, 98–103 *passim*, 106, 107 142, 147–151 *passim*, 216

Scott, M. W. 3, 4
self-mortification 99, 116–117
self-perpetuating mechanisms
   Ah Pek parties as 216
   alcohol as 8
   and Anxi Chenghuangmiao 11
   and *communitas* 101
   and communities sustaining a temple culture 30
   and Datuk Gong 114, 216
   fear of ghosts as 226 (note 27)
   as forms of adaptation 22
   and gambling 8, 60
   guanxi and godchildren as 132, 140, 226 (note 27)
   inversions of the Heaven–Underworld hierarchy as 216
   and money god temples 226 (note 27)
   multiple Tua Di Ya Pek as 98

self-perpetuating mechanisms (*cont.*)
   and new deities 20
   and new deity cults 227
   tang-ki as 64
   and temple-based community formation in Malaysia 161, 162
self-perpetuating technologies of religious synthesis 2, 21, 24, 217–225 *passim*
   causal explanations for differential patterns of religious evolution 218
   individual technologies of religious synthesis see technologies of religious synthesis
   in multiple locations 218–225 *passim*
sending off
   and cemetery rituals 93, 101–103
   Da Shi Ye 86, 97–98, 102–103, 203
   exorcised spirits 175, 177
   and transference see realms of existence, transference between realms through burning / immolation
Singapore
   Buddhist evangelism 104, 106
   cemeteries 25, 82, 87, 107
   cemetery rituals as forms of resistance 104, 107
   ceremonial circles 24, 27, 30, 222
   crime and corruption 137
   crypt burial system 108
   decennial census and religious identity 9, 105–107 *passim*, 148
   ethnic / racial integration policy 24, 50 161
   exhumation of graves / exhumations 26, 87–88, 108–109, 173, 220
   Housing Development Board (HDB) 24, 25, 26, 105, 161, 173, 210, 211, 222
   Japanese massacres during occupation 25, 218
   Maintenance of Religious Harmony Act 211, 212
   Master Plan 9, 23, 25, 107
   multi-ethnic / multi-religious 24, 50, 53, 80, 106
   multicultural / multiculturalism 23, 137, 161, 162
   National Environment Agency (NEA) 26, 87, 88, 107
   Nationalism and Singaporean identity 24, 162, 173
   orthodox Taoist and *tang-ki* cooperation 104
   People's Action Party (PAP) 23, 24, 59, 173
   and religious harmony 9, 24, 50, 53, 80, 113
   ritual / temple networks and temple landscape 24, 62–64, 222
   Sino-Singapore relations 221
   and urban redevelopment / renewal 9, 22, 62, 64, 107, 108, 145, 220
   urban relocation 24, 63, 222
Sinification
   of Buddhist cosmology 35
   of Datuk Gong 145, 161, 216
   of tradition 22, 217, 220
Sinology ix, 4, 6
societal catalysts to religious change 2, 9, 10, 17, 21–23 *passim*, 26, 109, 113, 138, 140, 142, 145, 150, 161, 162, 193, 216, 217–227 *passim*
soul (*hun* / *ling hun*)
   divisible nature of 18–19, 87, 97, 179, 182, 197
   entering and leaving body 42, 170, 170 (note 5)
   nature of the human soul 32, 229
   proxy self see human, proxy self (*tishen*)
   substitute 86
spirit possession see trance possession states
spiritual
   absorbing the spiritual essence of food offerings 131, 157
   beings and religious phenomena 78, 229
   deception 133
   the spiritual other 47
   a temple's spiritual efficacy 127, 129, 223
   a temple's spiritual protection 211
   traditions xi, 226–227
stem-branch calendar 51 (note 14), 89, 95

Taiwan 3, 11, 16, 54, 218–225 *passim*
   Anxi Chenghuangmiao 191, 192, 217
   belief circles 30, 219, 221, 223, 223 (note 20)
   ceremonial circles 24, 30
   control over potentially malicious spirits 219
   Da Shi Ye 86
   and foetus ghosts 10, 150, 219–220
   foetus ghost (appeasement) rituals / temples 74, 81, 219–221, 223
   ghost temples / venerated ghosts 8, 60–61, 218–219, 224
   Japanese influence 218, 219, 220, 221

KMT legislation and restrictions on
    tang-ki 221–222
money god temples 66, 224–225, 226
    (note 27)
money gods 66, 73
no comparable Underworld tradition
    in Taiwan 218–225 passim
religious tourism / pilgrims 223
temple building and gold 222–223
temple networks 30, 223
transnational flows of Japanese
    popular culture 219
Underworld deities, performance
    troupes and taboo 225
talismans
    to animate inanimate objects 95
    drawing and content 97
    and efficacy 80, 97, 155
    and exorcism 118, 175
    green 76–77, 94, 97, 118, 151, 166,
        175, 212
    'qi' talisman 166–169 passim
    to identify ancestral offerings 90
    yellow 48 (note 9), 212
tang-ki as deity incarnate 15, 80, Figures
    5.2 and 9.2, Plates 2, 3, 6 and 11
tang-ki bone 115
tang-ki's displaced soul 19, 42
Taoist
    cosmology 16, 33–35
    priests chanting scriptures 96, 98, 99,
        103, 127
    priests in rituals 102, 104–105,
        127–128, 133, 207
    priests working with Underworld
        tang-ki 96, 104–105, 128
Taoist schools
    Celestial Masters 33–34, 125
        Laozi 33
        Six Heavens 33
        Six Palaces 34
        Zhang Daoling 33
    Lingbao School 34
        earth prisons (diyu) 35
        Scripture of Karmic Retribution
            (Yinyuan jing) 35
        Taiyi Jiuku Tianzun 35
        torture chambers for the dead 35
        transmigration of the soul 35
    Shangqing School
        Chart of the ranks and functions
            of the real numinous beings
            (Zhenling weiye tu) 34
        Declarations of the Perfected'
            (Zhengao) 34

gaining merit 35
Palaces of Fengdu 34
Six Heavens of Fengdu 34
Tao Hongjing 34
Taoist scriptures
    Five Cinnabar Spells 127
    Tai shang ling bao ba du wang shan
        shishi keyi 99
    Tai shang qing shen ke 96
    Tai yi jiu ku miao jing 103
    True scripture of the Heavenly
        Worthy of Primordial
        Beginnings who saves Beings
        from the Blood Pond 123
technologies of religious synthesis 22,
    24, 73, 79, 226
    absorption 22, 217
    absorption from the orthodox
        traditions 36
    absorption of Buddhist cosmology
        32, 35, 62
    appropriation 22, 64, 217
        of authority from the orthodox
            traditions 128, 133, 141, 147,
            151
        of Buddhist cosmology into
            Taoism 35–36
        of Japanese malicious foetus ghosts
            in Taiwan 219–220
        of luk thep dolls and malicious
            foetus ghosts in Malaysia 150,
            173, 219
        of Taiwan's music culture 66
        of Thai coffin rituals 163, 171–172,
            173
    hybridisation 22, 217
        and foetus ghosts in Taiwan 220
        of ghosts with attributes of deities
            in Taiwan 218, 220
        of post-mortal cosmology and
            cemetery rituals as everyday
            forms of resistance in Singapore
            83, 87–88, 107, 108, 109
        of post-mortal cosmology in
            Malaysia 137
        of Tua Di Ya Pek's anonymity and
            identity 73, 98
    invention see invention
    inversion see inversion
    reinvention see reinvention
    reinversion see reinversion
    Sinification see Sinification
    transfiguration 22, 217
        of behavioural norms and ritual
            intoxication 10, 137, 139

technologies of religious synthesis, transfiguration (*cont.*)
   and cemetery rituals in Singapore 109
   and foetus appeasement rituals in Taiwan 81, 219–220
   and foetus assistance rituals in Singapore 81
   and intoxicants in temple settings 10, 137
   of the Heaven–Underworld hierarchy in Malaysia 134, 138
   and inversions of authority in the Heaven–human–Underworld hierarchy 10, 114, 138, 139
   and offerings to multiple Tua Di Ya Peks 73
  transfiguring hybridisation 22, 217
   and cemetery rituals in Singapore 107, 109
   of cosmology and practices and the Underworld recreation 114, 119–127 *passim*, 137
   and role inversion of Tua Di Ya Pek 79–80
temple networking / networks 9, 21, 222–223
temple networking based on past location in Singapore 62–63, 222
temples' reciprocal ritual networks 54, 62, 63, 152, 210, 222
temples in Malaysia
  Brickfields Chenghuangmiao in Kuala Lumpur 164–174 *passim*
  Dasheng City God Temple (Muar Dasheng Gong Chenghuang Dian) in Johor State 142, 152–160 *passim*, 184, Figure 8.2, Plates 10 and 11
  Difang Fu in Malacca 104 (note 8)
  Linghai Dian in Penang 192
  Muar City God Temple (Xinjiawang Chenghuangmiao) in Johor State 10, 142–152, 184, Figure 8.1
  Penang City God Temple (Penang Chenghuangmiao) 11, 171, 185, 203–210 *passim*, 214, Plate 16
  Qingyun Dian in Penang 210
  Tiandeyuan Xunyin Fu in Penang 208–209
  Tua Pek Kong Beo in Penang
  Sanbao Gong in Klang, Selangor State 115, 117, 133
  Xunyin Miao in Penang 209
  Yinfu Tan in Klang, Selangor State 113–140 *passim*, 174–182 *passim*, 184, 196–200 *passim*, 228–229, Figures 7.1, 7.2, 9.1 and 9.2, Plates 7 and 8
  Zhenlinshan Jieyuan Tang Chenghuangmiao in Johor State 192
temples in Singapore
  Choa Chu Kang Doumu Gong and Sanzhong Gong 62, 63, 65, 66, 68–72, 74–81, Figure 5.2
  Jin Shui Gang in Yio Chu Kang 63
  Jiucaiba Chenghuangmiao in Geylang 190, 192, 193, 203, 215–216
  Laisheng Gong in Bukit Batok 63
  Longde Tang 74
  Nanlai Dian in Yew Tee 63
  Shanlong Miao 192
  Shengan Temple in Jurong West
  Shenglian Gong 74
  Xuanhuang Dian in Bukit Merah 74
  Yu Feng Nan Fu Xuanshan Miao in Jurong East 49–60 *passim*, 83, 92–104 *passim*, Figure 6.3, Plates 1, 2 and 3
temples in Singapore (*cont.*)
  Yushan Dian in Woodlands 74, 89, 90, 98
  Zhenren Gong in Redhill 192
temples in Taiwan
  Beigang Chaotian Gong Yunlin County 223 (note 17)
  Dajia Zhenlan Gong Taichung City 223 (note 7)
  Dongshiliao Dongan Gong in Chaiyi county 192
  Guangtian Gong in Taichung City 224
  Longhu Gong in Miaoli County 220
  Nankunshen in Tainan City 218, 223
  Sheliao Zinan Gong in Nantou county 224
  Shenglin Gong in Chaiyi County 192
  Shengxian Tang in Taichung City 225
  Shiba Wang Gong in New Taipei City 60–61
  Shiding Wu Lu Caishen Miao in New Taipei City 224
  Zhongliao Anxi Chenghuangmiao in Chaiyi County 190, 192
Thai
  luk thep dolls and *kuman thong* 10, 150–151, 161, 221
  vernacular religion / traditions 10, 149, 150, 161, 172, 173

trance possession states 19–20
  alcohol in 79, 158–159
  and effects of opium 138, 158
  and emotions 80
  entering 42, 55, 66, 68, 74, 129–130, 155
  exiting 58, 60, 66, 147
  invocations 55, 66, 68
  involuntary 116
  mass synchronised channelling 130, 152, 155–156, 182
  and perception of time 181
  and physiological effects and sense perception 7, 8, 50, 59–60, 68, 77–79, 80–81, 158
  and transference of alcohol and opium to the Underworld 57–58, 159
  and transformation from human to deity 55, 68, 79, 80, 93
transmigration *see* reincarnation
transnational cultural flows 3, 10, 22
  and digitalised modernity 228
  from Japan 219, 221
  between Malaysia and Singapore 214, 216, 217
  from Thailand 141, 150–151, 161, 173
Tua Di Ya Pek 1, Plates 11 and 14
  and alcohol 82, 138, 158
  on altars 53, 68, 89, 153, 155, 164
  as Ba Ye Gong and Jiu Ye Gong 194, 196, 200, 215–216
  and cemeteries 82, 88
  and changing pantheonic hierarchies 130, 139, 140
  channelled from different courts 93, 98, 155–160 *passim*, 165–168 *passim*, 179
  control / power over ghosts and malicious spirits 25, 82, 119, 218, 219
  and digitalised modernity 107
  and divisible soul 179
  duties / roles in the Underworld 71, 82, 180, 218
  duties / roles when channelled through *tang-ki* 82, 87, 179, 216, 219
  and emotions 80
  as Fan Wujiu and Xie Bian 43, 47, 143, 179, 183, 200
  and gambling 81, 82, 206–207
  and Jade Record 37
  multiple Tua Di Ya Pek and family names 47, 73, 98, 183
  mythologies 43–47 *passim*

  see also Anxi Chenghuangmiao, Fan Wujiu and Xie Bian
  mythology and titles
  and opium 45, 138, 143, 158–159, 204–206, 212
  prior to Tua Di Ya Pek in the Underworld 182
  role / personality reversal 79
  and spirit armies 173
  statues 46–47, 94, 95, 115–117 *passim*, 143, 190, 191, 200, 203, Plate 14
  and Ten Courts of the Underworld 73, 152–160, 179, 183
  as Underworld enforcers 47, 53, 73
  and the vernacularisation of tradition 37
Tua Ya Pek
  conversations with Tua Ya Pek *see* dialogic approach, conversations with Tua Ya Pek
  in human form 206–207
  identifying features and names 46
  mythology, opium and modern Underworld tradition in Penang 204–207, Plate 16

Underworld
  for atheists, agnostics and followers of other religions 160
  ethnically inclusive / multi-ethnic 53, 125, 160–162 *passim*
  ethnically exclusive 125, 160–163 *passim*
  expanding pantheon 8, 62, 64, 65, 70, 72, 81, 210
  gates / gateway to xiii, 47, 55, 66, 85, 98, 116, 155
  gates are opened 85, 151, 155
  gates are closed 98
  human creation of 181–182
  language / spoken word 50, 53, 179
  time *see* relative time
Underworld cosmology 6, 8, 11, 32–40 *passim*
  avoiding punishments 137
  Buddhist hells 33
  chickens 181
  crimes and punishments 121–127
  deities and family names 47, 53, 73–74, 93, 95, 98, 179, 183
  earth prisons 35, 82
  Fengdu 34
  Jade Record *see* Jade Record
  karmic retribution *see* post-mortal, karmic retribution

INDEX

Underworld cosmology (*cont.*)
  Mount Tai 32, 34, 85
  promotion in 34–35, 70–71, 72, 73
  reincarnation in 36
  rank/status 70–71
  suicide 86, 121, 126
  women and childbirth in Buddhism and Taoism 122–123
  Yellow springs 16, 32
Underworld courts 121–127 *passim*
  Ten courts 9, 10, 33, 36, 73, 114, 119
  First Court 33, 36, 121
  Second Court 121–122
  Third Court 122
  Fourth Court 47, 93, 94, 116, 122–123, 179, 180
  Fifth Court 52, 98, 123–124
  Sixth Court 93, 124–125
  Seventh Court 53, 89, 98, 125
  Eighth Court 125–126
  Ninth Court 126–127
  Tenth Court 36, 73, 121, 127
Underworld deities 8, 43, 52
  Ang Ya Pek (Uncle Red) 210
  Bak Ya Pek (Uncle North) 210
  Bao Bei Ya 54, 62, 65–74 *passim*, 81, 212, 216, 224, Figure 5.1
  Da Shi Ye (Ghost King) see Da Shi Ye
  Dongyue Dadi 16, 32, 44, 52, 77, 153, 164
  Eight Generals 101
  generals 19, 51, 52, 85, 99, 151, 155
  Generals of the Five Directions 68, 85, 94–95, 155, 177, 210–211
  Ghost Emperors of the Five Directions 210
  Hao Zhu Ya (God of Filial Piety) 89, 153, 164, 165
  Kim Ya Pek (Uncle Gold) 210, 224
  Lang Pek (Rickshaw Uncle) 208
  Lo Qio Sian Pek (laughing God) 72, 72 (note 8), 209, 217
  Meng Po 36, 73
  Ox Head (Niutou) and Horse Face (Mamian) 42, 49, 55, 85, 117, 155, 164, 212, 225
  Pai Gu Pek (Bone God) 72, 72 (note 8), 209–210, 217
  Sa Ya Pek 71, 164, 210
  Siming Panguan 117
  Taishan Fu Jun (Lord of Mount Tai) 32, 125
  Tiger General 131
  Yama-Kings of Ten Tribunals (*Shi Dian Yenwang*) 36
  Zai Ya Pek (Uncle Wealth) 210, 224
Underworld external camps
  Generals of the Five Directions / Tua Di Ya Pek's combined ghost armies (*wai wu ying / wai ying*) 51, 211–212
Underworld kings
  first king, Qinguang Wang 36, 94, 121
  second king, Chujiang Wang 121
  third king, Songdi Wang 122
  fourth king, Wuguan Wang 122, 179
  fifth king, Yanluo Wang 52, 123, 164
  sixth king, Biancheng Wang 117
  seventh king, Taishan Wang 125
  eighth king, Dushi Wang 126
  ninth king, Pingdeng Wang 126
  tenth king, Zhuanlun Wang 36
Underworld locations
  Blood River 165–169 *passim*
  Bridge of Pain 36
  City of the Dead-by-Accident, *Wangsi Cheng* (9th Court) 121, 126
  Naihe Bridge 168
  Terrace of the Mirror of the Wicked, *Nie jingtai* (1st Court) 121
Underworld paraphernalia
  abacus 48, 68–70 *passim*, 80, 93, 128, 130, 156, 158, 159, 170
  children's coffins in Malaysia 164, 169, 172, 174
  demon summoning / expelling plaque 46, 47, 48, 70, 151
  fans 5, 48, 70, 76, 78, 80, 145, 151, 156
  flags 51, 94, 103, 155, 165–168 *passim*, 177
  miniature coffins in Singapore 118, 173 Plate 13
  smoking pipes 48, 69, 79, 129, 156, 158, 169, 177
  soul-catching chain / soul-chaining lock 44, 47, 48, 155–156 *passim*
  thrones 42, 68, 74, 99, 174, 212, Figure 11.1
  whips *see* ritual objects, whips
Underworld reconstruction / recreation 9, 11, 114–115, 117, 118, 119–127, 139, 140, 174–175, Figures 7.1 and 9.1, Plates 7 and 8
Underworld spirits
  bamboo 211–212
  demons and demon soldiers 1, 33, 34, 98, 122, 124, 179, 180

door guards 76
ghost / spirit armies / soldiers 51,
    82, 85, 88, 147, 149, 151, 173,
    211–212
ghosts 52, 68, 155, 164
shadow soul 126
Underworld sub-hells 9, 48, 114–115,
    119–127 *passim*
Blood Pond / Pool Hell 116–117,
    122–123, 180
Hell of Boiling Oil 119, 125
Hell of Eye Gouging 78
Hell of Flying Knives and Burning
    Stones 124
Hell of Lifting Sharp Rocks 123
Hell of Pus and Blood 122
Hell of Severing in Two 78, 119, 124,
    125, Plate 7
Hell of Sword Trees 119, 179
Hell of Tongue Removal and Cheek
    Piercing 125
Underworld tradition
    geographic diffusion / dissemination
        8, 11, 184, 214–217 *passim*
    origins *see* origins of the modern
        Underworld tradition

van der Veer, P. xii, xiv, 2, 23
vernacularisation of tradition 37, 183,
    228

Whitehouse, H. 226–227

yang 19
Yellow Springs 16, 32
yin 32, 94, 173, 212
yin and *yang* 19, 32, 51, 56, 145
Yuli chao chuan see Jade Record